Moncure Daniel Conway

The Sacred Anthology

A Book of Ethnical Scriptures

Moncure Daniel Conway

The Sacred Anthology
A Book of Ethnical Scriptures

ISBN/EAN: 9783744652773

Printed in Europe, USA, Canada, Australia, Japan

Cover: Foto ©ninafisch / pixelio.de

More available books at **www.hansebooks.com**

THE SACRED ANTHOLOGY.

PRINTED BY BALLANTYNE AND COMPANY
EDINBURGH AND LONDON

THE

SACRED ANTHOLOGY

A BOOK OF ETHNICAL SCRIPTURES.

COLLECTED AND EDITED BY

MONCURE DANIEL CONWAY,
AUTHOR OF " THE EARTHWARD PILGRIMAGE."

Φήμη δ' οὔ τις πάμπαν ἀπόλλυται, ἥντινα πολλοὶ
λαοὶ φημίζουσι· Θεοῦ νύ τις ἐστὶ καὶ αὐτή.
Hesiod.

LONDON:
TRÜBNER & CO., 57 & 59 LUDGATE HILL.
1874.

[*All Rights reserved*]

PREFACE.

'THE utterance does not wholly perish which many peoples utter; nay, this is the voice of God.'

A conviction somewhat like this of the Greek poet, transcribed on the title-page of this volume, led to its being undertaken. The purpose of the work is simply moral. The editor has believed that it would be useful for moral and religious culture if the sympathy of Religions could be more generally made known, and the converging testimonies of ages and races to great principles more widely appreciated. He has aimed to separate the more universal and enduring treasures contained in ancient scriptures, from the rust of superstition and the ore of ritual. He has omitted much, the value of which seemed chiefly local or temporary; much which appeared to him, though true, deficient in impressiveness of statement; much more, no doubt, because unknown to him: but he would be much misunderstood if his suppressions should be regarded as intended to disparage the many cherished passages of sacred writings not to be found in this book. Each nation has its full scriptures, and it is among the hopes with which this selection is offered to the public that it may lead to a more general and reverent study of them.

Under the necessary limitations of such a work, the editor has—beyond the Hebrew and Christian scriptures—confined his selections to those books of a moral or religious character which, having commanded the veneration of the races among whom they were produced, are still the least accessible to European readers.

LONDON, *December* 1873.

CONTENTS.

	PAGE
LAWS,	1
RELIGION,	33
THEISM,	63
WORSHIP,	96
WISDOM,	115
SUPERSTITION,	133
KNOWLEDGE,	158
ETHICS OF INTELLECT,	172
CHARITY,	215
LOVE AND FRIENDSHIP,	244
NATURE,	259
MAN,	277
CHARACTER,	286
CONDUCT OF LIFE,	301
HUMILITY,	320
GREATNESS,	337
JUSTICE AND GOVERNMENT,	352
ACTION,	378
SORROW AND DEATH,	387

	PAGE
SANCTIONS,	424
PRINCIPAL AUTHORITIES,	461
CHRONOLOGICAL NOTES,	466
ABBREVIATIONS EXPLAINED,	471
INDEX,	473

SACRED ANTHOLOGY.

LAWS.

I.

The Inward Sinai.

This commandment which I command thee this day, is not hidden from thee, nor is it far off. It is ^{Heb.} Deut. not in the heavens, that thou shouldst say, Who will go up for us to the heavens, and bring it to us, that we may hear it, and do it? Nor is it beyond the sea, that thou shouldst say, Who will go over the sea for us, and bring it to us, that we may hear it, and do it? But the word is very nigh to thee, in thy mouth, and in thy heart, that thou mayest do it.

II.

Laws.

Thou shalt not make for thyself a graven image, nor any likeness of what is in heaven above, or what ^{Heb.} Gen. is in the earth beneath, or what is in the water under ^{Lev.} the earth: thou shalt not bow down thyself to them, nor shalt thou serve them.

Honour thy father and thy mother.

A

Thou shalt not commit murder.
Thou shalt not steal.
Thou shalt not bear false witness against thy neighbour.
Thou shalt not covet anything which is thy neighbour's.
Thou shalt not injure a stranger nor oppress him.
Ye shall not afflict any widow or fatherless child.
Ye shall do no injustice in judgment, in meting, in weight, or in measure. Just balances, just weights, a just ephah, and a just hin, shall ye have.
Thou shalt love thy neighbour as thyself.

III.

Prohibitions.

<small>Siam.
Budh.</small>
Thou shalt abstain from acquiring or keeping, by fraud or violence, the property of another.
Thou shalt abstain from those who are not the proper objects of thy lust.
Thou shalt abstain from deceiving others by word or deed.
Thou shalt abstain from intoxication.

IV.

Four Virtuous Inclinations.

<small>Siam.
Budh.</small>
Seeking for others the happiness one desires for one's self.
Compassionate interest in the welfare of all beings.
Love for and pleasure in all beings.
Impartiality, preventing preference or prejudice.

V.

The Eightfold Path.

1, Correct religious ideas; 2, correct thought; 3, correct speaking (exactitude in words); 4, correct conduct; 5, correct life (free from sin and ambition); 6, correct application (or energy in seeking Nirvána, the supreme Felicity); 7, correct memory; 8, correct meditation in perfect tranquillity.

<small>Siam. Budh.</small>

VI.

False Reliances.

Be not presumptuous through any advantage in the world.

Be not too much world-adorning.

Be not reliant on much wealth.

Be not reliant on monarchs.

Be not reliant on excessive respect.

Be not reliant on kindred or great ancestry.

Be not reliant on life; for death comes at last.

<small>Parsi. Mainyó-i-Khard. 6th cent.</small>

VII.

Morality.

To a man contaminated by sensuality, neither the Vedas, nor liberality, nor sacrifices, nor observances, nor pious austerities will procure felicity.

A wise man must faithfully discharge all his moral duties, even though he does not constantly perform the ceremonies of religion. He will fall very low if he performs ceremonial acts only, and fails to discharge his moral duties.

<small>Hindu. Manu. comp.</small>

There are two roads which conduct to perfect virtue,—to be true, and to do no evil to any creature.

VIII.

Seed and Fruit.

<small>Hindu.
Manu.
(Brighu.)</small>

Brighu, whose heart was the pure essence of virtue, who proceeded from Manu himself, thus addressed the great Sages :—Hear the infallible rules for the fruit of deeds in this universe.

Action, either mental, verbal, or corporeal, bears good or evil fruit as itself is good or evil; and from the actions of men proceed their various transmigrations in the highest, the mean, and the lowest degree.

Of that threefold action, be it known in this world that the heart is the instigator.

Goodness is declared to be true knowledge; darkness, gross ignorance; passion, an emotion of desire or aversion : these qualities attend all souls.

Study of sacred knowledge, devotion, purity, self-control, performance of duty, meditation on the divine being, accompany the quality of goodness.

Interested motives for acts of religion or morality, perturbation of mind on slight occasions, commission of acts forbidden by law, and habitual indulgence in selfish gratifications, are attendant on the quality of passion.

Covetousness, ignorance, avarice, detraction, impiety, a habit of soliciting favours, and inattention to necessary business, belong to the quality of darkness.

To the quality of darkness belongs every act of which a man is ashamed : to passion, every act by which a man seeks exaltation and celebrity: to goodness every act by which he hopes to acquire divine knowledge, which he is never ashamed of doing, and which brings placid joy to his conscience.

Souls endued with goodness attain always the state of deities; those filled with ambitious passions, the condition of men; and those immersed in darkness, the nature of beasts: this is the triple order of transmigration.

IX.
Justice.

I have no control over what may be helpful or hurtful to me, but as God willeth. Had I the knowledge of his secrets I should revel in the good, and evil should not touch me. Arabic. Koran, s. 7, 'Al Araf.'

Make the best of things; and enjoin what is just, and withdraw from the ignorant.

Lay not burdens on any but thyself.

Be good to parents, and to kindred, and to orphans, and to the poor, and to a neighbour, be he of your own people or a stranger, and to a fellow-traveller, and to the wayfarer, and to the slave. S. 4, 'Women.' comp.

O ye who believe! stand fast to justice when ye bear witness before God, though it be against yourselves, or your parents, or your kindred; whether the party be rich or poor. God is nearer than you to both; therefore follow not passion, lest ye swerve from the truth.

Verily the hypocrites shall be in the lowest abyss.
God hath not given a man two hearts within him.
Clothe not the truth with falsehood, and hide not the truth when ye know it. S. 33. S. 2, 'The Cow.'

Will ye enjoin what is right upon others, and forget yourselves?

O believers! stand up as witnesses for God by righteousness: and let not ill-will to any induce you to act unjustly. Act uprightly: this will approach nearer unto piety.

Let every soul look well to what it sendeth on before for the morrow.

S. 59.

X.

Reciprocity.

The man of perfect virtue, wishing to be established himself, seeks also to establish others; wishing to be enlarged himself, he seeks also to enlarge others.

To be able to judge of others by what is in ourselves, may be called the Art of Virtue. He who requires much from himself and little from others, will shield himself from resentment.

It is only the virtuous man who can love or who can hate others. The Sage said, 'Sin, my doctrine is that of an all-pervading unity?' He went out, and the disciples said, 'What do these words mean?' Tsang said, 'The doctrine of our master is to be true to the principles of our nature, and the benevolent exercise of them to others,—this and nothing more.'

Some one said, 'What do you say concerning the principle that injury should be recompensed with kindness?' The Sage replied, 'With what then will you recompense kindness? Recompense kindness with kindness, and injury with justice.'

Tsze-Kung asked, 'Is there one word which may serve as a rule for one's whole life?' Confucius

Chinese.
Confucius.
Analects.
(600 B.C.)

answered, 'Is not Reciprocity such a word? What you do not wish done to yourself, do not to others.'

When you are labouring for others, let it be with the same zeal as if it were for yourself.

XI.
Duties.

Contentment, returning good for evil, resistance to sensual appetites, abstinence from illicit gain, purification, control of the senses, knowledge of sacred writings, knowledge of the Supreme Mind, veracity, and freedom from anger, form the tenfold system of duties. Hindu. Manu.

Let a man continually take pleasure in truth, in justice, in laudable practices, and in purity; let him keep in subjection his speech, his arm, and his appetite.

Wealth and pleasures repugnant to law, let him shun; and even lawful acts which may cause future pain, or be offensive to mankind.

Let him not have nimble hands, restless feet, or voluble eyes; let him not be crooked in his ways; let him not be flippant in his speech, nor intelligent in doing mischief.

Let him walk in the path of good men.

XII.
Laws.

Let none of you treat his brother in a way which he himself would dislike. Sabœan 'Book of the Law.'

Do not glory or boast. B.C. Preserved by El Wardi.

Adhere so firmly to the truth that your Yea shall be yea, and your Nay, nay. comp.

Do not talk much or vainly.

Do not entrust your affairs to the weak and frivolous.

Do not be fond of unseemly jesting, or of scandal, or of backbiting.

Let not your anger induce you to utter a word of abuse, which can only bring reproach and disgrace upon you, and expose you to retribution.

Whoso represses anger, and controls his tongue, and purifies his soul, has conquered every evil.

Be not hasty in punishing an evil-doer.

If any one among you has committed a sin, let him purge himself therefrom, and let not impunity induce him to commit the like again.

Place your whole trust in God, who knoweth every secret : he will suffice you as a just ruler, and pronounce a fair decision.

XIII.

Equity.

<small>Heb. Exod. comp.</small>

Thou shalt not raise a false report : thou shalt not join thy hands with a wicked man to be an injurious witness. Thou shalt not follow the great to do evil ; nor shalt thou incline towards the great so as to pervert judgment ; nor shalt thou be partial to a poor man in his cause.

When thou meetest the ox or the ass of thine enemy going astray, thou shalt surely bring it back to him. When thou seest the ass of him who hateth thee lying under his burden, and wouldst forbear to help him, thou shalt surely help him.

Thou shalt not pervert the judgment of thy poor

in his cause. Keep far from a false matter. And thou shalt not take a bribe; for a bribe blindeth the eye of the clear-sighted, and perverteth the words of the just. A stranger also thou shalt not oppress; for ye know the heart of a stranger, since ye were strangers in the land of Egypt.

Six days mayest thou do thy work; but on the seventh day thou shalt rest, in order that thine ox and thine ass may rest, and the son of thy handmaid and the stranger may be refreshed.

XIV.
Duties.

Speak to all the congregation of the children of Israel, and say to them, Ye shall be holy: every one of you shall revere his mother and his father. Turn ye not to idols, nor make for yourself molten gods. Heb. Lev. comp.

When ye reap the harvest of your land, thou shalt not wholly reap the corners of thy field, neither shalt thou gather the gleanings of thy harvest. And thou shalt not glean thy vineyard, neither shalt thou gather every grape of the vineyard; thou shalt leave them for the poor and stranger. Ye shall not steal, nor deal falsely, nor lie one to another. Thou shalt not oppress thy neighbour, nor rob him; nor shall the wages of a hired servant abide with thee all night until the morning.

Thou shalt not curse the deaf, nor put a stumbling-block before the blind.

Ye shall do no injustice in judgment: thou shalt not respect the person of the poor, nor honour the person of the mighty: in righteousness shalt thou judge thy neighbour.

Thou shalt not go about, a tale-bearer among thy people; nor shalt thou stand up against the blood of thy neighbour.

Thou shalt not hate thy brother in thy heart: thou shalt freely reprove thy neighbour, and not suffer sin upon him. Thou shalt not avenge, nor bear any malice against the children of thy people, but thou shalt love thy neighbour as thyself.

Nor shall ye use divination, or observe times.

In the presence of the hoary head thou shalt rise up, and honour the face of the old man.

Apply not to see necromancers, nor seek after wizards.

And when a stranger sojourneth with thee in your land, ye shall not vex him. As one born amongst you shall be the stranger that dwelleth with you, and thou shalt love him as thyself.

The land shall not be sold for ever.

XV.

Humanity.

<small>Heb.
Deut.
comp.</small>

Thou shalt not deliver up to his master the slave who hath escaped from his master unto thee: he shall dwell with thee, in the midst of thee, in that place which he shall choose in one of thy gates, whenever he pleases: thou shalt not oppress him.

Thou shalt not oppress a hired servant who is poor and needy, whether he be one of thy own brethren, or of thy strangers that are in the land, within thy gates. In his day thou shalt give him his

hire, and before the sun shall have gone down upon
him : because he is poor, and setteth his heart upon it
Thou shalt remember that thou wast a bondman in
Egypt.

Thou shalt not muzzle the ox when he is treading
the corn.

XVI.
Injustice.

By the heaven, and by the Night-comer !
But who shall teach thee what the Night-comer is ? <small>Arabic. Koran, s. 86, 'The Night-Comer.'</small>
'Tis the Star of piercing radiance.
Over every soul is set a guardian.
Ye honour not the orphan,
Nor urge ye one another to feed the poor ; <small>S. 89, 'The Daybreak.'</small>
And ye devour heritages, devouring greedily,
And ye love riches with exceeding love.
Woe to those who stint the measure :
Who when they take by measure from others, exact <small>S. 83, 'Those who stint.'</small>
    to the full ;
But when they mete to them, diminish.
Yet surely there are guardians over you—
Illustrious recorders— <small>S. 82, 'The Cleaving.'</small>
Cognisant of your actions.

XVII.
Justice.

Let him who is departing from justice consider
with himself, 'I shall perish.' <small>Hindu. Cural I.</small>

The great will not regard as poverty the low <small>3d cent.</small>
estate of that man who abides with equity.

Loss and gain come not without cause : it is the
ornament of the wise to preserve evenness of mind.

To rest impartial as the fixed balance is the ornament of the wise.

Forsake on the moment any advantage gained without equity. The true merchandise of merchants is to guard and do by the things of others as they do by their own.

<small>Cural II.</small>

The property which is acquired by fraud will perish in the ratio of its seeming increase.

That black knowledge called fraud is not in those who desire the greatness called rectitude.

Even their body will fail the fraudulent; but even the world of the gods will not fail the just.

XVIII.

Purposes.

The world was given us for our own edification,

<small>African inscription on a mosque in Is. of Johanna. Sir W. Jones.</small>

Not for the purpose of raising up sumptuous buildings;

Life for the discharge of moral and religious duties,

Not for pleasurable indulgence;

Wealth to be liberally bestowed,

Not avariciously hoarded;

And learning to produce good actions,

Not empty disputes.

XIX.

Excellencies.

<small>Ceylon. Páli. Budh. Khuddaka Pátha. comp. (250 B.C.)</small>

Buddha was residing at Jetavana. In the night a heavenly being, illuminating Jetavana with his radiance, approached him, saying—'Many gods and men, aspiring after good, have held divers things to be blessings; declare the things that are excellent.' Buddha said—

'To serve the wise, and not the foolish, and to honour those worthy of honour; these are excellencies.

'To dwell in the neighbourhood of the good, to bear the remembrance of good deeds, and to have a soul filled with right desires; these are excellencies.

'To have knowledge of truth, to be instructed in science, to have a disciplined mind, and pleasant speech; these are excellencies.

'To honour father and mother, to provide for wife and child, and to follow a blameless vocation; these are excellencies.

'To be charitable, act virtuously, be helpful to relatives, and to lead an innocent life; these are excellencies.

'To be pure, temperate, and persevering in good deeds; these are excellencies.

'Humility, reverence, contentment, gratitude, attentiveness to religious instruction; these are excellencies.

'To be gentle, to be patient under reproof, at due seasons to converse with the religious; these are excellencies.

'Self-restraint and chastity, the knowledge of the great principles, and the hope of the eternal repose;[1] these are excellencies.

'To have a mind unshaken by prosperity or adversity, inaccessible to sorrow, secure and tranquil; these are excellencies.

'They that do these things are the invincible; on every side they walk in safety; they attain the perfect good.'

[1] Nirvána.

XX.

Beatitudes.

Christian.
Matt.

And seeing the multitudes, Jesus went up into the mountain; and when he had sat down, his disciples came to him. And he opened his mouth, and taught them, saying:—

Blessed are the poor in spirit; for theirs is the kingdom of heaven.

Blessed are the meek; for they shall inherit the earth.

Blessed are they who mourn; for they shall be comforted.

Blessed are they who hunger and thirst after righteousness; for they shall be filled.

Blessed are the merciful; for they shall obtain mercy.

Blessed are the pure in heart; for they shall see God.

Blessed are the peace-makers; for they shall be called children of God.

Blessed are they who are persecuted for righteousness' sake; for theirs is the kingdom of heaven.

Blessed are ye, when men revile you, and persecute you, and say everything that is bad against you, falsely, for my sake. Rejoice, and be exceeding glad; for great is your reward in heaven; for so did they persecute the prophets that were before you.

XXI.

Beatitudes.

Heb.
Talmud.

This is the way of the wise—to be humble and of a contrite spirit. Be like the bed of the ocean, which retains its water; like the earthen vessel, which preserves the wine ; like the threshold, over which every one steps ; and like the peg on the wall, on which every one hangs his cloak. <small>Zotah.</small>

They that sow in tears shall reap in joy. <small>R. David.</small>

The meek shall possess the land. A benevolent eye, humility of spirit, and a mind free from pride characterise the true disciples of Abraham. <small>Ethics.</small>

Those who aspire after what is holy and pure shall have assistance from above.

He who is merciful towards his fellow-creatures shall receive mercy. <small>R. Gamaliel.</small>

With the pure thou wilt show thyself pure. <small>Nedarim.</small>

Love peace and pursue peace ; love mankind, and bring them near unto the law. The moral condition of the world depends on three things—Truth, Justice, and Peace. <small>Hillel.</small>

Those who are afflicted, and do not afflict in return, who suffer everything for the love of God, and bear their burden with a gladsome heart, shall be rewarded according to the promise, 'Those who love the Lord shall be as invincible as the rising sun in his might.' <small>Shabbat.</small>

XXII.

Offices and Duties.

I beseech you therefore, brethren, by the mercies of God, to present your bodies a living sacrifice, holy, well-pleasing to God, which is your reasonable worship ; and be not conformed to the fashion of this world, but be transformed by the renewal of your mind, that ye may learn by experience what is the will of God, what is good, and well-pleasing, and perfect. For through the grace given to me, I warn every one among you <small>Christian. Rom. comp.</small>

not to think of himself more highly than he ought to think, but to think soberly, according to the measure of faith which God hath imparted to each. For as in one body we have many members, and the members have not all the same office, so we, though many, form one body in Christ, and each of us is a member of it in common with the rest. Having then gifts which differ, according to that which hath been bestowed upon us, if we have prophecy, let us prophesy according to the proportion of our faith; or if service, let us attend to the service; he that teacheth, let him attend to teaching; or he that exhorteth, to exhortation; he that giveth, let him do it with liberality; he that presideth over others, with diligence; he that doeth deeds of mercy, with cheerfulness.

Let your love be unfeigned. Abhor that which is evil, cleave to that which is good. In brotherly love, be affectionate to one another; in honour, give each other the preference. Be not backward in zeal; be fervent in spirit, serving the Lord. Rejoice in hope; be patient in affliction; be given to hospitality. Bless those who persecute you; bless, and curse not. Rejoice with those who rejoice; weep with those who weep. Be of one mind among yourselves. Set not your minds on high things, but content yourselves with what is humble. Be not wise in your own conceit. Render to no one evil for evil; have regard to what is honourable in the sight of all men. If it be possible, so far as dependeth on you, live at peace with all men. Dearly beloved, avenge not yourselves, but rather make room for wrath; if thy enemy hunger, feed him; if he thirst, give him drink. Be not overcome by evil, but overcome evil with good.

XXIII.

The Law fulfilled in Love.

Render to all what is due to them; tribute to whom tribute is due; honour to whom honour. Owe no one anything but fraternal love; for he that loveth others hath fulfilled the law. For these, Thou shalt not commit adultery, Thou shalt not kill, Thou shalt not steal, Thou shalt not covet, and every other commandment, are summed up in this precept, Thou shalt love thy neighbour as thyself. Love worketh no ill to one's neighbour; therefore love is the fulfilling of the law. The night is far spent, the day is at hand; let us then throw off the works of darkness, and put on the armour of light. Let us walk becomingly, as in the day. Christian. Rom. comp.

XXIV.

Toleration.

Him that is weak in his faith receive with kindness, and not to pass judgment on his thoughts. Who art thou that judgeth the servant of another? To his own lord he standeth or falleth. Christian. Rom. comp.

One man esteemeth on day above another; another esteemeth every day alike: let each one be fully persuaded in his own mind. He that regardeth the day, regardeth it to the Lord; and he that regardeth not the day, to the Lord he doth not regard it. None of us liveth to himself, and no one dieth to himself. But thou, why dost thou judge thy brother? And thou, too, why dost thou despise thy brother? Let us no longer judge one another; but let this rather be your judgment, not to put a stumbling-block, or an occasion to fall, in a brother's way. Let us strive to promote peace, and the edification of each other. Happy is he who doth not condemn himself in that which he alloweth!

XXV.
The Law of Love.

<small>Heb. Talmud. R. Simeon.</small> Whosoever lifts up his hand against his neighbour, though he do not strike him, is called an offender and sinner.

<small>Yoma.</small> Sins committed against our fellow-creatures neither repentance nor the day of atonement can purge away, if amends have not been previously made, and the injured brother appeased.

<small>Nathan.</small> If thou hast done harm to any one, be it ever so little, consider it as much; if thou hast done him a favour, be it ever so great, consider it as little. Has thy neighbour shown thee kindness? do not undervalue it; and has he caused thee an injury? do not overrate it.

<small>Kalah.</small> Whoso looketh upon the wife of another with a lustful eye is considered as if he had committed adultery.

<small>R. Joshua.</small> Let thy Yea be just, and thy Nay be likewise just.

XXVI.
The Law of Love.

<small>Christian. Matt.</small> Think not that I came to destroy the law or the prophets: I came not to destroy, but to fulfil.

Ye have heard that it was said to them of old time, 'Thou shalt not kill; and whoever shall kill; shall be in danger of the judges.' But I say to you, that whoever is angry with his brother shall be in danger of the judges.

If thou bring thy gift to the altar, and there remember that thy brother hath aught against thee, leave there thy gift before the altar, and go away; first be reconciled to thy brother, and then come and offer thy gift.

Ye have heard that it was said, 'Thou shalt not commit adultery.' But I say to you, that whoever looketh on a woman to lust after her, hath committed adultery with her already in his heart.

Again, ye have heard that it was said to them of old time, 'Thou shalt not swear falsely, but shalt perform to the Lord thine oaths.' But I say to you, Swear not at all; but let your language be, Yea, yea; Nay, nay; for whatever is more than these cometh of evil.

XXVII.
Love of Enemies.

Rejoice not when thine enemy faileth, and let not thy heart be glad when he stumbleth. Heb.
Talmud.
Ethics.

Who can deservedly be called a conqueror? He who conquers his rancorous passions, and endeavours to turn his enemy into a friend. Nathan.

Thou shalt not say, 'I will love the wise, but the unwise I will hate;' but thou shalt love all mankind. R. Joshua.

Thou shalt love thy neighbour: even if he be a criminal, and has forfeited his life, practise charity towards him in the last moments. Perachim.

What thou wouldst not like to be done to you, do not to others: this is the fundamental law. Hillel.

XXVIII.
Love of Enemies.

Ye have heard that it was said, 'Thou shalt love thy neighbour and hate thine enemy.' But I say to Christian.'
Matt.

you, Love your enemies, and bless them that persecute you; that ye may become the children of your Father in heaven; for he maketh his sun to rise on the evil and the good, and sendeth rain on the just and unjust.

XXIX.
Hypocrisy.

Christian.
Matt.
comp.

Take heed that ye do not your righteousness before men, to be seen by them; otherwise ye have no reward with your Father who is in heaven. Therefore when thou doest alms, do not sound a trumpet before thee, as the hypocrites do in the synagogues and in the streets, that they may have glory of men. Truly do I say to you, they have received their reward. But when thou doest alms, let not thy left hand know what thy right hand doeth.

And when ye worship, ye shall not be as the hypocites are; for they love to pray standing in the synagogues and in the corners of the streets, that they may be seen by men. Truly do I say to you, they have received their reward. But enter thou, when thou worshippest, into thy closet, and, when thou hast shut thy door, adore thy Father who is in secret.

And use not vain repetitions, as the heathen do, in prayer; for they think that they shall be heard for the multitude of their words. Be not ye therefore like them; for your Father knoweth what things ye have need of, before ye ask him.

XXX.
Earthbound Vision.

Where thy treasure is, there will thy heart be also. The eye is the lamp of the body. If thine eye be clear, thy whole body will be in light; but if thine eye be disordered, thy whole body will be in darkness. If then the light that is within thee is darkness, how great that darkness! No one can serve two masters; for either he will hate one, and love the other; or else he will cleave to one, and despise the other. Ye cannot serve God and mammon. Therefore I say to you, Be not anxious for your life, what ye shall eat; nor yet for your body, what ye shall put on. Is not the life more than food, and the body than raiment? Who of you by anxious thought can add to his life one cubit? and why are ye anxious about raiment? Consider the lilies of the field, how they grow. They toil not, neither do they spin; and yet I say to you, that not even Solomon in all his glory was arrayed like one of these. Be not ye then anxious about the morrow; for the morrow will be anxious about itself. Sufficient for the day is the evil thereof.

Christian.
Matt.
comp.

XXXI.
Measure for Measure.

Judge not, that ye be not judged. For with what judgment ye judge, ye will be judged; and with what measure ye mete, it will be measured to you. And why dost thou look at the mote that is in thy brother's eye, and not perceive the beam in thine own eye? Or how wilt thou say to thy brother, Let me take the mote out of thine eye; when, lo! the beam is in thine own eye? First cast the beam out of thine own eye; and then wilt thou see clearly to take the mote out of thy brother's eye.

Give not that which is holy to dogs, lest they turn

Christian.
Matt.
comp.

and rend you ; neither cast ye your pearls before swine, lest they trample them under their feet.

All things, then, whatever ye would that men should do to you, do ye also so to them; for this is the law and the prophets.

XXXII.
Being and Seeming.

Christian.
Matt.
comp.

Beware of the false prophets, who come to you in sheep's clothing, but inwardly are ravening wolves. Ye may know them by their fruits. Do men gather grapes of thorns, or figs of thistles? So every good tree beareth good fruit; but a bad tree beareth bad fruit. A good tree cannot bear bad fruit, nor can a bad tree bear good fruit. Not every one that saith to me, Lord, Lord, will enter into the kingdom of heaven; but he that doeth the will of my heavenly Father.

XXXIII.
Hypocrisy.

One hand cannot expiate the wrong of the other.

Heb.
Talmud.
Talkut to
Proverbs.

Secret alms pacify anger. Rabbi Yanai said to one giving alms in a public manner, 'You had better not have given him anything; in the way you give it him, you must have hurt his feelings.'

Hagiga.

Nedarim.

Study not the law that thou mayest be called a wise man, a Rabbi, and a teacher; but study for love of the law.

Migella.

Silence is praise unto God. If speaking is worth a silang (coin), silence is worth two. As excessive eulogies cannot enhance the value of the diamond, so many praises cannot add to the glory of God.

XXXIV.
Measure for Measure.

Judge not thy fellow-man until thou be similarly situated. Heb. Talmud. Ethics. Perachyah.
Judge all men with leniency.

An itinerant trader in spices, who travelled in the neighbourhood of Ziporah, called aloud, 'Who will buy the balm of life?' A crowd thronged around him to buy the elixir, to whom he said, 'If you want to possess this life-prolonging balm, here it is;' and taking the Psalm from his pocket, read aloud—'Where is the man that desireth life? who loveth many days to live happy? Guard thy tongue from speaking evil, and thy lips from uttering guile.' Parasha.

At the beginning of the world, God instituted this just retribution—measure for measure; and if all the laws of nature should be reversed, this law would stand for ever. Parasha.

With the measure we mete we shall be measured again. R. Johanan.

It would greatly astonish me if there could be any one found in this age who would receive an admonition; if he be admonished to take the splinter out of his eye, he would answer 'Take the beam out of thine own.' R. Tarphon.

What is the meaning of the passage 'Examine yourselves and search?' He who will reprove others must himself be pure and spotless. B. Meziah.

So thy pupil be well-meaning and of good principles, let thy fountains of wisdom and law pour forth their supplies publicly; and if not, restrain thyself, and be reserved. Taanith.

XXXV.
The Golden Rule.

<small>Heb. Talmud. R. Akiba. Ethics.</small>

Love thy neighbour as thyself: this is a fundamental law in the Bible.

Let the honour of thy fellow-man be as dear to thee as thy own; be as careful of his property as of thine own. True charity, in order to brave every vicissitude of life, must be free from all worldly considerations, like the love Jonathan bore David.

<small>Sotah.</small>

Imitate God in his goodness. Be towards thy fellow-creatures as he is towards the whole creation. Clothe the naked; heal the sick; comfort the afflicted; be a brother to the children of thy Father.

XXXVI.
The Tree known by Fruits.

<small>Heb. Talmud. Parasha.</small>

Man is as the tree of the field. Why is the foliage of the fruit-tree less exuberant and less noisy than that of the forest-tree? 'We can well dispense with both,' answered the first; 'we are distinguished by the delicious fruits we bear, and need not noise about our existence.'

<small>Kidashin.</small>

Virtue alone is productive of goodly fruits, which yield abundance, not only for the time being, but for the future, bringing blessings upon posterity. But sin is barren.

<small>R. Eliezar.</small>

He whose knowledge surpasses his good deeds may be compared to a tree with many branches and a scanty root. Every wind shakes and uproots it. But he whose good deeds excel his knowledge, may be compared to a tree with few branches and strong roots; if all the hurricanes in the world should come and storm against it, they could not move it from its place.

XXXVII.
Appearances.

On a certain highway two roads branched off in opposite directions: the one, level and straight in the beginning, soon turned out rugged, and overgrown with thorns and briars; the other proved itself, when first taken, to be narrow, and beset with many difficulties, but ultimately led smoothly and without interruption to the desired goal.

Heb. Talmud. Yalkut to Deut.

XXXVIII.
Friends.

Three friends man has in his life—wealth, family, and his good actions. When in the hour of approaching death man calls on his friends to deliver him, wealth and family avail not; but his good actions respond, 'Even before thou hast asked us, we have preceded thee, and have smoothed thy way.'

Heb. Talmud. Medrash.

XXXIX.
Knowledge and Action.

A man who studies the law, and acts in accordance with its commandments, is likened to a man who builds a house, the foundation of which is made of freestone, and the superstructure of bricks. Storm and flood cannot injure the house. But he who studies the law, and is destitute of good actions, is likened unto the man who builds the foundation of his house of brick and mortar, and raises the upper storeys with solid stone. The flood will soon undermine and overturn the house.

Heb. Talmud. Elisha, son of Abuyah.

XL.
Knowledge and Action.

<small>Christian.
Matt.</small>

Every one then that heareth these sayings of mine, and doeth them, shall be likened to a wise man, who built his house upon a rock; and the rain descended, and the streams came, and the winds blew, and beat upon that house; and it fell not; for it was founded upon a rock. And every one that heareth these sayings of mine, and doeth them not, shall be likened to a foolish man, who built his house upon the sand; and the rain descended, and the streams came, and the winds blew, and beat upon that house; and it fell; and great was its ruin.

XLI.
The Golden Rule.

<small>Hindu.
(Albitis.)</small>

Do not force on thy neighbour a hat that hurts thine own head.

He that hath true faith hath formed himself in reverence, zeal, and charity.

<small>Bha. Gita.
Par.</small>

Fools torment the spirit of their body. He who neglecteth the duties of life is unfit for this, much less for any higher, world.

XLII.
Principles.

<small>Old English
Proverbs.</small>

Who hath God, hath all; who hath him not, hath less than nothing.

Too much cunning undoes.

Power weakeneth the wicked. God arms the harmless.

Man's best candle is his understanding.

Deep lies the heart's language.

God stays long, but strikes at last.
What God made he never mars.
No wisdom equals silence.
The hand that gives gathers.
The higher the fool, the greater the fall.
Wise and stout never want a staff.
Truth is the best buckler.
Better God than gold.
To-day gold, to-morrow dust.
In every fault there is folly.
What is not wisdom is danger.

XLIII.
Royal Duties.

O my children! praise God and love men. For it is not fasting, nor solitude, nor monastic life, that will procure you eternal life, but only doing good. Forget not the poor, nourish them; remember that riches come from God, and are given you only for a short time. Do not bury your wealth in the ground. Be fathers to orphans. Be judges in the cause of widows, and do not let the powerful oppress the weak. Put to death neither innocent nor guilty. Do not fear the lot of the impious. Desert not the sick. Drive out of your heart all suggestions of pride, and remember that we are all perishable; to-day full of hope, to-morrow in the coffin. Abhor lying, drunkenness, and debauchery. Endeavour constantly to obtain knowledge.

Russian.
Vladimir II.
12th cent.

XLIV.
Old and New.

There are those that offer the gifts according to the law, who serve the mere delineation and shadow of the heavenly things, as Moses was admonished—'See that thou make all things according to the pattern which was shown thee in the mount.'

> Christian.
> Ep. to Heb.
> comp.

If that first covenant had been faultless, then a place would not have been sought for a second. For finding fault therewith, he saith, 'Behold, the days are coming, saith the Lord, when I will make with the house of Israel and with the house of Judah a new covenant; not according to the covenant which I made with their fathers: I will put my laws into their mind, and on their hearts will I write them; and I will be to them a God, and they shall be to me a people. And they shall not teach every one his fellow-citizen, and every one his brother, saying, Know the Lord; for all shall know me, from the least to the greatest.' In that he saith, 'a new covenant,' he hath made the first old; but that which is becoming old, and worn out with age, is ready to vanish away.

XLV.
Rules of Life.

> Parsi.
> Mainyô-i-Khard
> (Spirit of Wisdom).
> 6th cent.
> Ab.

The sage asked the Spirit of Wisdom, 'How is it possible to seek the preservation and prosperity of the body, without injury to the soul, and the deliverance of the soul without injury of the body?'

The Spirit of Wisdom replied :—

'Do not slander, that ill-fame and wickedness may not come to thee therefrom; for it is said every other demon attacks in the front, but Slander, which assaults from behind.

'Form no covetous desire, that avarice may not deceive thee, and that the benefit of the world may not be tasteless to thee, and that of the spirit unheeded.

'Practise not wrathfulness, since a man, when he practises wrath, becomes then forgetful of his duties and good works.

'Suffer not anxiety, since he that is anxious is heedless of the enjoyment of the world and of the spirit, and decay results to his body and soul.

'Commit no lustfulness, that, from thine own actions, injury and regret may not come to thee.

'Bear no envy, that life may not be tasteless for thee.

'Commit no sin through shame.

'Practise not slothful sleep, that the duties and good works which it is necessary for thee to do may not remain undone.

'Utter no ill-timed gossip.

'Be diligent and discreet, and eat of thine own regular industry; and form a portion for God and the good. This practice, in thy occupation, is the greatest good work.

'Plunder not from the wealth of others, that thy own industry may not become unheeded; since it is said that whoever eats anything not from his own regular industry, but from another, is as one who devours men's heads.

'With enemies, struggle with equity.

'With friends, proceed with their approbation.

'With a malicious man, carry on no conflict, and molest him not, even in any way.

'With the covetous man, be not a partner, and trust him not with the leadership.

'With an ignorant man, be not a confederate; with

a foolish man, make no dispute; from an ill-natured man, take no loan.

'With a slanderer, go not to the door of kings.'

XLVI.
Saving Virtues.

Persian.
Enwari.
(d. A.D. 1152.)

Man of to-day, be thou wise or foolish, three things above all take to heart. If thou hopest to break thy chain, with these thou shalt be rescued. Reason withholds its guidance from those who possess them not. Whatever sect thou mayest embrace, with these alone thou canst resign thyself to any suffering. Know them: rectitude, judgment, inoffensiveness.

XLVII.
Health.

Hindu.
Manu.
(Laws collected about 4th cent. B.C.)

Let the student honour his food, and eat it without contempt. Food eaten with constant respect gives muscular force and generative power; but, eaten irreverently, destroys both. Excessive eating is prejudicial to health and virtue.

When one among all the student's organs fails, by that single failure his divine knowledge passes away, as water flows through one hole in a leathern bottle.

XLVIII.
Sowing and Reaping.

Persian.
Sádi.
Gul.

I was sitting in a boat, in company with some persons of distinction, when a vessel near us sank, and two brothers fell into a whirlpool One of the company promised a mariner a hundred dinars if he would save both the brothers. The mariner came and saved one, and the other perished. I said, 'Of a truth, the other had no longer to live, and therefore he was taken out of the water the last.' The mariner laughing, replied, 'What you say is true; but I had also another motive for saving this, in preference to the other; because once, when I was tired in the desert, he mounted me on a camel; and from the hand of the other I received a whipping in my childhood.' I replied, 'Truly the great God is just, so that whosoever doeth good shall himself experience good, and he who committeth evil shall suffer evil.' As far as you can avoid it, distress not the mind of any one, for in the path of life there are many thorns. Assist the exigencies of others, since you also stand in need of many things.

XLIX.
Lives that are Laws.

Devout men are the title and inscription of the Book of the Law. They are the demonstration of all the truths, the solution of all the mysteries. Their outward life bears us to the path of obedience; their hidden life wins us to self-denial. They began their career before the ages, and they work for eternity. They have effaced from their hearts and minds every trace of pride and hypocrisy. They have trodden the ways of God, even when they appeared powerless to move, so feeble were they. These are the friends of God: they have discovered divine secrets: they guard them with devout silence.

^{Arabic.} Kashf-al-afrár. (D'Herb.

L.
Laws Universal.

The rays of intelligence make the order of venerable teachers. They are all and equally born to unite science and virtue.

32   SACRED ANTHOLOGY.

Nepaul.
Buddhist.
'White Lotus
of the Good
Law.'
comp.

The Great Repose (Nirvána) results from the comprehension of the equality of all laws; there is only one, not two or three. I explain the law to creatures, after having recognised their inclinations. It is as a cloud, with a garland of lightning, spreads joy on the earth; the water falls on all creatures, herbs, bushes, trees; and each pumps up to its own leaf and blossom what it requires for its several end. So falls the rain of the law upon the many-hearted world. The law is for millions; but it is one and alike beautiful to all: it is deliverance and repose.

LI.

Heb.
Deut.
comp.
From last
words of
Moses.

Give ear, O ye heavens! while I speak,
And let the earth hear the words of my mouth.
Let my doctrine drop as the rain,
And my speech distil as the dew,
As showers on the tender herb,
And as copious rain on the grass:
For I proclaim the name of God.
Ascribe ye greatness unto our God;
He is the Rock, perfect is his work;
For all his ways are just:
A God of truth and without iniquity,
Just and right is he.
Remember the days of old,
Consider the years of successive generations;
Ask thy father, and he will declare to thee:
Truly, God loveth the people:
All its saints are in thy hand:
And at thy feet sat down,
That they might receive thy commands.

RELIGION.

LII.
Sympathy of Religions.

If thou art a Mussulman, go stay with the Franks; if a Christian, join the Jews; if a Shuah, mix with the schismatics: whatever thy religion, associate with men of opposite persuasion. If in hearing their discourses thou art not in the least moved, but canst mix with them freely, thou hast attained peace, and art a master of creation. [Sufi and Parsi.]

Háfiz says, 'The object of all religions is alike. All men seek their beloved; and all the world is love's dwelling: why talk of a mosque or a church?'

Nánac says, 'He alone is a true Hindu whose heart is just; and he alone a true Mussulman whose life is true.'

The Parsi sentence says, 'Each prophet who appears is not to be opposed to his predecessors, nor yet complacently to exalt his law.'

LIII.
Religion.

Wherewith shall I come before the Lord,
And bow myself before God on high?

Shall I come before him with burnt-offerings,
With calves of a year old?
Will he be pleased with thousands of rams?
With ten thousand rivers of oil?
Shall I, then, give my first-born for my transgression,
The fruit of my body for the sin of my soul?
He hath declared to thee, O man, what is good;
And what doth the Lord thy God require from thee,
But to do justice, and to love mercy,
And to walk humbly with thy God?

Heb. Micah.

LIV.

Toleration.

There is no doubt in this Book : it is a direction to the devout,

Who believe in the unseen, and out of what is bestowed upon them bestow to others :

These are guided by their Lord, and with these it shall be well.

O men of Mecca, adore your Lord!

Announce to those who believe and do the things that are right, that for them are gardens through which rivers flow : so oft as they eat of the fruit therein they shall say, 'This same was our sustenance of old.'

The Jews say, 'The Christians lean on nought :'

'On nought lean the Jews,' say the Christians.

Yet both read the same Scriptures. So with like words say they who have no knowledge.

The east and the west belongeth to God; therefore whichever way ye turn, there is the face of God.

But until thou follow their religion, neither Jews nor Christians will be satisfied with thee. Say to them, 'The direction of God is the true direction.

Arabic. Koran, s. 2, 'The Cow.' comp.

'We believe in God, and that which hath been sent to us, and that which hath been sent to Abraham and Ismael and Isaac and Jacob, and the tribes; and that which hath been given to Moses and to Jesus, and that which was given to the prophets from their Lord. No difference do we make between any of them: and to God are we resigned.

'Will ye dispute with us about God? He is our Lord and your Lord. We have our works, and you have your works; and unto him we are sincerely devoted.'

LV.

Old Paths.

Thus saith the Lord: \
Stand ye in the ways, and see, Heb. Jer. comp. \
Ask for the old paths,— \
Which is the good way? walk therein, \
And ye shall find for yourselves rest. \
To what purpose cometh to me incense from Sheba? \
Your sacrifices are not pleasant to me. \
They have not heeded my law, but rejected it. \
Trust ye not in lying words, saying, \
'The temple of God, the temple of God are these;' \
But thoroughly amend your ways, \
And do justice between man and man.

LVI.

The True Man.

A man does not become a Brahmana by his platted hair, by his family, or by both; in whom there is truth and righteousness, he is the true Man.[1] Burm. Budh. Dhammapada, comp.

He who has cut all fetters, and who never trembles; [1] Lit. Brahmana.

he who is independent and unshackled, him I call indeed a Man.

He who is free from anger, dutiful, virtuous, without weakness and subdued; he who utters true speech, instructive, and free from hardness, so that he offend no one, him I call indeed a Man.

He whose knowledge is deep, who possesses wisdom, who knows the right way; he who is tolerant with the intolerant, mild with fault-finders, free from passion among the passionate, him I call indeed a Man.

The manly, the noble, the hero, the great sage, the guileless, the master, the awakened, him I call the right and true Man.

LVII.
Attainment.

<small>Hindu. Vishnu. Pur. (Wilson MS.) comp.</small>

Whatever the Mind longs for, whatever the hands reach, whatever the Reason considers, these, O Lord, are thy forms! I am pervaded by thee; thou containest me; and I have sheltered me under thy protection. Thou art scriptures and laws, planets and suns, the formed and the formless; and the Day and Night are thy eyes. Those who possess knowledge, and whose minds are pure, see the whole world as the form of Wisdom, which is thine!

Holy acts of sacrifice are performed by those who are devoted to their own duties, whose conduct is right and free from blemish, who are good, and tread in good paths.

Men attain the joy of heaven in their human form: they attain beatitude. These are absorbed with the desire for good conduct; they are free from all impediments; they are pure. When the intellect is pure as well as the heart, to it the region of the Deity becomes visible.

LVIII.

Catholicity.

When therefore Jesus knew that the Pharisees had heard that Jesus made and baptized more disciples than John (though Jesus himself did not baptize, as did his disciples), he left Judea, and went again to Galilee. And he must necessarily pass through Samaria. He cometh therefore to a city of Samaria called Sychar, near the piece of land which Jacob gave to his son Joseph. And Jacob's well was there. Jesus, being wearied with the journey, was sitting by the well. It was about the sixth hour.

Christian.
John.
comp.

There cometh a woman of Samaria to draw water. Jesus saith to her, Give me to drink. For his disciples had gone away into the city to buy food. The Samaritan woman saith to him, How is it that thou, who art a Jew, askest drink of me, who am a Samaritan woman? For Jews have no dealings with Samaritans. Jesus answered and said to her, If thou hadst known the gift of God, and who it is that saith to thee, Give me to drink, thou wouldst have asked of him, and he would have given thee living water. The woman saith to him, Sir, thou hast nothing to draw with, and the well is deep. Whence hast thou the living water? Art thou greater than our father Jacob, who gave us the well, and drank thereof himself, and his sons and his cattle? Jesus answered and said to her, Every one that drinketh of this water, will thirst again; but whosoever drinketh of the water that I shall give him, will never thirst; but the water that I give him shall become within him a well of water springing up to everlasting life. The woman saith to him, Sir, I perceive that thou art a prophet. Our fathers worshipped on this mountain; and ye say, that in Jerusalem is the place where men ought to worship. Jesus saith to her, Believe me, woman, the hour is coming, when ye shall neither on this mountain, nor in Jerusalem, worship the Father. But the hour is coming, and now is, when the true worshippers will worship the Father in spirit and in truth, for such worshippers the Father seeketh God is spirit; and they who worship him must worship in spirit and in truth.

LIX.
The Present Time.

<small>Christian. John.</small>

The disciples asked him, saying, Rabbi, eat. But he said to them, I have food to eat that ye know not of. The disciples therefore said to one another, Hath any one brought him anything to eat? Jesus saith to them, My food is to do the will of him that sent me, and to finish his work. Do ye not say, There are yet four months, and the harvest cometh? Lo! I say to you, lift up your eyes, and look on the fields, that they are white for harvest. Already is the reaper receiving wages, and gathering fruit into everlasting life, that both the sower and the reaper may rejoice together. And herein is fulfilled the true saying, One soweth, and another reapeth. I have sent you to reap that whereon ye have not laboured. Others have laboured, and ye have entered into their labour.

LX.

The Heart.

Thou wilt be asked, 'By what dost thou know God?' Say, 'By what descendeth on the heart.' For could that be proved false, souls would be utterly helpless. <small>Persian. Desátír. Jemshíd.</small>

There is in thy soul a certain knowledge, which, if thou display it to mankind, they will tremble like a branch agitated by a strong wind.

The choicest effulgence is the shining of knowledge on men of understanding.

O Jemshíd! thou seest God in his servant, and the servant in God.

Say unto mankind, 'Look not upon the self-existent with this eye; ask for another eye—the eye of the heart.

'How can he who knoweth not himself know the Lord?

'True self-knowledge is knowledge of God.'

LXI.

Obedience.

The first time that I was called to the world above, the heavens and stars said unto me, 'O Sásán! we have bound up our loins in the service of the Most High, and never withdrawn from it, because he is worthy of praise; and we are filled with astonishment how mankind can wander so wide from the commands of God!' <small>Sásán. Persian. Desátír.</small>

LXII.

Inner Light.

Walk as children of light,—for the fruit of the light is in all goodness, and righteousness, and truth,

—proving what is acceptable to the Lord; and have no fellowship with the unfruitful works of darkness, but rather reprove them. For the things done in secret by them it is a shame even to speak of. But all things, when reproved, are made manifest by the light; for whatever maketh manifest is light.

See then that ye walk circumspectly; not as unwise men, but as wise; buying up for yourselves opportunities, because the days are evil. Wherefore be not unwise, but understanding what the will of the Lord is. And be not drunk with wine, in which is dissoluteness, but be filled with the Spirit, speaking to one another in psalms, and hymns, and spiritual songs, singing and making melody in your heart to the Lord.

LXIII.

Sentiment and Principle.

Nathan came unto David, and said unto him, 'There were two men in one city; the one rich, the other poor. The rich man had exceeding many flocks and herds; but the poor man had nothing, save one little ewe-lamb, which he had bought and nourished, and it grew up together with him and his children; it did eat of his own food, and drank of his own cup, and lay in his bosom, and was as a child unto him. And then came a traveller unto the rich man, and he spared to take of his own flock to dress for the wayfarer, but he took the poor man's lamb, and dressed it for the man that was come to him.'

And David's anger was greatly kindled, and he said, 'As God liveth, the man that hath done this thing deserveth to die; and he shall restore the lamb fourfold, because he did this thing, and because he had no pity.'

And Nathan said unto David, 'Thou art the man!'

LXIV.
Practical Religion.

Let patience have its perfect work.

A double-minded man is unstable in all his ways.

Let no one when he is tempted say, 'I am tempted by God.' Each one is tempted when he is led away by his own lust. ^{Christian. James. comp.}

Every good gift and every perfect gift cometh from the Father of Lights, with whom is no change, nor shadow of turning.

Let every man be swift to hear, and slow to speak.

Be doers of the word, and not hearers only, deceiving yourselves. For if any one is a hearer of the word, and not a doer, he is like a man beholding his face in a glass, who goes away, and immediately forgets what manner of man he was. But he who looks into the perfect law of liberty, and remains there, being not a forgetful hearer, but a doer of the work, this man will be blessed in his deed. If any one thinks that he is religious, and bridles not his tongue, he deceives his own heart; this man's religion is vain. Pure religion and undefiled before the Father is this—to visit the fatherless and widows in their affliction, and to keep one's self unspotted from the world.

What doth it profit, my brethren, if any one say that he hath faith, and have not works? Can his faith save him? If a brother or sister be naked, and destitute of daily food, and one of you say to them

'Depart in peace, be warmed and be filled;' notwithstanding ye give them not the things needful for the body, what doth it profit? Faith, if it hath not works, is in itself dead.

LXV.

The Prophet.

<small>Persian. Desátír. Siámer. comp.</small>

The paths to God are more in number than the breathings of created beings.

Every prophet whom I send goeth forth to establish religion, not to root it up.

O my prophet! the sun is thy supporter.

O Siámer! I will call thee aloft and make thee my companion. Many times daily thou escapest from the body, and comest near unto me; therefore will I make thee sit in my company.

The doers of good shall reach me through this religion for ever and ever.

LXVI.

The Good Man.

<small>Heb. Ps.</small>

Happy the man
Who walketh not in the counsel of the wicked,
And standeth not in the way of sinners,
And sitteth not in the seat of scorners;
But his delight is in the law of the Lord;
And in his law both he meditate day and night.
He shall be like a tree planted by streams of water,
That yieldeth its fruit in its season,
And whose leaf doth not wither:
All that he doeth shall prosper.

Not so the wicked;
But they are like chaff, which the wind driveth
away.

LXVII.

Truthfulness.

Lo! thou desirest truth in the inmost parts;
Therefore, in the hidden parts teach me wisdom! Heb. Ps.
Create in me a pure heart, O God,
And renew a right spirit within me,
And let a free spirit sustain me.
For thou delightest not in sacrifice;
A burnt-offering thou acceptest not.
The sacrifices of God are a lowly spirit;
A lowly and contrite heart, O God, thou wilt not
despise.

LXVIII.

Asceticism.

Religious exercises performed to obtain reputation, Hindu. Mahábhárat. or for an air of sanctity, are of little worth, and come from inferior influences on the soul. Penances performed by a man attached to foolish doctrines, self-tormentings, or exercises tormenting to others, these have their source in the region of shadows. The penance of the body is to be chaste; the penance of the words is to speak always with truth and kindness; the penance of thought is to control self, to purify the soul, to be silent, and disposed to benevolence.

LXIX.

Asceticism.

The Grand Being (Buddha) applied himself to practise asceticism of the extremest nature. He ceased to eat; he held his breath, and the air, unable to pass through his nostrils, turned upward into his head, causing exceeding pain.

Then it was that the royal Mara sought occasion to tempt him. Pretending compassion, he said, 'Beware, O Grand Being! Your state is pitiable to look on; you are attenuated beyond measure, and your skin is dark and discoloured. You are practising this mortification in vain. I can see that you will not live through it.'

Him the Grand Being answered: 'Thou, O Mara! hast eight generals. Thy first is Delight in Lust; thy second is Wrath; thy third is Concupiscence; thy fourth is Desire; thy fifth is Impudence; the sixth is Arrogance; thy seventh is Doubt; and thine eighth is Ingratitude. These are thy generals, who cannot be escaped by those whose hearts are set on honour and wealth. But I know that he who can contend with them shall escape beyond all sorrow, and enjoy the most glorious happiness. Therefore I have not ceased to practise mortification, knowing that even were I to die while thus engaged, it would still be a most excellent thing.

Then Mara fled in confusion.

After he had departed, the Grand Being reflected as to why this extreme mortification failed to bring him into the path of perfect knowledge. Then in a vision came Indra, bringing a three-stringed guitar, and sounded it at a short distance from him. One string, too tightly strained, gave a harsh and unpleasant sound; the second, not strained enough, had no resonance; the third, moderately stretched, gave forth the sweetest music. Having thus done, Indra returned to his abode; and the Grand Being having pondered on the meaning of the vision, drew a lesson from the string moderately stretched, and determined for the future to practise asceticism with moderation. He resumed his practice of sitting contemplatively under a tree; in order that he might have sufficient bodily strength to effect his purpose, he again collected alms, and ate enough for his needs, and so regained his health and his beauty.

But the five Brahmins who had followed him saw this, and they were offended, and left him.

LXX.
The Middle Path.

Five Brahmins followed the Prince Gotama when he left his father's palace, into the forest of Uruwela. There they remained with him six years, hoping to see him obtain perfection through his austerities; but when, instead of increasing, his austerities ceased, and Gotama regained his health and beauty by eating sufficient food, they deserted him. When Gotama had become Buddha, he searched for these five Brahmins, and found them at Benares. To them he addressed this his first discourse:— From the first discourse delivered by Buddha. Gogerly.

'O priests! these two extremes should be avoided —an attachment to sensual gratifications, which are degrading and profitless; and severe penances, which produce sorrow, and are degrading and useless.

'O priests! avoiding both these extremes, Buddha has perceived a middle path for the attainment of mental vision, true knowledge, subdued passions, and the perception of the paths leading to the supreme good.

'O priests! this middle path has eight divisions—

namely, correct doctrines, correct perceptions of those doctrines, speaking the truth, purity of conduct, a sinless occupation, perseverance in duty, holy meditation, and mental tranquillity.'

LXXI.
Goodness.

<small>Chinese. Budh. Catena.</small>

Buddha said, 'Who is the good man? The religious man only is good. And what is goodness? First and foremost, it is the agreement of the will with the conscience (reason). Who is the great man? He who is strongest in the exercise of patience. He who patiently endures injury and maintains a blameless life—he is a man indeed! And who is a worshipful man? A man whose heart has arrived at the highest degree of enlightenment.'

LXXII.
The Undefiled.

<small>Heb. Ps. comp.</small>

Happy are the undefiled in the way,
Who walk in the law of the Lord.
Happy they that keep his testimonies;
Who with their whole heart seek him:
They also do not iniquity;
They walk in his ways.
Wherewith shall a young man make pure his way?
By observing thy laws.
I will walk at liberty, for I seek thy precepts:
I will speak of thy testimonies before kings, and
    not be ashamed.
It hath been good for me that I have been afflicted,
That I might learn thy statutes.
Had not thy law been my great delight,
I should long ago have perished in mine affliction.

Thy statutes are my songs in the house of my pilgrimage.
I have seen a limit to all perfection:
Thy commandment is exceedingly wide.
How I love thy law!
It is my meditation all the day.
Thy law is a lamp unto my feet,
And a light unto my path.
The opening of thy law enlighteneth,
Giving understanding to the simple.
Thou hast commanded righteousness in thy testimonies,
And perfect truth.
Thy law is very pure;
Therefore thy servant loveth it.
Thy righteousness is everlasting,
And thy law is Truth.

LXXIII.
The Stronghold.

They who trust in God shall be like Mount Zion: It cannot be moved, it remaineth for ever. Heb. Ps.
Mountains are around Jerusalem,
And God is round his people.
The rod of the wicked shall not rest
Upon the lot of the righteous;
Lest the righteous should put forth their hands to iniquity.

LXXIV.
Love without Repentance.

Up, my soul! a friend greets thee; and with the joyless joy is fellow-traveller. Through love is my heart made crystal-pure, an offering to the great heart. Ye pious! tell me not of love's repentance. What good is there in mourning? Falsehood says, 'Repent;' Truth says only, 'Love!' That which is away from God remaineth not: put away from thee all remembrance of it. We are troubled with traditions. O show me the way to harmony! Heavy laden, the heart must journey on; yet depart not from the path to harmony, for there is the beginning and the end: glory not till thou hast attained it. Yet, as thou journeyest, speak not of the past, but only of the future; recall not even tears of blood if thou hast shed them: sing only of the great secret! Nor think thou of fleeing the world, which wastes the soul. Abide in Love's shadow; let all else pass on.

Persian.
Seid Kassim-
ol-Euwar.
(d. 1431.)

LXXV.
Ideals.

The Father disseminated symbols in souls. He has concealed himself, but not shut up his proper fire and his wisdom. Nothing imperfect proceeds from the paternal principle. The holy powers build up the body of a holy man. To the persevering mortal the blessed immortals are swift. Every intellect apprehends Deity. You should not defile the spirit, nor give depth to the superficial. In the centre of the celestial sphere sits the holy woman; from her right hand springs the fountain of souls, from her left hand the fountain of virtues. The celestial orbs repeat above the movements of wise spirits on the earth.

Chaldæan
Oracles.

LXXVI.
Truth.

The fruit of every virtuous act which thou hast done, O good man, since thy birth, shall depart from thee to the dogs, if thou deviate from the truth. O friend to virtue! that supreme spirit, which thou believest one and the same with thyself, resides in thy bosom perpetually, and is an all-knowing inspector of thy goodness or of thy wickedness.

Hindu. Manu.

LXXVII.
Interior Life.

Amid Shastras, prayers, and penances I roamed, but found not many jewels. Daily and nightly ablutions have left the mind's impurity. Among all men he is the chief whose pride the society of the good has effaced. He who knows his own lowness is higher than all. God removes all stain from him whose mind is clear of ill. He who has rooted evil from his heart sees his whole nature renewed. Of all places, that is the best where God dwells in the mind.

Hindu. Ashtápáda.

LXXVIII.
Self-surrender.

Let not then sin reign in your mortal body, bringing you into subjection to its lusts, nor yield up your members to sin as instruments of unrighteousness; but yield up yourselves to God, as being alive from the dead, and your members to God, as instruments of righteousness.

Whomsoever ye choose to obey as a master, his bondsmen ye are, whether of sin, whose fruit is death, or of obedience, whose fruit is righteousness.

Christian. Rom. comp.

Having been delivered from the slavery of sin, and having become the servants of God, ye have holiness as the fruit, and eternal life as the end.

LXXIX.
Love.

[Persian. Faizi. 10th cent. comp.]

I am the simple heart: if you do not believe it, look into my breast through the glass of my external form.

The flame of my broken heart rises upwards: to-day a fiery surge rages in my breast.

O heart! thou dost not possess what people call gold; but yet the alchemist knows how to extract gold from thy pale cheek.

O travellers on the right road! do not leave me behind. I see far, and my eye espies the resting-place.

I walk on a path where every step is concealed. I speak in a place where every sigh is concealed.

The birds in the meadow melt away in love, and are yet silent.

For me there is no difference between the ocean of love and the shore of safety.

I am the man in whose ear melodies attain their perfection.

Desires are not to be found within my dwelling-place: when thou comest, come with a content heart.

Come, let us turn towards a pulpit of light; let us lay the foundation of a new Kaaba[1] with stones from Mount Sinai.

[1] The Holy Temple at Mecca.

The wall of the sacred Kaaba is broken, and the basis of the sanctuary is gone; let us build a faultless fortress on a new foundation.

I will burn this heart, and make a new, another heart.

In the desert love builds triumphal arches with shifting sands.

O Love! am I permitted to take the banner of thy grandeur from off the shoulder of heaven, and put it on my own?

LXXX.
Progression.

Every one that feedeth on milk is unacquainted with the word of righteousness; for he is a babe; but solid food belongs to those who are of full age, who by use have their senses exercised to discern both good and evil. Let us then, leaving the first principles of the doctrine of Christ, press on to perfection. Christian. Ep. to Heb.

LXXXI.
The Heart.

Whoever hath this world's goods, and seeth his brother having need, and shutteth up his compassion from him, how dwelleth the love of God in him? Christian. 1 John. comp.

My children, let us not love in word, nor in tongue, but in deed and in truth. And hereby we know that we are of the truth, and shall assure our hearts before him; because if our heart condemn us, God is greater than our heart, and knoweth all things. Beloved, if our heart condemn us not, we have confidence towards God. Beloved, believe not every spirit, but try the spirits, whether they are of God; because many false prophets have gone forth into the world.

LXXXII.
Love.

<small>Christian.
1 John.</small>
Beloved, let us love one another; for love is from God, and every one that loveth hath been born of God, and knoweth God: he that loveth not hath not known God; for God is love. No one hath ever seen God. If we love one another, God dwelleth in us, and his love is perfected in us. Hereby we know that we dwell in him, and he in us, because he hath given us of his Spirit. And we have known and believed the love that God hath in regard to us. God is love; and he that dwelleth in love dwelleth in God, and God in him.

There is no fear in love, but perfect love casteth out fear; because fear hath torment; and he that feareth is not made perfect in love. We love, because he first loved us. He that loveth not his brother, whom he hath seen, how can he love God, whom he hath not seen?

LXXXIII.
The Divine Father.

<small>Christian.
1 John.
comp.</small>
Behold the love the Father hath bestowed upon us, that we should be called God's children. If ye know that he is just, ye know that whoso doeth justice hath been born of him.

Now are we children of God, and it hath not yet been manifested what we shall be. We know that, when it shall be manifested, we shall be like him; because we shall see him as he is. And every one that hath this hope in him purifieth himself, even as he is pure.

My children, let no one deceive you; he that doeth righteousness is righteous.

LXXXIV.
The Essence of Religion.

All have a quarter of the heavens to which they turn them; but wherever ye be, hasten emulously after good: God will one day bring you all together. _{Arabic. Koran, s. 3, 'The Family of Imran.' comp.}

Mohammed is no more than an apostle; other apostles have already passed away before him. If he die, therefore, or be slain, will ye turn back? But he who turneth back shall not injure God at all.

God loveth those who endure with steadfastness. _{S. 2.}

And say not of those who are slain on God's path that they are dead. Nay, they are living!

Say the Christians and Jews, 'Sons are we of God, and his Beloved.' Nay, ye are but a part of the men whom he hath made.

O ye who believe, worship God! Desire union with him. Contend earnestly on his path, that you may attain to happiness. _{S. 5, 'The Table.'}

In the footsteps of the prophets caused we Jesus, the son of Mary, to follow, confirming the law which was before him.

To thee have we sent the Koran, with truth confirmatory of previous scriptures, and their safeguard. Judge therefore between them by what God hath sent, and follow not their desires by deserting the truth which hath come to thee. To every one of you have we given a rule and a beaten road.

If God had pleased, he would surely have made you all one people; but he would test you by what he hath given to each. Be emulous then in good deeds. To God shall ye all return, and he will tell you concerning the subjects of your disputes.

The Messiah, the son of Mary, is but an apostle:

other apostles have flourished before him; and his mother was a just person: they both ate food.

<small>S. 112,
'The
Unity.'</small>

Say, He is God alone!
God the eternal!

LXXXV.

Optimism.

<small>Persian.
Sheik Saad
of Homa.
(*d.* A.C.
1152.)</small>

I am an aged child; Reason is my nurse. To me belong all things that exist. Creation and destruction are my constant will. The world is but a shell; I am the kernel. Why shall I fear when dust returns to dust? I am not dust. Submit thyself to God, and live in peace. Take no merit for thy good, or guilt for thy error. Good and ill dispose of thee, not thou of them. Intellect inquires how or why. Love beholds everything in the Divine.

LXXXVI.

Pauline Sayings.

<small>Christian.
2 Cor.</small>

Who is weak and I am not weak?
Prove your own selves.
We have no power against the truth, but (only) for the truth.

<small>Phil.</small>

Finally, brethren, farewell! Be perfect, be of good comfort, be of one mind, live in peace, and the God of love and peace shall be with you.

Work out your own salvation with fear and trembling; for it is God that worketh in you.

Do all things without murmuring or doubts, that ye may be blameless and pure, children of God, without reproach, in a crooked and perverse generation.

Not that I have already attained, or have been perfected; but I press on, if I may also lay hold of that for which I was laid hold of by Christ. Brothers,

I do not reckon myself to have laid hold of it; but one thing I do—forgetting the things that are behind, and stretching forth to the things that are before, I press toward the mark for the prize of the heavenly calling of God in Christ.

Whereto we have reached in that let us walk.

Rejoice in the Lord always; again I will say it, Rejoice! Let your moderation be known to all men. Be anxious about nothing. The peace of God, which passeth all understanding, will keep your hearts and minds in Christ.

LXXXVII.
The Ideal Christ.

We henceforth know no one according to the flesh; and if we have even known Christ according to the flesh, yet now we no longer know him. Therefore, if any one is in Christ, he is a new creation; the old things have passed away; behold, all things have become new. Christian. 2 Cor.

LXXXVIII.
Courage.

But we have this treasure in earthen vessels, that the exceeding greatness of the power may be of God, and not of us; being troubled on every side, yet not distressed; perplexed, but not in despair; persecuted, but not forsaken; cast down, but not destroyed; always bearing about in the body the dying of Jesus, that the life also of Jesus may be manifested in our body. Christian. 2 Cor. comp.

For which cause we are not faint-hearted; but though our outward man is perishing, yet the inward man is renewed day by day. For our light affliction, which is but for a moment, worketh out for us, in a higher and still higher degree, an everlasting weight of glory ; while we look not at the things which are seen, but at the things which are not seen; for the things which are seen are but for a time ; but the things which are not seen endure.

LXXXIX.
Conscience.

<small>Christian.
Rom.
comp.</small>

There is no respect of persons with God. As many as have sinned without a law, will die without a law ; and as many as have sinned under a law, will be judged by a law ; for it is not the hearers of a law who are righteous before God, but the doers of a law will be accounted righteous. When the nations who have no law do by nature what is required by the Law, these are a law to themselves ; since they show that what the Law requireth is written in their hearts, their conscience bearing witness, and their thoughts in turn accusing or defending them.

For he is not a Jew who is one outwardly, nor is that circumcision which is outward in the flesh ; but he is a Jew who is one inwardly ; and circumcision is of the heart, spiritual, not literal, whose praise is not of men, but of God.

XC.
The New Heaven and New Earth.

<small>Christian.
Rev.
comp.</small>

And I saw a new heaven and a new earth ; for the first heaven and the first earth had passed away, and the sea was no more. And I saw the holy city, New Jerusalem, coming down out of heaven from God, prepared as a bride adorned for her husband. And I heard a loud voice out of the throne, saying, Behold, the tabernacle of God is with men, and he will dwell with them, and they will be his people, and God himself will be with them, their God; and God will wipe away every tear from their eyes, and death shall be no more, neither shall mourning, nor crying, nor pain be any more; for the former things are passed away.

And he that sat upon the throne said, Behold, I make all things new. To him that thirsteth I will give of the fountain of the water of life freely. He that overcometh shall inherit these things, and I will be his God, and he shall be my son.

And the twelve gates were twelve pearls; every several gate was of one pearl. And the street of the city was pure gold, like transparent glass. And I saw no temple therein; for the Lord God is its temple. And the nations will walk by the light of it; and the kings of the earth bring their glory into it; and the gates of it shall not be shut by day, for there will be no night there; and they will bring the glory and the honour of the nations into it. And there shall not enter into it anything unclean, or that worketh abomination and falsehood.

And he showed me a river of water of life, clear as crystal, coming out of the throne of God. Between the street of the city and the river, on one side and on the other, is the tree of life, bearing twelve kinds of fruit, and yielding its fruit every month; and the leaves of the tree are for the healing of the nations.

XCI.
Pious Selfishness.

A certain holy man having quitted a monastery, and a society of religious men, became a member of a college. I asked what was the difference between being a learned or a religious man, that could induce him to change his society? He replied, 'The devotee saved his own blanket out of the waves, and the learned man endeavours to rescue others from drowning.'

<small>Pers. Sádi Gul.</small>

XCII.
Pious Selfishness.

<small>Sádi Gul. 12th cent.</small>

The liberal man who eats and bestows, is better than the religious man who fasts and hoards. Whosoever hath forsaken luxury to gain the approbation of mankind, hath fallen from lawful into unlawful voluptuousness. The hermit who sitteth in retirement not for the sake of God, what shall the hopeless wretch behold in a dark mirror? A little and a little, collected together, become a great deal; the heap in the barn consists of single grains, and drop and drop form an inundation.

XCIII.
Union with God.

<small>Hindu. Bhágavat. Gita. comp.</small>

A man endued with a purified intellect, having humbled his spirit by resolution; who hath freed himself from passions and dislike; who worshippeth with discrimination, eateth with moderation, and is lowly of speech, of body and of mind; who preferreth the devotion of meditation, and who constantly placeth his confidence in dispassion; who is freed from ostentation, tyrannic strength, vainglory, lust, anger, and avarice; and who is exempt from selfishness, and in all things temperate, is formed for union with God.[1]

<small>[1] Lit. 'for being Brahm.'</small>

XCIV.
The Friend.

He my servant is dear unto me who is free from enmity, the friend of all nature, merciful, exempt from pride and selfishness, the same in pain and pleasure, patient of wrongs, contented, constantly devout, of subdued passions, and firm resolves. He also is my beloved of whom mankind are not afraid, and who of mankind is not afraid; and who is free from the influence of impatience, and the dread of harm. He my servant is dear unto me who is unexpecting, just and pure, impartial, free from distraction of mind; who is the same in friendship and hatred, in honour and dishonour; who is unsolicitous about the event of things; to whom praise and blame are as one; who is of little speech, pleased with whatever cometh to pass, and who is of a steady mind. Hindu. Bhágavat. Gítá. comp.

XCV.
The Inner Life.

Children only, and not the learned, speak of the speculative and the practical doctrines as two. Hindu. Bhágavat.

Self is the friend of self, and in like manner, self is its own enemy. A man should raise himself by himself; he should not suffer his soul to be depressed. Gítá. comp.

The holy man planteth his own seat firmly on the spot that is undefiled, neither too high nor too low, and sitteth upon the sacred grass.

A man is devout when his mind is regulated within himself, and he is exempt from lust and every inordinate desire.

He delighteth in his own soul. He becometh

acquainted with that boundless pleasure which is far more worthy of the understanding than that which ariseth from the senses; depending upon which, the mind moveth not from its principles; which having obtained, he respecteth no other acquisition so great as it.

It is to be obtained by resolution, by the man who knoweth his own mind. Wheresoever the unsteady mind roameth, he should subdue it, bring it back, and place it in his own breast. Supreme happiness attendeth the man whose mind is thus at peace. Endued with this devotion, and looking on all things alike, he beholdeth the supreme soul in all things and all things in the supreme soul.

XCVI.
Fate Inward.

Arabic.
Koran, s. 17,
'The Night-
Journey.'
comp.
[1] Lit. Bird; whose flight was believed to indicate future events.

Verily thy Lord is round about mankind. Man prayeth for evil as he prayeth for good. Every man's fate[1] hath God fastened about his neck.

Read thy book: thou needest none but thyself to make out an account against thee this day.

For his own good only shall the guided yield to guidance, and to his own loss only shall the erring err; and the heavy-laden shall not be laden with another's load. Not to any shall the gifts of thy Lord be denied.

Give full measure when you measure, and weigh with just balance.

Follow not that of which thou hast no knowledge. Of knowledge only a little to you is given. Walk not proudly in the earth.

Speak kindly.

To him who is of kin render his due, also to the poor and to the wayfarer : yet waste not.

If ye do well, to your own behoof will ye do well : and if ye do evil, against yourselves will ye do it.

Guided indeed is he whom God guideth. And he whom God guideth shall have none to mislead him. S. 18, 19.

Nothing hath been said to thee which hath not been said of old to apostles before thee.

Thou shalt see every nation kneeling : to its own book shall every nation be summoned. S. 41. comp.

XCVII.
Toleration.

For a week Abraham would scarce break his fast for fear some hungry traveller might pass needing his store. Daily he looked out upon the desert, and on a day he beheld the bent form of an aged man, his hair white as snow, tottering toward his door. 'Guest of mine eyes,' said Abraham, 'enter thou with welcome, and be pleased to share my bread and salt.' The stranger entered, and to him was given the place of honour. When the cloth was spread, and the family had gathered round the board, each uttered 'Bismillah' ('In the name of God') save one: the aged guest uttered no word. Abraham said, 'Old man, is it not right when thou dost eat thy food to repeat the name of God?' The stranger said, 'My custom is that of the fire-worshipper.' Then Abraham arose in wrath, and drove the aged Geber from his house. Even as he did so a swift-winged spirit stood before the patri- Persian Sádi. Bóstán. comp.

arch and said—'Abraham! for a hundred years the divine bounty has flowed out in sunshine and rain, in bread and life, to this man: is it for thee to withhold thy hand from him because his worship is not thine?'

THEISM.

XCVIII.
God.

Moses cried, 'Where, O Lord, shall I find thee?' God said, 'Know that when thou hast sought, thou hast already found me.' Arabic.
(D'Herb.)

One asked a Bedouin, 'How knowest thou that God exists?'

He answered, 'Does the dawn then need a torch to be seen?'

The Methnevi says, 'Supreme Being soars above thought and imagination: we are lost when we would comprehend or even suspect that which he is. How vain then to seek words worthy of that being! Let it suffice us to adore in reverent silence.'

XCIX.
The Supreme Soul.

Soul of the Soul! Neither thought nor reason comprehend thy essence, and no one knows thy attributes. Souls have no idea of thy being. The prophets themselves sink in the dust of thy road. Although intellect exists by thee, has it yet ever found the path Persian.
Attar.
Mantic.

of thy existence? O thou who art in the interior and in the exterior of the soul! thou art and thou art not that which I say. At thy court reason grows dizzy; it loses the thread that would direct it in thy way. I perceive clearly the universe in thee, and yet discover thee not in the world. All beings are marked with thy impress, but thyself hast no impress visible; thou reservest the secret of thine existence.

C.

Hymn to Brahma.

<small>Hindu.
Vishnu.
Purána.
(Wilson MS.)
comp.
8th cent.</small>

Thanks to thee, O Lord, whose form is unknown, who art the soul of all beings!
Whose purposes are not understood,
Whose appellations are not known,
Whose name cannot be spoken!
Thou art unchangeable, and nothing in this world exists independently of thee.
Thou preservest the world in the form of sunbeams:
The word True is indicative of thy form.
Thanks to thee whose heart is full of wisdom,
The visible, the invisible!

CI.

Delusion.

<small>Hindu.
Vishnu
Purána.
(Wilson MS.)
comp.</small>

It is the ignorant who take for a God that which is not so. Men will boast of consciousness, and of their right to a property. This is the delusion of those unacquainted with the great Good.

O Lord of all creatures! destroy the conceitedness of ignorant people who deem themselves learned!

Thou residest in the pure heart.

CII.

Hymn to Vishnu.

Thou, O Lord, art one with Supreme Wisdom, and with the lower wisdom! Hindu. Vishnu.
All knowledge is thy form! Puránа. Par.
Thou art hidden, indescribable, without name, inconceivable!
Thou art pure, eternal, and very great!
Thou art smaller than the smallest, and greater than the greatest.
Seeming many, thou art one.
All things are in thee:
Like the many-hued fire, lurking in endless forms, thou dost quicken the world and answer the need of each.
Unknown, all-knowing!
Thou art the true one.
Thou art the part and the whole.
Thou art above concealment.
The preserver of all regions,
Thy abode is the excellence of the earth, and to thee earth flies for refuge.
O universal pervader!
Where need of thee is, there art thou!

CIII.

The Unknowable.

Inscription on a temple of Isis at Saïd:—'I am that which has been, which is, which will be, and no one has yet lifted the veil that covers me.' Egypt.

CIV.

The Unknowable.

Rig-Veda.

Ye know not him who produced these things: Something else is within you. The chanters of hymns go about enveloped in mist, unsatisfied with idle words.

CV.

The Unsearchable.

Christian. Rom.

O the depth of the riches, and of the wisdom, and of the knowledge of God! How unsearchable are his purposes, and his ways past finding out! For who hath known the mind of the Lord? or who hath been made his counsellor? or who first gave to him, and shall receive a return? From him, and through him, and to Him are all things.

CVI.

Seeking God.

Heb.
P's.

When thou saidst, Seek ye my face,
My heart replied, Thy face, Lord, will I seek.
Though my father and mother forsake me,
Yet the Lord will receive me.
I have believed that I shall behold the goodness of the Lord
In the land of the living.
Wait then for the Lord; be of good courage,
And he shall strengthen thy heart:
Wait, then, for the Lord!

CVII.

The Unknowable.

In the thirtieth year after the ruin of the city, I was in Babylon, and lay troubled upon my bed, and my thoughts came up over my heart: for I saw the desolation of Sion, and the wealth of them that dwelt in Babylon. My spirit was sore moved, so that I began to speak words full of fear to the Most High, and said: O Lord, who bearest rule ! thou spakest at the beginning, when thou didst plant the earth, and that thyself alone, and commandedst the people ... and yet tookest thou not from them a wicked heart. Are their deeds then any better that inhabit Babylon, that they should therefore have the dominion over Sion ? ^{Apoc. 2 Esd. Ab.}

And the messenger that was sent unto me, whose name was Uriel, said, Go thy way, weigh me the weight of the fire, or measure me the blast of the wind, or call me again the day that is past.

Then answered I and said, What man is able to do that ?

And he said, I have asked thee only of the fire and wind, and of the day wherethrough thou hast passed, of things from which thou canst not be separated, and yet canst thou give me no answer of them: how then shouldst thou comprehend the way of the Highest ?

Then said I, It were better that we were not at all, than that we should live in wickedness, and suffer, and know not wherefore.

Then he said, I went into a forest and the trees took counsel, and said, Come, let us go and make war against the sea, that it may depart away before us, and that we may make us more woods. The floods of the sea in like manner took counsel, saying, Let us go up and subdue the woods, that there we may make us another country. The thought of the wood was vain, for the fire consumed it. The thought of the floods came to naught, for the sand-stopped them. If thou wert judge betwixt these two, which wouldst thou justify, or which wouldst thou condemn?

I said, Verily it is a foolish thought that they both have devised, for the ground is given to the wood, and the sea hath his place to bear his floods.

Then answered he me, Thou hast given a right judgment, but why judgest thou not thyself also? As the ground is given to the wood, and the sea to his floods, even so they that dwell upon the earth may understand nothing but that which is upon the earth; and he alone that dwelleth above the heavens can understand things above the height of the heavens.

Then answered I and said, I beseech thee, O Lord, let me have understanding : for it was not my mind to be curious of high things, but of such as pass by us daily.

Then answered he me and said, The more thou searchest, the more shalt thou wonder.

CVIII.

Hindu.
(Tamil.)
Pattanathu.
10th cent.

In my heart I place the feet,
The golden feet of God.
If he be mine, what can I need?
My God is everywhere :
Within, beyond man's highest word,
My God existeth still :
In sacred books, in darkest night,
In deepest, bluest sky,
In those who know the truth, and in
The faithful few on earth.

CIX.

The Unrecognised.

The height and depth of all the world is centred in thee, Lord: I know not what thou art; thou art what thou alone canst be. Persian.
Firdausi.

Once upon a time the fishes of a certain river took counsel together, and said, 'They tell us that our life and being is from the water, but we have never seen water, and know not what it is.' Then some among them wiser than the rest said, 'We have heard that there dwelleth in the sea a very wise and learned fish who knoweth all things; let us journey to him, and ask him to show us water, or explain unto us what it is.' So several of their number set out upon their travels, and at last came to the sea wherein this sage fish resided. On hearing their request he answered them thus: Sufi.
Parable.
(Palmer.)

'O ye who seek to solve the knot!
Ye live in God, yet know him not.
Ye sit upon the river's brink,
Yet crave in vain a drop to drink.
Ye dwell beside a countless store,
Yet perish hungry at the door.'

CX.

Pantheism.

Foolish are they who are perpetually inquiring where the Deity resides. God dwells in all things in his fulness. Kine are of divers colours, but all milk is alike; altar-flowers are of many species, but all worship is one; systems of faith are different, but God is one. Hindu.
Vemana.
12th cent.

If a man knows not himself, how should he know the Deity?

CXI.

The Nearest.

God best knoweth the impious.

Arabic. Koran. comp. S. 6, 'Cattle.'
With him are the keys of the secret things; none knoweth them but he: he knoweth whatever is on the land and in the sea; and no leaf falleth but he knoweth it: neither is there a grain in the darknesses of the earth, nor a green thing or sere, but it is noted in his decree.

S. 50, 'Kaf.'
We created man: and we know what his soul whispereth to him, and we are closer to him than his neck-vein.

S. 20.
Thou needest not raise thy voice: he knoweth the secret whisper, and the yet more hidden.

S. 6.
No vision taketh in him, but he taketh in all vision.

CXII.

The Living Deity.

Persian. Khéyam. 11th cent.
O friend! to what good occupy thyself with the mystery of Being? Why trouble thy heart thus, and thy soul with soaring speculations? Live happily, pass thy time with joy; in the end thy advice will not be asked about the making of that which is.

Behold the morning! Rise up, O youth, and quickly fill thyself with this rosy wine sparkling in the crystal cup of the dawn! The time will come when thou shalt seek long, but never recover, this moment of existence which hath surprised us in this illusive world.

The morning has already thrown off the veil of darkness. Wherefore thy sadness? Rise up! Let us breathe again the morning air before having to long for it; for, alas! long enough will the morning breathe when we breathe not.

They say that on the last day there will be settlements, and that the dear God will give himself up to wrath. But from goodness itself only good can emanate. Fear not; the end shall be full of sweetness.

Diversity of worship has divided the human race into seventy-two nations. From among all their dogmas I have selected one,—Divine Love.

O thou who art master of the most hidden secrets! give me faith if thou wouldst have me betake myself to prayer.

CXIII.
God as the Dawn.

We meditate on the adorable light of the divine Parent. May he direct our minds! Sáma Veda.
B.C. 800.
Ab.

Lord, thou art every day manifested with the rays of morning, imparting life to the torpid and giving form to the shapeless masses of beings.

Heaven and earth take refuge with thee as a child with its mother.

I celebrate the thought of the beneficent Father and the sovereign Mother, from whom all creatures have proceeded, an offspring sharing their immortality. Rig-Veda.
Par.

CXIV.
The Spirit of the Age.

The Supreme One said:—I am made evident by my own power; and as often as there is a decline of virtue, and an insurrection of vice and injustice in the world, I make myself evident; and thus I appear from age to age, for the preservation of the just, the Hindu.
Bhágavat.
Gíta.

destruction of the wicked, and the establishment of virtue.

CXV.
Divine Love.

Rig-Veda.

When will you take us as a dear father takes his son by both hands, O ye gods, for whom the sacred grass has been trimmed?

On what errand of yours are you going in heaven, not on earth?

If you were mortals and your worshipper an immortal, then never should your praiser be without welcome, as the deer to the pasture, nor should he go on the path of death.

CXVI.
The Divine Mother.

Heb.
Isa.

But Zion saith, God hath forsaken me.

And the Lord hath forgotten me.

Can a women forget her sucking-child,

So as not to have compassion on the son of her womb?

Yea, she may forget; yet will I not forget thee.

CXVII.
The Best.

Zendavesta.
Spenta
M. Gâtha.

God appears in the best thought, the truth of speech, and the sincerity of action, giving through his pure Spirit health, prosperity, devotion, and eternity to this universe. He is the Father of all truth.

CXVIII.
The Veil of God.

God hath made all atoms in space mirrors, and fronteth each one with his perfect face.

Wouldst know where I found the Supreme? One step beyond myself. <small>Persian Aphorisms.</small>

Behind the veil of self shines unseen the beauty of the Loved One.

CXIX.

Ignorant Certainty.

The souls are seething, the hearts beat high to know what will there be looked upon as good and true. O God! before thy knowledge our own doth vanish. <small>Persian. Omar. Khèyam. 11th cent.</small>

Seest thou two or three imbeciles who hold the world between their two hands, and who, in their candid ignorance, believe themselves the wisest of the universe? Be not disturbed that, in their extreme contentment, they regard all as heretics who are not simpletons.

Some people there are who by presumption suffer the fall of pride, others are carried away in the search for the luxuries of a celestial palace : when the riddles of existence are solved they will appear to have equally fallen far, far, far from thee, O God!

No one has ever penetrated the secret of the great principle; no one has ever taken a step beyond himself. I observe, and I have seen only inadequacy, since a pupil looking up to his master—inadequacy in all of woman born.

O thou, in the search for whom a world is in dizziness and in distress! the saintly mendicant and the rich man are equally far from the means of reaching thee: thy name blends with the existence of all, but all are deaf; thou art present under the eyes of all, but all are blind.

O devotee! it is by humility, and not by prayers,

that thy spiritual affairs will take a favourable turn; for what is a prayer without sincerity and without humility?

The flame of my love burns to its height. The beauty of that which has captivated me is perfect. My heart speaks, my tongue is dumb. O God,—how strange! I am devoured with thirst, and before me springs a fountain fresh and clear!

CXX.
The Ineffable.

Persian.
Anwarí.
Palinodia.
comp.

All nations and languages repeat the name of God, even infancy lisps it,—Allah, Taugarí, Yezdán, Elohim. Yet cannot his praise be duly expressed by mortal till the dumb man shall be eloquent, and stocks and stones find a voice; till the silent universe rejoices in language.

The sun sinks down in the ocean, and azure-hued vapours arise; it is Nature's incense of devotion perfuming the heavens.

Ride thou on for eternity through the empyrean, mounted on thy ideal, thou shalt not stride beyond his threshold!

Soar thou beyond all limit to the roof of the universe, thou shalt behold one tile of his dwelling,— one tile, no more.

CXXI.
God.

Sabœan
Litany,
attributed to
Enoch.
Preserved by
El Wardi.
comp.

Thou art the eternal One, in whom all order is centred; Lord of all things visible and invisible; Prince of mankind; Protector of the universe!

From thee doth intellect descend upon the rulers of the earth!

Thou dost embrace all things!
Thou art the Infinite and Incomprehensible, who standest alone, ruler of the eternal fountains of light!
The ordainer of all good things!
Who givest inspiration and guidance unto all!
From thee cometh light!
Merciful One, exalted above all defects, descend into our intellects, and purge us of every ill!
Turn our sorrow into joy!
To thee do we cling!
From thee all things seek their light!
Thou art the hope of the worlds!
Thou art the helper of mankind, one and all!

CXXII.
God.

Which is the great name of God?

Communicate to me his least name and I will return to thee his greatest. Every day he is in action: one day of his is equal to a thousand years of man's. O thou whose light manifests itself in the vesture of the world! thy names are manifested in the nature of man; thy knowledge shows itself in the science of thy prophets; thy bounty is manifested in the bounty of great hearts. Recognise the mark of God in every place, and never place the foot without its own limit. The world is the image of God.

Sufi Oracles.

CXXIII.
God in All.

In thee, in me, in every other, the Lord of Life resides: in vain art thou angry with me, not bearing my approach: this is perfectly true, all must be

Hindu. Móhadmudguta.

esteemed equal: be not, therefore, proud of thy estate, however magnificent.

CXXIV.

God.

<small>Hindu. Rig-Veda. B.C. 1500.</small>

On that effulgent power which is God himself, and is called the Light of the radiant Sun, do I meditate; governed by the mysterious light which resides in me for the purposes of thought.

I myself am an irradiated manifestation of the Supreme Being.

There is only one Deity, the great soul. He is called the Sun, for he is the soul of all beings.

That which is One, the wise call it in divers manners. Wise poets make the beautiful-winged, though he is One, manifold by words.

CXXV.

Mind in Nature.

<small>Hindu. Isavasgam. (An Upanishad from Yagur Veda.)</small>

There is one supreme Mind which transcends all other intelligences. Moving, it cannot be shaken; distant, yet near; it pervades the system of worlds, and is yet infinitely beyond it.

The man who considers all beings as existing even in the Supreme Spirit, and the Supreme Spirit as pervading all beings, henceforth views no creature with contempt.

In him who knows that all spiritual beings are the same in essence with the Supreme, what room is there for delusion of mind or for sorrow?

They who are ignorantly devoted to the mere ceremonies of religion are fallen into thick darkness, but they have a thicker gloom who are solely attached to fruitless speculation.

That diviner Sun, hid in the golden vase of visible light, even the same in essence am I. As my form sinks to ashes, may this flame pass by adoration to beatitude!

CXXVI.

Divine Love.

And all the publicans and the sinners were drawing near to Jesus to hear him. And the Pharisees and the scribes murmured, saying, This man receiveth sinners, and eateth with them. And he spoke to them this parable, saying: Christian.
Luke.

A certain man had two sons, and the younger of them said to his father, Father, give me the portion of the property that falleth to me. And he divided to them his living. And not many days after, the younger son gathered all together, and went abroad into a far country; and there wasted his substance in riotous living. And when he had spent all, there arose a great famine in that country; and he began to be in want. And he went and joined himself to one of the citizens of that country; and he sent him into his fields to feed swine. And he longed to fill himself with the husks that the swine ate; and no one gave to him. And when he came to himself, he said, How many hired servants of my father's have bread enough and to spare, and I perish here with hunger! I will arise and go to my father, and will say to him, Father, I have sinned against heaven and before thee; I am no longer worthy to be called thy son; make me as one of thy hired servants.

And he arose, and went to his father. But when he was yet a great way off, his father saw him, and was moved with compassion, and ran and fell on his neck, and kissed him. And the son said to him, Father, I have sinned against heaven, and before thee; I am no longer worthy to be called thy son. But the father said to his servants, Bring out the best robe, and put it on him, and put a ring on his hand, and sandals on his feet. And bring the fatted calf; kill it, and let us eat and make merry. For this my son was dead, and is alive again; he was lost, and is found. And they began to make merry.

Now his elder son was in the field; and as he came and drew near to the house, he heard music and dancing. And calling one of the servants, he inquired what these things meant. And he said to him, Thy brother is come; and thy father hath killed the fatted calf, because he hath received him safe and sound. But he was angry, and would not go in; and his father came out, and entreated him. And he answering said to his father, Lo! for so many years have I served thee, and never transgressed thy command; and yet to me thou never gavest a kid, that I might make merry with my friends. But as soon as this thy son came, who devoured thy living with harlots, thou didst kill for him the fatted calf. And he said to him, Son, thou art ever with me, and all that I have is thine. It was meet that we should make merry and be glad; for this thy brother was dead and is alive again; he was lost, and is found.

CXXVII.

Ignorant Devotion.

Now while Paul was waiting at Athens, his spirit was stirred within him when he saw the city full of idols. Therefore he reasoned in the synagogue with the Jews and the devout [Greeks], and in the market daily with those that met him. And some of the Epicurean and Stoic philosophers also conversed with him. And some said, What doth this babbler mean to say? and others, He seemeth to be a setter forth of foreign gods. And they took him and brought him to Mars' hill, saying, May we know what this new doctrine is, of which thou speakest? For thou bringest certain strange things to our ears. We would know therefore what these things mean. Now all the Athenians, and the strangers residing among them, spent their leisure for nothing else but to tell or to hear something new. Then Paul stood in their midst on Mars' hill, and said, Men of Athens, in all things I perceive that ye are very devout. While passing along and observing your objects of worship, I found also an altar with this inscription, 'To an unknown God.' What therefore ye, without knowledge of it, worship, that do I make known to you. The God of heaven and earth dwelleth not in temples made with hands; nor doth he receive service at the hands of men, as though he needed anything, since it is he that giveth to all life and breath and all things. And he made of one blood every nation of men to dwell on all the face of the earth, having fixed appointed times, and the bounds of their habitation; that they should seek God, if haply they might feel after him, and find him, though he is not far from every one of us. For in him we live, and move, and have our being; as also some of your own poets have said: 'We are his children.'

<small>Christian. Acts.</small>

CXXVIII.
Light.

<small>1 John. comp.</small> This is the message which we have heard from him, and announce to you, that God is light, and in him is no darkness at all. If we say that we have fellowship with him and walk in darkness, we speak not and do not the truth; but if we walk in the light, as he is in the light, we have fellowship one with another. He that saith he is in the light, and hateth his brother, is in the darkness until now. He that loveth his brother abideth in the light.

CXXIX.
Divine Love.

<small>Persian. Khèyam.</small> O thou who burnest in heart for those who burn in hell, how long wilt thou then be crying, 'Have compassion on them, God!' Who art thou to teach and he to learn?

We (heretics) seek not to torment men in their dreams; we do not cause them to burthen the midnight with cries—'O my God! O my God!'

Has thy empire, O Lord, gained in splendour by my obedience? and my sins, have they diminished thy immensity? And if because I have done ill thou shouldst do ill to me, what were the difference between thee and me?

CXXX.
Pantheism.

If I myself upon a looser creed
Have loosely strung the jewel of good deed,
Let this one thing for my atonement plead
That Two for One I never did misread.

CXXXI.

Theism.

A religious act proceeding from selfish views in this world, as a sacrifice for rain, or in the next, as an oblation in hope of future reward, is concrete and interested; but an act performed with a knowledge of God, and without self-love, is abstract and disinterested.

<small>Hindu. Code of Manu. (Brighu.)</small>

Equally perceiving the supreme mind in all beings, and all things in the supreme mind, the true worshipper sacrifices his own spirit by fixing it on the Spirit of God, and approaches the nature of the One, who shines by his own effulgence.

Let every Brahmin with fixed attention consider all nature, visible and invisible, as existing in the divine mind; for when he contemplates the boundless universe existing in the divine mind, he cannot give his heart to iniquity.

The divine mind alone is the whole assemblage of gods: all worlds are seated therein: and the divine mind no doubt produces the connected series of acts performed by embodied beings.

He may contemplate earth, air, fire, water, the subtile ether, in his own body and organs; in his heart the Star; in his motion, Vishnu; in his vigour, Hara; in his speech, Agni; in excretion, Mitra; in procreation, Brahma: but he must consider the supreme omnipresent Reason as sovereign of them all.

Him some adore as transcendently present in elementary fire; others in Manu, the lord of creatures; some as more distinctly present in Indra, the sun; others in pure air; others as the most high eternal Thought.

The man who perceives in his own mind the Supreme Mind present in all creatures, acquires equanimity toward them all, and shall be absorbed at last in the highest essence, even the eternal One himself.

—Here ended the sacred instructor; and every twice-born man who by attentive study of these laws shall become habitually virtuous, will attain the beatitude which he seeks.

CXXXII.

Nature a Mirror of God.

Persian.
(Palmer.)

The varied pictures I have drawn on space,
Behold what fair and goodly sights they seem;
One glimpse I gave them of my glorious face,
And lo! 'tis now the universal theme.

CXXXIII.

The Divine Unity.

Persian.
Sufi.
(Palmer.)

Look not askance; the Holy One will ever be the same,
The God of all, though oft invoked by many a different name.

CXXXIV.

Inner Light.

Persian.
Sufi.
(Palmer.)

All the earth I'd wandered over, seeking still the beacon light,
Never tarried in the daytime, never sought repose at night;
Till I heard a reverend preacher all the mystery declare,
Then I looked within my bosom, and 'twas shining brightly there.

CXXXV.

God.

O thou the cool shade at the door of weariness!
   Even the wicked are panting for thee.
A drop of the rain of thy compassion
   Cleanses me from all my blackness.
Do thou accept me with the children,
   O thou my God, and the God of all!
Show us the road that we may reach thy door.
   O thou towards whom is the way of all men!
Our days thou increasest beyond measure;
   Thy mercy purifies us from all sins:
Khusraü with thee seeks refuge,
   O thou my shade and the shade of all!

<small>Persian. Amír Khusraü. 13th cent. Miss Manning. MS.</small>

CXXXVI.

Gods.

The gods that have not made the heavens and the earth shall perish from the earth and from under these heavens.

<small>Heb. Jer.</small>

CXXXVII.

Supreme Reason (called Heaven).

I know that one must watch incessantly over himself; that Heaven has an intelligence which nothing escapes, and that its decrees are without appeal. I know that it regards all things; that it enters into all; that it is present incessantly to all.

Heaven penetrates to the depth of all hearts, as daybreak illumines the darkest room. We should strive to reflect its light, as two instruments in full accord respond to one another.

<small>China. She-King.</small>

CXXXVIII.

Ecstasy.

<small>Persian.
Abulfazl.
A.D. 1595.</small>

O Lord, whose secrets are for ever veiled,
And whose perfection knows not a beginning!
End and beginning both are lost in thee;
No trace of them is found in thy eternal realm.
My words are lame; my tongue, a stony tract;
Slow wings my foot, and wide is the expanse.
Confused are my thoughts; but this is thy best praise—
In ecstasy alone I see thee face to face!

CXXXIX.

The Sun.

<small>Heb.
Apoc.
Ecclesiasticus.
comp.</small>

The pride of the height, the clear firmament, the beauty of heaven, with his glorious show: the sun when it appeareth, declaring at his rising, a marvellous instrument, the work of the Most High.

The sun that giveth light looketh upon all things, and the work thereof is full of the glory of God.

He seeketh out the deep and the heart.

He revealeth the steps of hidden things.

He hath garnished the excellent works of his wisdom, and he is from everlasting to everlasting.

All these things live and remain for ever for all uses, and they are all obedient.

All things correspond one to another: and he hath made nothing imperfect.

One thing establisheth the good of another, and who shall be satisfied in beholding his glory?

CXL.

God the Blinding Glory.

O thou who existest from eternity, and abidest for ever ! sight cannot bear thy light, praise cannot express thy perfection.

Persian.
Faizí.
10th cent.
Blochmann.
Ab.

Thy light melts the understanding, and thy glory baffles wisdom : to think of thee destroys reason ; thy essence confounds thought.

Science is like blinding desert sand on the road to thy perfection ; the town of literature is a mere hamlet compared with the world of thy knowledge.

My foot has no power to travel on this path which misleads sages : I have no power to bear the odour of this wine ; it confounds my knowledge.

Man's so-called foresight and guiding reason wander about bewildered in the streets of the city of thy glory.

Human knowledge and thought combined can only spell the first letter of the alphabet of thy love.

CXLI.

Supreme Beauty.

In eternity without beginning, a ray of thy beauty began to gleam, when Love sprang into being, and cast flames over all nature.

Persian.
Háfiz.
14th cent.

On that day thy cheek sparkled even under thy veil, and all this beautiful imagery appeared on the mirror of our fancies.

Rise, my soul ! that I may pour thee forth on the pencil of that Supreme Artist, who comprised in a turn of his compass all this wonderful scenery.

From the moment that I heard the divine sentence,

'I have breathed into man a portion of my Spirit,' I was assured that we were his and he ours.

Where are the glad tidings of union with thee, that I may abandon all desire of life? I am a bird of holiness, and would fain escape from the net of this world.

Shed, O Lord, from the cloud of heavenly guidance one cheering flower, before the moment when I must rise up like a particle of dry dust!

The sum of our transactions in this universe is nothing; bring on the wine of devotion, for the possessions of this world vanish.

The true object of heart and soul is the glory of union with our beloved: that object really exists, but without it heart and soul would have no existence.

Oh! the bliss of that day when I shall depart from this desolate mansion, shall seek rest for my soul, and shall follow the traces of my beloved:

Dancing with love of his beauty, like a mote in a sunbeam, till I reach the spring and fountain of delight, whence yon sun derives all his lustre!

CXLII.

The Most Just.

Persian.
Desátír.
Sásán.
comp.

Every soul that maketh choice of justice shall attain unto God.

The Most Just raised me aloft, and I beheld the place of bodies like a drop in the ocean of souls; and I saw the place of souls like a drop in the place of intelligences, and the place of intelligences like a drop in the ocean of the Divine Essence.

CXLIII.
The Sustainer.

O God, the portion of my inheritance and of my cup !
Thou sustainest my lot. _{Heb. Ps.}
The lines have fallen for me in pleasant places;
Truly I have a goodly inheritance.
I will bless the Lord who giveth me counsel;
By night also my reins instruct me.
I place the Most High before me continually;
Because he is at my right hand I shall not be moved.
Therefore my heart rejoiceth, and my glory exulteth;
My flesh also dwelleth in security.
For thou wilt not abandon my soul to the lowermost world,
Nor suffer thy devoted one to see corruption.
Thou wilt show me the path of life :
In thy presence is fulness of joy;
At thy right hand are pleasures for evermore.

CXLIV.
Divine Goodness.

The Lord is my shepherd, I shall not want.
He maketh me to lie down in green pastures; _{Heb. Ps.}
He leadeth me beside still waters.
He refresheth my soul; he leadeth me
In straight paths, for his name's sake.
Even though I should walk through a valley of the shadow of death,
I would fear no evil; for thou wouldst be with me;
Thy staff and thy crook would comfort me.

Thou spreadest before me a table in the sight of mine
    enemies :
Thou anointest my head with oil ;
My cup overfloweth.
Surely goodness and loving-kindness will follow me
    all the days of my life ;
And I shall dwell in the house of the Lord for ever.

CXLV.
Fountain of Joy.

<small>Heb.
Ps.</small>

O God! thy loving-kindness is in the heavens ;
Thy faithfulness reacheth to the clouds.
Thy righteousness is as the lofty mountains ;
Thy judgments are a great deep :
Man and beast thou preservest.
How precious is thy loving-kindness, O God!
Therefore the children of men take refuge in the
    shadow of thy wings ;
They are satisfied with the plenteousness of thy house ;
And of the river of thy pleasures thou givest them to
    drink.
For with thee is the fountain of life :
In thy light we see light.

CXLVI.
Repose on Rectitude.

<small>Heb.
Ps.</small>

If God build not the house,
In vain do they labour who build it ;
If God keep not the city,
In vain doth he watch who keepeth it.
Vain is it for you to rise up early,
To go late to rest,

To eat the bread of sorrows :
He giveth to his beloved in their sleep.

CXLVII.
The Near God.

O God ! thou hast searched me and known me :
Thou knowest my down-sitting and mine up rising ; _{Heb. Ps.}
Thou understandest my thoughts from afar.
Thou surroundest my path and my bed,
And art acquainted with all my ways.
When there is not a word on my tongue,
Lo, thou knowest perfectly my thought.
Thou enclosest me behind and before,
And layest thy hand upon me.
Thy knowledge is too wonderful for me ;
It is high, I cannot attain unto it.
Whither can I go from thy spirit ?
Or whither can I flee from thy presence ?
If I should ascend the heavens, thou art there ;
And if I should make my bed in the lower world, lo!
    thou art there.
Should I take the wings of the morning,
Should I dwell in the farthest part of the sea,—
Even there thy hand would lead me,
And thy right hand would hold me.
Should I say, Surely darkness will conceal me,—
Even the night would be light about me.
Even darkness maketh nothing dark to thee ;
But the night enlighteneth as the day :
Darkness is to thee as light.
I will give thanks to thee, for I am fearfully, wonder-
    fully made :
How precious, therefore, are my thoughts of thee, O God !

How great is the sum of them!
When I awake, I am still with thee.

CXLVIII.
The Refuge.

Heb.
Ps.

When my spirit fainteth within me,
Then thou knowest my path.
I look on my right hand and see,
But there is no one that knoweth me:
Refuge faileth me;
No one careth for my soul.
I cry unto thee, O God!
I say, Thou art my refuge,
My portion in the land of the living.

CXLIX.
The Near God.

Persian.
Jeláleddín
Rúmí.

Rabia, footsore and weary, followed the pilgrims to Mecca, but when she saw them praying around the holy temple Kaaba, she beat her breast and cried, 'O heart! weak follower of the weak! Thou hast traversed land and sea to seek in this far-off place the God who had long ago come to thee!'

CL.
The Unchangeable.

Koran, s. 6,
'Cattle.'
comp.

When the night overshadowed Abraham, he beheld a star. 'This,' said he, 'is my Lord;' but when it set, he said, 'I love not gods which set.'

And when he beheld the moon uprising, 'This,' said he, 'is my Lord;' but when it set, he said, 'Surely if my Lord guide me not, I shall surely be of those who go astray.'

And when he beheld the sun uprise, he said, 'This is my Lord; this is the greatest.' But the sun too went down.

And Abraham said, 'O my people! I turn my face to the Father of the heavens and the earth!'

CLI.
The Light.

In the name of God, the Compassionate, the Merciful. _{Koran, s. 57, 'Iron.' comp.}

All that is in the heavens and the earth praiseth God, and he is the mighty, the wise:

He is the first and the last; the seen and the hidden; and he knoweth all things!

He will bestow on you light to walk in.

God is the light of the heavens and of the earth. His light is like a niche in which is a lamp—the lamp encased in glass—the glass as it were a glistening star. From a blessed tree is it lighted—the olive neither of the East nor of the West, whose oil would well-nigh shine out even though fire touched it not. It is light upon light. _{S. 24, 'Light.'}

Hast thou not seen how all in the heavens and in the earth uttereth the praise of God?—the very birds as they spread their wings? Every creature knoweth its prayer and its praise!

The East and the West are God's: therefore whichever way ye turn, there is the face of God. _{S. 2.}

He will guide to himself him who turneth to him, those who believe, and whose hearts rest securely on the thought of God. What! shall not men's hearts repose in the thought of God? They who believe and do the things that be right, blessedness awaiteth them. _{S. 13, 'Thunder.'}

CLII.
The Supreme Study.

<small>Persian.
Dábistan.</small> O thou whose name is the beginning of the book of the child at school! thy remembrance is to the eldest sage the torch of his mighty meditation.

Without thee the tongue fails the barbarians though they know the language of Arabia.

Having the heart full of thy remembrance, the novice as well as the adept in contemplation becomes a king of beatitude, and attains the throne of gladness.

Whatever road I take joins the highway that leads to thee.

The desire to know thy being is the life of those who meditate.

The world is a school, the philosopher a teacher of thy truth; and he who has found that there is nothing but thee has attained the final knowledge.

CLIII.
The Rejected Stone.

<small>Heb.
Ps
comp.</small>
God reigneth; let the earth be glad;
Let the multitude of lands beyond the sea rejoice.
Clouds and darkness are round about him;
Righteousness and justice are the foundation of
    his throne.
His lightnings enlighten the world;
The heavens declare his righteousness.
Light is sown for the righteous,
And joy for the upright in heart.
The stone which the builders refused
Is become the chief corner-stone.
This hath been from the Most High:

It is wonderful in our eyes.
This is the day which God hath made;
We will exult and rejoice in it.

CLIV.
Morning.
Behold the dawn approaching from the East! Evil shadows depart; health comes with her glow. The purple-tinted radiance streams into every dwelling, and the sacred mother gently unseals the eyelids of her sleeping children. Over land and sea she passes swiftly, restoring all living things to consciousness. The bird rises from its nest, and man passes to his task. Now let all pure flames ascend; let the dawn kindle sacred fires in every dwelling. The altar-fire is born of the rubbed stick, and man begets the immortals.

<sub>Hindu.
Rig-Veda.
(Par.)</sub>

CLV.
The Fire-Worshipper.
Think not that our fathers were adorers of fire; for that element was only an exalted object on the lustre of which they fixed their eyes: they humbled themselves before God; and if thy understanding be ever so little exerted, thou must acknowledge thy dependence on the being supremely pure.

<sub>Persian.
Firdausi.
(b. A.C. 916.)</sub>

CLVI.
The Soul's Thirst.
O God, thou art my God; early will I seek thee:
My soul thirsteth for thee,
My flesh longeth for thee,
In a land dry and weary, where is no water.
As with rich dainties my soul is satisfied,

<sub>Heb.
Ps.</sub>

While with joyful lips my mouth praiseth thee,
When I call thee to mind on my bed,
When in the watches of the night I meditate on thee.
Because thou hast been my help,
Therefore in the shadow of thy wings I will rejoice.

CLVII.

Ascription.

<small>Egyptian.
Hermes Trismegistus.</small>
Who can bless thee, or give thanks for thee or to thee? When shall I praise thee, O Father; for it is neither possible to comprehend thy hour nor thy time? Wherefore shall I praise thee,—as being something of myself, or having anything of mine own, or rather as being another's? Thou art what I am, thou art what I do, thou art what I say. Thou art all things, and there is nothing which thou art not. Thou art thou, all that is made, and all that is not made — the mind that understandeth; the Father that maketh; the good that worketh; the good that doeth all things. Of matter, the most subtile and slender part is air; of the air, the soul; of the soul, the mind; of the mind, God. By me the truth sings praise to the truth, the good praiseth the good. O All! receive a reasonable homage from all things. Thou art God; thy man crieth these things unto thee, by the fire, by the air, by the earth, by the water, by the spirit, by all beings.

CLVIII.

Waiting.

<small>Heb.
Ps.
comp.</small>
I wait for God, my soul waiteth;
And in his word I hope.
My soul watcheth for the Lord,

More than they that watch for the morning—
Than they that watch for the morning.
Lord my heart is not haughty,
Nor are mine eyes lofty;
Neither do I employ myself in great things,
Or in things too wonderful for me.
Truly I have composed and quieted my spirit,
As a weaned child towards its mother:
As a weaned child is my spirit within me.

CLIX.

God.

Thou pure and perfect God! thine is the world's beauty and dominion. Thy beauty transcends the sun, and thy completeness the universe of forms. I call thee not high nor low, recognising no limit to thy being: thou art highest, thou art deepest: all beings' essence. How can I know thee who art beyond the vision of reason? So concealed, thou art the more revealed to the eye of the heart. The world were an empty tablet but that thou hast written thereon thy eternal thought. Of thy divine poem the first word is Reason, and the last is Man. And whoso shall trace the words from first to last shall find them the unbroken series of thy favours, the varied names of thy love. Antagonistic natures blend in sweet accord: in fine ether, behold the solid sphere suspended; fire and water work together for that great harmony from which the good sprang into being. Such harmony is the sign of the best. In mines gleam the gems, and the earth hath its green vesture; but deep within me shall that harmony be found singing praises, with the revolving spheres, to the fairest and best.

Persian.
Jámí.
15th cent.

WORSHIP.

CLX.
The Rosary.

Persian.

He needs no other rosary whose thread of life is strung with beads of love and thought.

CLXI.
Worship of Wisdom.

Hindu.
Bhágavat.
Gítá.
comp.

This world is not for him who doth not worship. Know that the worship of spiritual wisdom is far better than the worship with offerings of things. In wisdom is to be found every work without exception.

Although thou wert the greatest of offenders, thou shalt be able to cross the gulf of sin with the bark of wisdom.

There is not anything in this world to be compared with wisdom for purity.

Wisdom is all hands and feet, and all ear; it sitteth in the midst of the world, possessing the vast whole. It is the reflected light of every faculty. It standeth at a distance and is yet present. It is that which now destroyeth, now produceth. It is the light of lights. It presideth in every breast.

He who is perfected by practice, in due time findeth it in his own soul.

CLXII.

Worship.

Keep silence well! Mean praise is not valued among the munificent.

Gotama made a new song for the old god,

Hindu.
Rig-Veda
Sanhita,
comp.

To the ancient guide of man, disappointing no desires, a friend to friends,—to him we address this song.

This earth belongs to Varuna (the king of heaven) and the wide sky: he is also contained in this drop of water.

He who should flee far beyond the sky, even he would not be rid of Varuna.

Thou art true; thou searchest out sin; thou art without blemish.

Let us be sinless before Varuna, who is gracious even to him who has committed sin.

No real foe of God is known in heaven nor on earth.

The storm-gods (Maruts) are thy allies.

His path is easy and without thorns who does what is right.

Many snares pass by him who is with God (Indra) in his work.

To the giver thou givest.

The shelter which thou affordest to him who praises thee, grant them threefold to the man that gives.

Formerly, and now, and also in the future, let us give praise to thee, O Varuna! for in thee, O unconquerable! are all laws grounded, immovable as a rock!

CLXIII.
The Intelligible.

<small>Oracles by the Theurgists. comp.</small>

Our voluntary sorrows germinate in us as the growth of the particular life we lead.

On beholding yourself, fear.

Believe yourself to be above body, and you are.

Those robust souls perceive truth through themselves, and are of a more inventive nature; such a soul being saved through its own strength.

We should fly from the multitude of men going along in a herd.

The powers build up the body of a holy man.

Not knowing that every god is good, ye are faithlessly vigilant. Fiery hope should nourish you in the angelic region.

To the persevering mortal the blessed immortals are swift.

All things are governed and subsist in faith, truth, and love.

The oracle says, Divinity is never so much turned away from man, and never so much sends him in novel paths, as when we make an ascent to the most divine of speculations or works, in a confused and disordered manner (as it were), with unhallowed lips or unbathed feet. For of those who are thus negligent, the progressions are imperfect, the impulses are vain and the paths are blind.

The orders prior to heaven possess mystic silence. Every intellect apprehends deity.

The intelligible is food to that which understands. You will not apprehend it by an intellectual energy as when understanding some particular thing. It is not proper to understand that intelligible with vehemence, but with the extended flame of an extended intellect; a flame which measures all things, except that intelligible. But it is requisite to understand this. For if you incline your mind, you will understand it, though not vehemently. It becomes you, therefore, bringing with you the pure convertible eye of your soul, to extend the pure intellect to the intelligible, that you may learn its nature because it has a subsistence above intellect.

CLXIV.

Observances.

Without purity of mind, to what end is the worship of God? <small>Hindu. Vémana. 17th cent.</small>

Why say, 'I will go to Benares?' why long for the sacred wells? How shall the true Benares be attained by the evil-doer?

Though we roam the wilds, sanctity is not in them; nor is it in the sky; nor on earth at the confluence of holy streams. Make thy body pure and thou shalt behold the King.

The devout man by the gradual progress of his soul shall attain his desire. He who is converted into pure mind knows the great secret.

Convert thy body into a temple, and restrain thyself: give up evil thoughts, and see God with thy internal eye. When we know him we shall know ourselves.

Without personal experience, the mere savour of the scripture will not remove the fears of the aspirant; as darkness is never dispelled by a painted flame.

Though he roam to sacred Concan, no dog will turn

into a lion; going to holy Benares will make no pig an elephant; and no pilgrimage will make a saint of one whose nature is different.

Be thy creed or thy prayers what they may, unless thou hast a little truth thou shalt not attain the path to happiness. He who possesses the truth is the twice-born.

The source of final happiness is inherent in the heart; he is a fool who seeks it elsewhere: he is like the shepherd who searched for the sheep which was in his bosom.

Why should you collect stones from the hills, and build fine temples? Why torment yourselves so, while the God as a living being constantly dwells within you?

Better the house-dog than the inanimate household goddess; and better than all demigods is the Lord of the universe.

That light, like the morning star, that dwells in the inmost heart of every man, is our refuge.

CLXV.
Worship.

Zendav.
Old Yasna.
comp.

We worship the pure; the Lord of purity.

We worship the universe of the true spirit, visible, invisible, and all that sustains the welfare of the good creation.

We praise all good thoughts, all good words, all good deeds, which are and will be, and keep pure all that is good.

Thou true happy Being! we strive to think, to speak, to do only what, of all actions, may promote the two lives,—the body and the mind.

We beseech the spirit of earth, by means of these best works (agriculture), to grant us beautiful and fertile fields, for believer and unbeliever, for rich and poor.

We worship the Wise One who formed and furthered the spirit of earth.

We worship him with our bodies and souls.

We worship him as being united with the spirits of pure men and women.

We worship the promotion of all good, all that is very beautiful, shining, immortal, bright, everything that is good.

CLXVI.
Temples.

Mussulmans say that after the form of the tabernacle of God in heaven, made out of a single ruby, is built the holy temple of Kaaba. As angels move around that holy seat above, so move the pilgrims seven times round that sacred house in Mecca.

<small>Second Divan of Jelaleddin Rúmi.</small>

Once when some pilgrims journeyed to Kaaba, they found themselves in a fruitless vale beholding a lofty house of stone. They sought with zeal to find God, but found him not. Long had they the house of stone encircled with their march, when from within a voice was heard saying, 'Why stand ye here to worship stone ? Go and adore in God's true house—the house of truth, home of the heart! Blessed is he who enters there!' Tebrísi, leaving the desert, made a pilgrimage to his own home, and found it a temple.

CLXVII.
The House of God.

Nának lay on the ground, absorbed in devotion, with his feet towards Mecca. A Moslem priest seeing

Persian Tradition.

him cried, 'Base infidel! how dar'st thou turn thy feet towards the house of Allah?' Nánác answered, 'And thou—turn them if thou canst towards any spot where the awful house of God is *not!*'

CLXVIII.

Worship.

Abulfazl.
A.C. 1595.
Ab.

He is a man of high understanding and noble aspirations who, without the help of others, recognises a ray of the divine power in the smallest things of the world; who shapes his inward and outward character accordingly, and shows due respect to himself and to others. True greatness, in spiritual and in worldly matters, does not shrink from the minutiæ of business, but regards their performance as an act of divine worship.

Every man of sense and understanding knows that the best way of worshipping God is in allaying the distress of the times, and in improving the condition of man.

Have the religions of the worldly tendencies of mankind no common ground? Is there not everywhere the same enrapturing beauty which beams forth from so many thousand hidden places? Broad indeed is the carpet which God has spread, and beautiful the colours which he has given it.

The lover and the beloved are in reality one.

Idle talkers speak of the Brahmin as distant from his idol.

There is but one lamp in this house, in the rays of which, wherever I look, a bright assembly meets me.

CLXIX.

God.

Let us adore the supremacy of that divine sun, the Deity, who illumines all, from whom all proceed, are renovated, and to whom all must return; whom we invoke to direct our intellects aright in our progress toward his holy seat. Gáyátrí.
(Holiest verse
of the Vedas.)

CLXX.

Meditation.

May that soul of mine, which mounts aloft in my waking and my sleeping hours, an ethereal spark from the light of lights, be united by devout meditation with the Spirit supremely blest and supremely intelligent! Hindu.
Vedas.

May that soul of mine, the guide by which the lowly perform their menial work and the wise versed in science, worship that soul which is the primal oblation within all creatures, be united by devout meditation with the Spirit supremely blest and supremely intelligent!

May that soul of mine, which is a ray of perfect wisdom, pure intellect, and permanent existence, the inextinguishable light set in mortal bodies, without which no good act is performed, be united by devout meditation with the Spirit supremely blest and supremely intelligent!

May that soul of mine, in whose eternal essence is comprised whatever has past, is present, or will be hereafter, be united by devout meditation with the Spirit supremely blest and supremely intelligent!

May that soul of mine, which contains all sacred

scriptures and texts, as spokes held in the axle of the chariot-wheel, and into which the essence of all created forms is interwoven, be united by devout meditation with the Spirit supremely blest and supremely intelligent!

May that soul of mine, which, distributed also through others, guides mankind as the charioteer guides his steeds,—the soul fixed in my breast, exempt from old age, swift in its course,—be united by divine meditation with the Spirit supremely blest and supremely intelligent!

CLXXI.

Litany.

>Persian.
>Desátír.

Preserver of preservers!
Maker of the pure!
Thou adored by the free intelligences, who have found felicity and proximity to thee, and shed illumination on bodies!

Who recallest from evil to good, of spotless purity!
Lord of the revolutions of time,
Accomplishment of desires!
Thou art exalted above all that is visible through thy resplendence;
And nothing can be detached from thee!
Mankind cannot duly appraise, in respect of their excellence, those who are low in degree;
How then can they worthily extol that Being, hidden by his brilliance, who melts them in his effulgence?
Thy worshippers are dejected from their inability to attain that height:

All pure things are moved by affection towards thee;
Pure souls repose their hope in thee!

CLXXII.

Ancient Prayers.

The prayer for the afflicted in King Solomon's temple was, 'Thou, O Lord, knowest the heart; grant him that which thou in thy wisdom knowest would be best for his good, and no more!' <small>Heb. Talmud. Semachoth.</small>

Our Father who art in heaven, proclaim the unity of thy name, and establish thy kingdom perpetually, and reign over us to all eternity! <small>Jewish Evening Prayer.</small>

Our Father who art in heaven, thy will be done on high; vouchsafe to bestow a peaceful and tranquil mind to those who honour thee on earth: but do, O Lord, what seems good in thy sight. Give me only bread to eat and raiment to put on! <small>Berachoth.</small>

Forgive, O Lord, those who have this day offended me! <small>Parasha.</small>

Let us, O Lord, not fall into the power of sin, transgression, or iniquity, and lead us not into temptation. Subdue our inclinations that they may be subservient to thee! <small>Jewish Morning Prayer.</small>

Thine O Lord is the greatness, power, glory, and majesty.

Our Father in Heaven! Hallowed be thy name! Thy kingdom come! Thy will be done in the earth as it is done in heaven! Give us this day our daily bread. Forgive us our trespasses, since even we forgive those who trespass against us. Lead us not into temptation, but deliver us from evil! <small>Christian.</small>

CLXXIII.

The Spiritual Pilgrimage.

Persian.
Attar.
Mantic.
comp.

The birds of the world gathered together and said, 'How can we form a nation without a king? This state of things cannot endure; we should join our efforts to find for ourselves a king.'

Into their assembly came the lapwing, bearing on its breast the sign that it had entered on the sacred path, and on its head the crown of truth. It claimed to have been the companion of Solomon, who knew the language of birds, and said, 'I know well my king, but alone cannot find him. If you will accompany me, I will bring you into his presence. His name is Simorg; he is the true king of birds. He dwells on a high tree, situated on the summit of a mountain, and before him are thousands of veils of light and darkness. The journey to him is long, it is over the firm earth and the deep sea, and there is need of a brave heart for those who shall voyage thither.'

To this prophet the nightingale first replied, 'The secrets of love are known to me. All the night I chant its songs. In my care are the roses and the hearts of lovers. If I am deprived of the sight of my beloved rose, I am desolate, and my songs cease. Lost in the love of the rose, I dream not of my own existence. To attain unto Simorg is beyond my energies; the love of the rose suffices the nightingale.'

The lapwing said, 'O thou who remainest behind, clinging to the external form of things! cease to find thy delight in that which hath charmed thee. The love of the rose has already pierced thy heart with thorns; it has brought thee anxiety, and yet rules over thee. The rose is beautiful, but in a few days it fades, and thou fillest the air with thy plaints. Leave the rose; each spring it smiles for thee, but it does not sigh with thee.'

Then came forward the parrot, its wings bearing the verdure of the fields, on its beak a morsel of sugar. 'The wicked people,' it said, 'have imprisoned me in an iron cage. In this prison I have longed for the water of immortality. Thither I would repair to quench my thirst; but I have no ambition to raise myself to the wing of Simorg.'

'Thou hast not,' said the lapwing, 'the true idea of happiness. To attain that, one must know how to renounce life, and desire something more than immortality, thinking only of finding the Beloved One.'

Next the peacock presented itself, adorned with a thousand colours. 'To form me,' it said, 'the painter of the invisible world gave his pencil to the genii. Once I lived in Paradise, but for my friendship with the serpent was driven thence, and sent to mourn in solitude at the ugliness of my feet. But I have always hoped to recover that fair abode. Can Simorg raise me to it? I have nothing to do in this world; I can find repose only in Paradise.'

The lapwing replied, 'O thou who hast wandered from the true path! know that the palace of this king is far above that of any earthly monarch. It is the eternal habitation of a soul filled with aspirations, the dwelling-place of the heart, the foundation of Truth. That height is an ocean of which Eden is but one drop. Paradise? Can one sharing the secrets of the sun pause for an atom of dust?'

Then came the duck. 'In the two worlds,' it said,

'there is no creature more pure than me. I bathe myself punctually at all the canonical hours ; I behold in water the carpet of prayer. Among birds I am a penitent of pure vows, of pure vestment, and pure habitation. Saith not the Koran "All that lives, lives by water?" As for me, I cannot pass by water, and so I cannot cross the valleys nor raise myself to Simorg.'

'And what are the two worlds of which thou speakest?' said the lapwing. 'Two drops of water, thy past and future, with no difference between them.'

The partridge said, 'I live among stones. The reign of the mountain-rock is eternal, and I find no essence in nature superior to gems.'

The lapwing said, 'He who has found the jewel of knowledge will not be content with a pebble.'

The bird of Paradise said, 'By me Féridoun and Jámshíd attained their glory ; it is by the influence of my shadow that monarchs reign. Why should I seek the friendship of the high Simorg when I dispose of crowns at my will ?'

The lapwing replied, 'Temporal royalty is often gained at the cost of spiritual royalty. Amid all his splendours Máhmud said, "I had rather be a gleaner in the fields than a monarch."'

The falcon presented himself, with his gay cap, prepared for the chase. 'I sit on the hand of the king,' he said, 'and disdain to look upon other beings in the world.'

'The favour of kings is capricious,' said the lapwing ; 'apprehension waits on the prince. It will be safer for thee to avoid that fire.'

The heron spoke of its dread to part from its

streams to attempt the lofty flight to Simorg; the wagtail complained of its feebleness. Other birds, in chorus, said, 'We cannot attain unto this great king. How shall such insects as we rise to Simorg?'

Then spake the prophet-bird, 'O feeble ones! 'tis the passionless heart rather than the weak wing which prevents your ascent. Know, ye ignorant ones, that when Simorg unveils his face, brilliant like the sun, millions of shadows are born throughout the earth. Such shadows are ye. All the birds of the world are but shadows of Simorg. Meditate on this mystery with intelligence. They who are filled with such thoughts lose themselves in that Supreme One, as shadows are lost in the shining light. He hath made thee, O heart! a mirror to reflect himself. If thou lovest the beauty of thy soul, fill thy heart with contemplation of its beauty. Make it a mirror to reflect the light of thy soul. It is thy king; its habitation is like the sun in its beauty. Behold in thine own heart thy king: behold his throne in an atom. Then shall the shadow thou art lose itself in the light which had caused it, and to which it had ever pointed.'

CLXXIV.

The Mystical Dance.

Among the religious customs of the dervishes is an astronomical dance, in which the dervish imitates the movements of the heavenly bodies, by spinning on his own axis, whilst at the same time he revolves round the sheikh in the centre, representing the sun; and, as he spins, he sings the song of Seid Nimetollah of Kuhistan.

Song of Nime-tolah of Kuhistan. (Emerson.)

Spin the ball! I reel, I burn,
Nor head from foot can I discern,
Nor my heart from love of mine,
Nor the wine-cup from the wine.
All my doing, all my leaving,
Reaches not to my perceiving;
Lost in whirling spheres I rove,
And know only that I love.

I am seeker of the stone,
Living gem of Solomon;
From the shore of souls arrived,
In the sea of sense I dived;
But what is land or what is wave
To me, who only jewels crave?
Love is the air-fed fire intense,
And my heart the frankincense;
As the rich aloes' flames, I glow,
Yet the censer cannot know,
I'm all-knowing yet unknowing;
Stand not, pause not, in my going.

Ask not me, as Muftis can,
To recite the Alcoran;
Well I love the meaning sweet,—
I tread the book beneath my feet.
Lo! the God's love blazes higher,
Till all difference expire.
What are Moslems? What are Giaours?
All are Love's and all are ours.
I embrace the true believers,
But I reck not of deceivers.

Firm to Heaven my bosom clings,
Heedless of inferior things;
Down on earth there underfoot,
What men chatter know I not.

CLXXV.
Devoutness.

Devoutly look, and nought
But wonders shall pass by thee;
Devoutly read, and then
All books shall edify thee;
Devoutly speak, and men
Devoutly listen to thee;
Devoutly act, and then
The strength of God acts through thee.

<small>Wisdom of the Brahmins. Rückert. (Tr. C. T. Brooks.)</small>

CLXXVI.
Love in Nature.

The rain of his infinite mercy refresheth all places, and the table of his bounty is spread far and near. O merciful God, who out of thine hidden treasures affordest daily sustenance to the Guebre and the infidel, how canst thou exclude thy friends, thou who deignest thus favourably to regard thine enemies? Clouds and wind, the moon, the sun, and the sky are all busied, that thou, O man, mayst obtain thy bread, and eat it not in neglect. For thy sake, all these revolve and are obedient: it is not therefore consistent with the rules of justice that thou only shouldst not obey.

<small>Persian. Sádi. Gul. comp.</small>

CLXXVII.
The Unknowable.

Those who constantly reside at the temple of his glory confess the insufficiency of their worship, saying,

'We have not worshipped thee in the manner that thou oughtest to be served.' And they who would describe the form of his beauty are wrapt in amazement, declaring, 'We have not known thee as thou oughtest to be known.' If any one should require me to describe him, how shall the disheartened describe that which hath no form? A devout man in deep contemplation, with his head reclined on the bosom of meditation, was immersed in the ocean of vision. When he recovered from that state, one of his companions, by way of pleasantry, said, 'What miraculous present have you brought us from this garden which you have been visiting?' He answered, 'It was my intention that, when I reached the rosebush, I would fill my lap with flowers, for presents to my friends; but when I came to the spot, the odour so overpowered my senses, that my skirt dropped out of my hands.' O bird of the desert! learn thou love of the moth, who, being burnt, expireth without a sigh. They who pretend to be informed are ignorant, for they who have known him have not yet recovered their senses. Oh! thou art beyond the reach of imagination, thought, or conjecture; surpassing all that has been related, and excelling all that we have heard or read: the banquet is ended, the assembly dismissed, and life draws to a close, and we still rest in our first encomium of thee!

CLXXVIII.

Adoration.

Hindu.
Vishnu.
Puráńa.
(Wilson MS.)

He who adores the highest (Vishnu), pride vanishes from his heart as fire becomes invisible under the shining of the full moon.

He whose heart is pure and good, who is without

pride, is mild, persevering, simple and plain, who considers every creature as his friend, and who loves every soul as his own, who behaves uniformly to every one with kindness and love, who wishes to do good, and has abandoned vanity,—in his heart resides the Lord of Life.

As the earth is adorned by the beautiful plants it puts forth, so is he beautified in whose heart dwells the Lord of Life.

Hold that person sacred whose heart knows no more than two things—that he himself and all others consist in the Deity.

CLXXIX.

Mystical Altar-Flowers.

That is the best worship which is made without the expectation of the attainment of any particular object; the worst is that which is performed for the accomplishment of a particular end.

Hindu. Agní. Paránа. (Wilson MS.) comp.

He who adores the Supreme Being should behold him in every creature and every creature in him.

The worshipper shall do homage to himself. He shall think in himself that the spirit which exists in the crown of his head has dispelled the darkness of his body, internal and external, and endowed the whole form and the sense, so that he may consider and say, 'I am divine,'[1] and lay hold on the sword of knowledge.

[1] Lit. 'I am Siva.'

The Lord of Life (Vishnu) should not be worshipped with flowers that have faded. Those that grow in thine own garden are far better than those of any other. With the flowers gathered there must be reverence—itself a flower.

There is in the intellect a sacred lotus to which every breath is wafted, and in it lost. He who shall contemplate this flower in the intellect shall find it full of splendour, beyond the collective light of many moons, and near unto the Deity.

WISDOM.

CLXXX.
Wisdom.

Whoso seeketh wisdom shall have no great travail; for he shall find her sitting at his door. She goeth about seeking such as are worthy of her, showeth herself favourably to them in the highways, and meeteth them in every thought. Love is the keeping of her laws. The multitude of the wise is the welfare of the world. *Wisdom of Solomon. Apoc. Ab.*

Wisdom is the worker of all things: for in her is an understanding spirit, holy, one only, manifold, subtile, lively, clear, undefiled, simple, not subject to hurt, loving the thing that is good, quick, which cannot be letted, ready to do good; kind to man, steadfast, sure, free from care, having all power, overseeing all things; and going through all understanding, pure and most subtle spirits. Wisdom is more moving than any motion: she passeth through all things by reason of her pureness. For she is the breath of the power of God, and a pure influence flowing from the glory of the Almighty: therefore can no defiled thing fall into her. For she is the brightness of the everlasting light, the unspotted mirror of the power of God, and the image of his goodness. And being but one, she can do all things; and remaining in herself, she maketh all things new: and in all ages entering into holy souls, she maketh them friends of God and prophets. She is more beautiful than the sun, and above all the order of the stars: being compared with the light, she is found before it; for after day cometh night, but vice shall not prevail against wisdom.

CLXXXI.
Wisdom.

As a solid rock is not shaken by the wind, wise people falter not amidst blame and praise.

Burmese.
Budh.
Dhammapada.
comp.
(Müller).

Good people walk on whatever befall; the good do not murmur, longing for pleasure.

Those whose mind is well grounded in the elements of knowledge, those whose frailties have been conquered, and who are full of light, are free (even) in this world.

Such a one, who does his duty, is tolerant like the earth.

His thought is quiet, quiet are his word and deed, when he has obtained freedom by true knowledge.

CLXXXII.
Folly.

Long is the night to him who is awake; long is a mile to him who is tired; long is life to the foolish.

Burmese.
Budh.
Dhammapada.
comp.
(246 B.C.)

If a traveller does not meet with one who is his better or his equal, let him firmly keep to his solitary journey; there is no companionship with a fool.

'These sons belong to me, and this wealth belongs to me,' says the fool. He himself does not belong to himself.

The fool who knows his foolishness is wise, at

least so far; but a fool who thinks himself wise, he is called a fool indeed.

If a fool be associated with a wise man all his life, he will perceive the truth as little as a spoon perceives the taste of soup.

CLXXXIII.
Wisdom.

The sage asked the spirit of wisdom thus, 'Is wisdom good, or skill?' The spirit of wisdom answered, 'Wisdom that has not goodness with it, is not to be considered as wisdom; and skill that has no wisdom in it, is not to be considered as skill.'

<small>Parsi. Mainyo i-Khard. 6th cent.</small>

CLXXXIV.

Vishnu spake, 'O Bal! take thy choice : with five wise men shalt thou enter hell, or with five fools pass into paradise.' Gladly answered Bal, 'Give me, O Lord, hell with the wise; for that is heaven where the wise dwell, and folly would make of heaven itself a hell!'

<small>Hindu Fable.</small>

CLXXXV.
Forethought.

There is nothing too difficult to be obtained by those who, before they act, reflect well themselves, and thoroughly consult with chosen friends.

<small>Hindu. Cural II.</small>

There are failures even in acting well. The work not done by suitable methods will fail, although many stand up to protect it. The chariot is weak at sea, and the ship on land.

There will be an end to his life who, having climbed out to the end of a branch, ventures to go farther.

A crow will overcome an owl in the daytime. Is there anything difficult for him who acts with right instruments at the right time?

The self-restraint of the energetic, is like the drawing back of the foot of a ram in order to butt.

If a rare opportunity come, let a man do that which is rarely done.

They may successfully meditate the conquest of the world who can think silently and wait for the right time.

CLXXXVI.

Wisdom.

<small>Hindu.
Cural II.</small>

No weapon has yet pierced the fortress of wisdom. To discern truth in everything, and by whomsoever spoken, this is wisdom.

To speak so that the meaning may easily enter the mind; to discern the subtilest thought in the words of others; this is wisdom.

To secure the friendship of the great is true wisdom, and it is wisdom to keep it unchanged, and not opening and closing like the lotus flower.

It is folly not to fear what ought to be feared; it is wisdom to fear what should be feared.

No terrifying calamity surprises the wise, who can see far.

Those who possess wisdom possess everything; those who have not wisdom, whatever they may possess, have nothing.

CLXXXVII.

Wisdom.

<small>Heb.
Prov.</small>

Happy the man who findeth wisdom,
And the man who obtaineth understanding!

For the merchandise of it is better than the
merchandise of silver,
And the gain of it than fine gold.
More precious is it than pearls,
And all thou canst desire is not equal to it.
Length of days is in her right hand;
In her left hand are riches and honour.
Her ways are ways of pleasantness,
And all her paths are peace.

CLXXXVIII.
Intellect.

Though high-born, and decked with every favour
of fortune, without intelligence no man is exalted. <small>Singh.
Muhándiram.</small>

Though he be in poverty, though of lowly birth
and uncouth form, kings shall bend before the wise
thinker.

To wisdom's sceptre every crown must bow; a
king sways an estate: genius commands an immeasurable realm.

CLXXXIX.
Wisdom and Folly.

The heart of a wise man is in his right hand;
The heart of a fool in his left. <small>Heb.
Ecclesiastes.</small>

CXC.
Hidden Wisdom.

For consider, brethren, who ye are that have been
called; not many wise men after the fashion of the <small>Christian.
1 Cor.
comp.</small>
world, not many mighty, not many noble; but the
foolish things of the world did God choose, to put to
shame the wise; and the weak things of the world
did God choose, to put to shame the things which are

strong; and the mean things of the world, and the things which are despised, the things which are not, to bring to nought things that are.

We do speak wisdom among the perfect; not, however, the wisdom of this world, nor of the rulers of this world, who are coming to nought; but we speak God's wisdom in a mystery, the hidden wisdom, which God determined on before the world was, for our glory; which none of the rulers of this world comprehended; for had they comprehended it, they would not have crucified him worthiest of honour; but, as it is written: 'The things which eye hath not seen, and ear hath not heard, and which have not entered into the heart of man, the great things which God hath prepared for those that love him.' For God hath revealed them to us by his spirit; for this spirit searcheth all things, even the depths of God. For who among men knoweth the things of a man, but the spirit of the man which is in him? even so the things of God knoweth no one but the spirit of God. But the unspiritual man receiveth not the things of the spirit of God; they are foolishness to him, and he cannot know them, because they are spiritually discerned. But he that is spiritual judgeth of all things, yet he himself is judged by no one.

I was not able to speak to you as to spiritual men, but as to babes. I fed you with milk, not with meat; for ye were not yet able to bear it. Nor indeed are ye able even now. For while there is among you rivalry and strife, are ye not unspiritual, and walking after the manner of men? For while one saith, I am of Paul, and another, I am of Apollos, are ye not like common men?

Who then is Apollos, and who is Paul, but ministers through whom ye believed, and that as the Lord gave to each? I planted, Apollos watered; but God gave the growth. So then, neither he that planteth nor he that watereth is anything, but God that giveth the growth. Ye are God's building. According to the gift of God to me, I have laid the foundation, and another buildeth thereon; but let every one take heed, how he buildeth thereon. If any one build upon this foundation with gold, silver, precious stones, wood, hay, stubble, the work of every one will be made manifest; the day will show it; it shall be revealed as by fire what every one's work is.

Know ye not, that ye are God's temple, and that the breath of God dwelleth in you? If any one defaceth the temple of God, God will deface him; for the temple of God is holy, and such are ye. All things are yours; whether Paul, or Apollos, or Cephas, or the world, or life, or death, or things present, or things to come,—all are yours.

CXCI.
Speech.

My deficiency and backwardness in the strenuous discharge of personal service at the palace of sovereignty resembles the story told of Buzerchemeher, how that, when a number of the sages of Hind were discoursing of his virtues, they could discover in him only this fault, that he hesitated in his speech, so that his hearers were kept a long time in suspense before he delivered his thoughts. Buzerchemeher overheard their conversation, and observed, ' It is better to deliberate before I speak, than to repent of what I

Persian.
Sádi.
Gul.

have said.' Old men of experience, who know the value of words, reflect and then speak. Expend not your breath in talking idly; speak to the purpose, and mind not if your delivery should be slow. First think, and then speak, but stop before they say, 'It is enough.' Man excelleth the brute creation by the faculty of speech, but you are beneath the brute if you make an improper use of that gift.

They asked Lókman of whom he had learned philosophy: he answered, 'Of the blind, because they never advance a step until they have tried the ground.' Try your way before you stir your foot.

CXCII.
Sloth.

Sádi.
Gul.

One night, in the desert of Mecca, from the great want of sleep, I was deprived of all power to stir; I reclined my head on the earth, and desired the camel-driver not to disturb me. How far shall the feet of the poor man proceed when the camel is weary of his load? Whilst the body of the fat man is becoming lean, the lean man may die of fatigue. He replied: 'O brother! Mecca is in front, and robbers in the rear; by proceeding you escape, and if you sleep you die. It is pleasant to sleep on the road in the desert under the acacia-tree in the night of decampment, but you must consider it as abandoning life.'

CXCIII.
Common Sense.

A firmer friend no one gets than sagacity.
He is happy who in himself possesses fame and

wit while living; for bad counsels have often been received from another's breast. <small>Scand. Sæmund's Edda.</small>

A better burthen no man bears on the way than good sense: this is thought better than riches in a strange place; such is the recourse of the indigent. <small>Havamal</small>

Harm seldom befalls the wary.

Silent and prudent, joyous and liberal, should everyone be until his hour of death.

CXCIV.
Wisdom.

They asked Lókman from whom he had learnt urbanity; he replied, 'From those of rude manners; for whatsoever I saw in them that was disagreeable, I avoided doing the same.' Not a word can be said, even in the midst of sport, from which a wise man will not derive instruction; but if an hundred chapters of philosophy are read to an ignorant person, it will seem to his ears folly and sport. <small>Sádi. Gul.</small>

Listen to the discourse of the learned man with the utmost attention, although his actions may not correspond with his doctrine. It behooveth a man to receive instruction, although the advice be written on a wall.

CXCV.
Ears that hear.

Once I travelled to Hejáz along with some young men of virtuous disposition, who had been my intimate friends and constant companions. Frequently, in their mirth, they recited spiritual verses. There happened to be in the party an Abid, who thought unfavourably of the morals of Durwaishes, being ignorant of their sufferings. At length we arrived at <small>Sádi. Gul. comp.</small>

the grove of palm-trees of Bení Hullal, when a boy of a dark complexion came out of one of the Arab families, and sang in such a strain as arrested the birds in their flight through the air. I beheld the Abid's camel dancing, and after flinging his rider, he took the road of the desert. I said, 'O Sheik! those strains delighted the brutes, but made no impression on you: knowest thou what the nightingale of the morning said to me? What kind of a man art thou, who art ignorant of love? The wind blowing over the plains causes the tender branches of the ban-tree to bend before it, but affects not the hard stone. Everything that you behold is exclaiming the praises of God, as is well known unto the understanding heart: not only the nightingale and the rosebush are chanting praises to God, but every thorn is a tongue to extol him.'

CXCVI.

Silence and Speech.

Ecclesiasticus.
Apoc.
Ab.

There is one that keepeth silence and is found wise; and another by much babbling becometh hateful. To slip upon a pavement is better than to slip with the tongue. A wise sentence shall be rejected when it cometh out of a fool's mouth; for he will not speak it in due season. The heart of fools is in their mouth; but the mouth of the wise is in their heart.

CXCVII.

Wisdom and Folly.

Sádi.
Gul.

Galen, on seeing a blockhead lay hold of the collar of a wise man, and disgrace him, said, 'If this man had been really wise, matters would not have come to this pass with the ignorant. Strife and contention will not happen between two wise men, and a wise man will not contend with a blockhead. If an ignorant fellow in his brutality speaks rudely, the wise man will answer him with mildness. Two wise men will not break a hair; it is the same case between an obstinate person and one of a mild disposition; but if they are both ignorant, they will break a chain.'

CXCVIII.

Learning from Enemies.

A preacher, who had a detestable voice, but thought he had a very sweet one, bawled out to no purpose. The people of the town, on account of the respectability of his office, submitted to the calamity, and did not think it advisable to molest him, until one of the neighbouring preachers, who secretly was ill-disposed towards him, came once to see him, and said, 'I saw a dream, may it prove good!' He asked, 'What did you see?' He replied, 'I thought you had a sweet voice, and that the people were enjoying tranquillity from your discourse.' The preacher, after reflecting a little on the subject, said, 'What a happy dream this is that you have seen, which has discovered to me my defect, in that I have an unpleasant voice, and that the people are distressed at my preaching! I have vowed that, in future, I will read only in a low tone. The company of friends was disadvantageous to me, because they look on my bad manners as excellent; my defects appear to them skill and perfection; and my thorn is regarded as the rose and the jasmine. Where is the enemy, with an impudent and piercing eye, who shall point out my fault?'

<small>Sádi.
Gul.</small>

CXCIX.

Illumination.

<small>Chinese. Budh.</small> Buddha said, A man who devotes himself to religion is like a man who takes a lighted torch into a dark house; the darkness is at once dissipated, and here is light! Once persevere in the search after wisdom, and obtain knowledge of truth—error and delusion entirely rooted out—Oh! what perfect illumination will there be!

Buddha said, In reflection, in life, in conversation, in study, I never for a moment forget the supreme end, Reason.

Let one behold heaven and earth, and think, 'These are impermanent'—and so the mountains and rivers, the varied forms of life and the productions of nature, all passing away! Attaining to this condition of mind, in a moment there will be illumination. Throughout an entire day's conduct to keep the thought steadily on Reason, and from this religious conduct to realise a deep principle of faith; this indeed is blessedness without measure!

CC.

Harmful Help.

<small>Sâdi. Gul.</small> A man with a disagreeable voice was reading the Koran aloud, when a holy man passing by asked what was his monthly stipend. He answered, 'Nothing at all.' He resumed, 'Why then do you take so much trouble?' He replied, 'I read for the sake of God.' The other rejoined, 'For God's sake read not.'

CCI.

Fitness.

A little man, being struck with a pain in his eyes, went to a farrier, desiring him to apply a remedy. The farrier, applying to his eyes what he was used to administer to quadrupeds, the man became blind; upon which he complained to the magistrate. The magistrate said, 'Get away, there is no plea for the damages; for if this fellow had not been an ass, he would not have applied to the farrier.' The application of this story is, that whosoever employs an inexperienced person on a weighty matter, besides suffering repentance, will, in the opinion of the wise, be considered of a weak understanding. The wise man, of enlightened mind, entrusts not an important business to one of mean abilities. The mat-maker, although a weaver, yet is not employed in the silk manufactory.

<small>Sádi. Gul.</small>

CCII.

Inward Fortune.

Out of mud springs the lotus flower; out of clay comes gold and many precious things; out of oysters the pearls; brightest silks, to robe fairest forms, are spun by a worm; bezoar from the bull, musk from the deer are produced; from a stick is born flame; from the jungle comes sweetest honey. As from sources of little worth come the precious things of earth, even so is it with hearts that hold their fortune within. They need not lofty birth or noble kin. Their victory is recorded.

<small>Singh. Budh.</small>

CCIII.
Fruitless Toil.

Sádi. Gul.

Two persons took trouble in vain, and used fruitless endeavours,—he who acquired wealth, without enjoying it, and he who taught wisdom, but did not practise it. How much soever you may study science, when you do not act wisely, you are ignorant. The beast whom they load with books is not profoundly learned and wise : what knoweth his empty skull whether he carrieth firewood or books?

Whosoever acquired knowledge, and did not practise it, resembleth him who ploughed, but did not sow.

A learned man without works is a bee without honey. Say to the austere and uncivil bee, 'When you cannot afford honey, do not sting.'

CCIV.
Use of Knowledge.

Sádi. Gul.

Science is to be used for the preservation of religion, and not for the acquisition of wealth. Whosoever prostituted his abstinence, reputation, and learning for gain, formed a granary and then consumed it entirely.

A learned man without temperance is a blind man carrying a link : he showeth the road to others, but doth not guide himself. He who through inadvertency trifled with life, threw away his money without purchasing anything.

CCV.

Reason.

The reason which can be reasoned is not the Eternal Reason, the name which can be named is not the Eternal Name. <small>Lao-Tsze. China. B.C. 17th cent. comp.</small>

Reason is great; heaven is great; earth is great.

Man takes his law from the earth; the earth takes its law from heaven; heaven takes its law from reason; reason takes its law from what it is in itself.

That which in its depth seems the first ancestor of all things, may be regarded as the mother of the universe. I know not its name, but give it the title of Reason.

Virtue in its grandest aspect is neither more nor less than following reason.

Reason is indefinite; yet therein are forms; impalpable, yet therein are things; profound and dark, yet therein is essence. This essence is most true; and from of old until now it has never lost its name. It passes into all things that have a beginning.

To have such an apprehension of the reason that was of old as to regulate present things, and to know their beginning in the past, this I call having the clew of reason.

Great reason is all-pervading. It can be on the right hand, and at the same time on the left. All things wait upon it for life, and it refuses none.

In love it nourishes all things, and it is ever free from ambitious desires. It may be named with the smallest. It may be named with the greatest.

Lay hold on the great form of reason, and the whole world will go to you. It will go to you and suffer no injury ; and its rest and praise will be glorious.

Use the light to guide you home to its own brightness.

CCVI.

Silence.

Sádi.
Gul.
Nothing is so good for an ignorant man as silence ; and if he was sensible of this he would not be ignorant. When you possess not perfection and excellence, you had better keep your tongue within your teeth. The tongue brings men into disgrace. The nut without a kernel is of light weight. A stupid man was training an ass, and spent all his time upon it. Somebody said, ' O blockhead ! what art thou endeavouring to do ? for this foolish attempt expect reprehension from the censorious. Brutes will not acquire speech from thee ; learn thou silence from them.' Whosoever doth not reflect before he giveth an answer, will generally speak improperly. Either arrange your words as a man of sense, or else sit quiet like a brute.

Whosoever interrupts the conversation of others to make a display of his own wisdom, certainly betrays his ignorance. The sages have said, that a wise man speaketh not until they ask him a question. Although the temperament of the discourse may be true, yet it is difficult to admit his pretensions.

CCVII.

Thought.

All that we are is the result of what we have thought : it is founded on our thoughts, it is made up of our thoughts. If a man speaks or acts with a pure thought, happiness follows him, like a shadow that never leaves him. <small>Burmese. Budh.</small>

'He abused me, he beat me, he defeated me, he robbed me,'—hatred in those who harbour such thoughts will never cease. <small>Dhammapada. comp. (Müller).</small>

For hatred does not cease by hatred at any time: hatred ceases by love; this is an old rule.

As rain breaks through an ill-thatched house, passion will break through a well-reflecting mind.

These wise people, meditative, steady, always possessed of strong powers, attain to Nirvána (the supreme condition).

By rousing himself, by reflection, by restraint and control, the wise man may make for himself an island which no flood can overwhelm.

The wise man possesseth reflection as his best jewel.

A Bhikshu who delights in reflection, who looks with fear on thoughtlessness, moves about like fire, burning all his fetters, small or large.

As a fletcher makes straight his arrow, a wise man makes straight his trembling and unsteady thought, which is difficult to keep, difficult to turn.

If a man's thoughts are unsteady, if he does not know the true law, if his peace of mind is troubled, his knowledge will never be perfect.

Whatever a hater may do to a hater, or an enemy to an enemy, a wrongly directed mind will do us greater mischief.

CCVIII.

Silence and Speech.

To what shall be likened the tongue in a man's mouth? It is the key of the treasury of wisdom:

Persian.
Sádi.
Gul.
comp.

when the door is shut, who can discover whether he deals in jewels or in small ware? Although, in the estimation of the wise, silence is commendable, yet at a proper season free speech is preferable. Two things indicate an obscure understanding,—to be silent when we ought to converse, and to speak when we should be silent.

SUPERSTITION.

CCIX.
Old and New.

Then came to him the disciples of John, saying, Why do we and the Pharisees fast, and thy disciples fast not? And Jesus said to them, No one putteth a patch of undressed cloth on an old garment; for the piece that filleth in teareth away from the garment, and a worse rent is made. Nor do men put new wine into old skins; else the skins burst, and the wine runneth out, and the skins are spoilt. But they put new wine into new skins, and both are preserved together.

Christian.
Matt.
comp.

CCX.
Pure Intention.

One night Gabriel from his seat in paradise heard the voice of God sweetly responding to a human heart. The angel said, 'Surely this must be an eminent servant of the Most High, whose spirit is dead to lust and lives on high.' The angel hastened over land and sea to find this man, but could not find him in the earth or heavens. At last he exclaimed, ' O Lord! show me the way to this object of thy love.' God answered, 'Turn thy steps to yon village, and in that pagoda thou shalt behold him.' The angel sped to the pagoda, and

Persian.
Attar.

therein found a solitary man kneeling before an idol. Returning, he cried, 'O master of the world! hast thou looked with love on a man who invokes an idol in a pagoda?' God said, 'I consider not the error of ignorance: this heart, amid its darkness, hath the highest place.'

CCXI.

Sects.

<small>Sabœan.
Ahmed Ben Soliman.
10th cent.
(D'Herb.)</small>

Jesus came and abolished the law of Moses: Mahomet followed him, and introduced his five prayers a day. The followers of both of these say that after their Prophet no other is to be expected, and they occupy themselves talking thus idly from morning to evening. But meanwhile tell me, since you are living under one of these dispensations, do you enjoy more than others, or less, the sun and moon?

CCXII.

Ancient Heresy.

<small>Padma
Purâna.
Bhúmí
Khanda.
(Wilson MS.)
comp.</small>

King Vena was devoted to austere religion, and possessed of a mild disposition and greatness of mind. A certain person of splendid form entered where the king sat in his assembly surrounded by the priests, and moved on silently before them all, reading a book. To him the king spoke, saying, 'Who art thou? What is the object of thy devotion and meditation? Why art thou here? Speak thou the truth.'

Then did this stranger say, 'O king! in vain art thou governing thy kingdom with justice. Know thou me as one adoring Virtue, before which even gods must bow. I speak truth and never falsehood.'

King Vena said, 'But what is thy virtue and thy religion, and what works dost thou perform?'

The stranger thus spoke, 'That object—virtue—worshipped by the gods, is the source of all honour. Mercifulness is above all those virtues which are performed to obtain salvation.

'Attend, O king, unto me! I perform no ceremonies, nor study the Vedas, nor practise austerities, nor incantations. What are offerings to the gods? Our highest work is to reverence the holiest man.'

King Vena said, 'What is the nature of this thy virtue of mercifulness?'

The stranger answered, 'O king! when the life of a human being ends, the body has no longer a separate existence, but re-unites with the elements of which it was composed. The friends of that person are afflicted with grief, and they perform a sacrifice, and afterwards continue to offer sacrifices on the day of that person's death. This, O best of kings, is delusion. Where do these deceased ones dwell, and on what do they subsist? Who has seen them, or knows their form? The priests are satisfied by eating the sweetmeats offered for the dead, but what can the dead derive from them?

'This token of love is surely vain.

'And concerning the ceremonies and austere devotions in honour of your gods, hear what I shall say. In all these rites innocent animals are sacrificed, and in one a man is slain on the altar. This is called the bestowal of gifts. But he who destroys an innocent being, even in the most solemn ceremony, has effected only evil. What virtue can there be in a ceremony where even innocence is not a barrier against (deified) vanity? What fruit does the performer derive from it? He eats the dust of the ground. Know this well,

O king, that whatever ceremonies prescribed in the Vedas bring needless pain or death, contain no virtue and conduct to no beatitude. A Vedas void of mercy is a holy scripture only in name.

'O king! not even a god could possess virtue did he not also possess mercy. And he alone is the true worshipper of God—be he Brahmin or Pariah—who cherishes all beings with generosity and compassion.

'King Vena, attend thou, while I relate the virtues by which the people with whom I dwell attain earthly happiness and seek eternal beatitude. The first virtue is mercifulness, which they exercise with a tranquil heart, and a mild and cheerful disposition. Their second virtue is to worship the God from whom are all beings.'

The king interrupted the stranger, saying, 'These rivers, like the Ganges, which are said to be holy, and productive of great virtues, thinkest thou they are truly such?'

The stranger replied, 'O king! if great virtues could be found in holy streams, in whom would they not be found? But in truth, virtue and eternal sanctity dwell not in the inanimate pond of water or mountain of rock, but where God lives. And he is the Supreme in all things. Do thou, O king, accept this pure faith, which shall bring with it happiness!'

From that time King Vena ceased to care for the Vedas, and ceased to perform ceremonies or sacrifices, and went no more on any pilgrimage. Sorrowing for this, his father and mother retired from their splendour, and from the world, and dwelt in the woods. Following their king, the people forsook the temples, and offered no more sacrifices. Seeing this, and that the bestowal of gifts to the gods was ceasing in the land, seven Rishis or holy persons came to King Vena, and entreated him to return to their faith. They said, 'These acts, O great king, that thou art performing, are not of our sacred traditions, nor fit for our religion, but are such as shall be performed by mankind at the entrance of Kali, or last and sinful age, when thy new faith shall be received by all, and the service of the gods be entirely relinquished.'

But the king dismissed the seven saints, saying he found in himself that which he held higher than their traditions.

This excited the wrath of the Munis, the seven powerful priests called sons of Brahma: these spread out the sacred grass, and having performed a holy Mantra over it, thereon burned King Vena to ashes.

NOTE.

A Puránic myth says that when King Vena thus perished, there sprang from his right hand one who milked the earth of wealth and wisdom, the very great Prithu, lord of the earth, versed in virtue, through whom Vena was raised to the blessed seat of Vishnu.

CCXIII.

Knowledge.

Mahomet said, Instruct in knowledge! He who instructs, fears God; he who speaks of knowledge, praises the Lord; who disputes about it, engages in holy warfare; who seeks it, adores the Most High; who spreads it, dispenses alms to the ignorant; and who possesses it, attains the veneration and good-will of all. Knowledge enables its possessor to distinguish what

Mahomet, as reported by Muádz-ibn-Jabal. comp.

is forbidden from what is not; it lights the way to heaven; it is our friend in the desert, our society in solitude; our companion when far away from our homes; it guides us to happiness; it sustains us in misery; it raises us in the estimation of friends; it serves as an armour against our enemies. With knowledge, the servant of God rises to the heights of excellence. The ink of the scholar is more sacred than the blood of the martyr. God created Reason, and it was the most beautiful being in his creation: and God said to it, 'I have not created anything better or more perfect or more beautiful than thou: blessings will come down on mankind on thy account, and they will be judged according to the use they make of thee.'

CCXIV.
Divination.

Persian. Zoroastrian Oracles. (Apoc.) comp.

Seek not to divine by the measures of the earth, nor by the dimensions of the sun. Dismiss the sounding course of the moon, for it perpetually runs through the forces of necessity. The advancing procession of stars is not for your sake. The wide-spread aerial wing of birds, and the sections and viscera of victims, are never true: all these are mere puerile sports, the foundation of fraud and mercantile religion. Fly from these if you intend to open the Paradise of piety, where virtue, wisdom, and equity are collected together.

Explore the river of the soul, whence or in what order having become a servant to the body, you may again rise to that order from which you flowed, uniting earthly work to sacred reason.

Verge not downward.

The world possesses intellectual, inflexible sustainers.

Attain thou to the sphere of intelligence, at whose centre is the fountain of virtue, which is all within you.

The immortal depth of the soul should be the leader; but vehemently extend all your eyes upward.

The soul being a splendid fire, through the power of the Father remains immortal, is the mistress of life, and combines in it the perfections of the world.

The Supreme Intelligible is to be apprehended with the flower of the intellect.

CCXV.
Necromancy.

Bind up the testimony;
Seal the commandment among my disciples!   Heb. Isa. comp.
I will wait for God,
And in him will I trust.
Behold, the children of God
Are for signs and symbols to the people.
And when they shall say unto you,
' Seek unto them that have familiar spirits,
And unto wizards that chirp and mutter,'
Shall not a people seek unto their God?
For the living shall they resort unto the dead?
To the law and to the testimony!
Shall they not speak according to this word,
Who have no dawning light?
They shall turn their faces upward;
And they shall look unto the earth;
And find trouble, obscurity, and thick darkness.

CCXVI.

Religious Exercises.

<small>Hindu. Hitopadesa. comp.</small>

When Caundilya, the warrior, saw his son dead, he fainted through grief: as he lay on the ground his kinsmen sat down by him. A holy man named Capila said to him, 'There is no stability. Youth, beauty, life, collected wealth, dominion, the society of friends, are all uncertain: in this the wise are not deceived. Whither are the lords of the world gone, with their armies, their valour, and their equipage? The earth itself remains to this day a witness of their separation from it. In the transient world, which never affords permanent pleasure, let the wise strengthen devotion and multiply the delights of holiness.'

Caundilya, hearing this, rose up, and said, 'What then have I to do with my vain palace? I will go as a pilgrim into the desert.'

Capila rejoined, 'He who has controlled his own spirit and desires, who has knowledge, piety, and a good character, gathers the fruit of a pilgrimage. Even in the sacred forest inflamed passions cause crime; and in the mansion, self-control brings piety to dwell. The virtuous man's home is his desert of devotion. They whose food is only to sustain life, whose voice is only to speak truth, make hardships easy. Thyself art the sacred river,—its waters truth; its banks, right conduct; its waves, benevolence. Here wash thy lips, O son of Pandu! for the interior soul is not purified by holy water! If truth be placed in a balance with a thousand sacrifices of horses, truth will outweigh a thousand sacrifices.

CCXVII.
Convention.

At that time Jesus went on the sabbath through the grain-fields; and his disciples were hungry, and began to pluck the ears of grain, and to eat. But the Pharisees, seeing it, said to him, Lo! thy disciples are doing that which it is not lawful to do on the sabbath. But he said to them, Have ye not read what David did, when he and those who were with him were hungry? how he went into the house of God, and they ate the shewbread, which it was not lawful for him to eat, nor for those who were with him, but for the priests alone? Or have ye not read in the Law, that on the sabbaths the priests of the temple profane the sabbath, and are blameless? But I say to you, that something greater than the temple is here. If ye had known what this meaneth, 'I desire mercy and not sacrifice,' ye would not have condemned the guiltless.

And he said to them, Who of you that owneth one sheep, if it fall into a pit on the sabbath, will not lay hold of it, and lift it out? Of how much more worth now is a man than a sheep! (When the Jews persecuted Jesus again for violating the sabbath, he said, My Father is working up to this time, and I work.)

CCXVIII.
Traditions.

Then come to Jesus Pharisees and scribes from Jerusalem, saying, Why do thy disciples transgress the tradition of the elders? for they wash not their hands when they eat bread. But he answered and said to them, Why do ye transgress the commandment of God for the sake of your tradition? Hypocrites! well did Isaiah prophesy concerning you, saying, 'This people honoureth me with their lips, but their heart is far from me. But in vain do they worship me, teaching as doctrines the commandments of men.'

He said to his disciples, Every plant which my heavenly Father did not plant will be rooted up.

Out of the heart proceed evil thoughts, murders, adulteries, fornications, thefts, false testimony, blasphemies. These are the things which defile a man; but to eat with unwashed hands defileth not a man.

CCXIX.
Marvels.

<small>Christian. Matt. comp.</small>

And the Pharisees and Sadducees came to try him, and asked him to show them a sign from heaven, And he answering said to them, When it is evening, ye say, Fair weather! for the sky is red. And in the morning, A storm to-day! for the sky is red and lowering. Ye know how to judge of the face of the sky, and can ye not discern the signs of the times?

CCXX.
Priest and Prophet.

<small>Christian. Matt. comp.</small>

And the Pharisees, hearing that he had put the Sadducees to silence, assembled together; and one of them, a lawyer, asked, trying him, Teacher, which commandment is great in the law? And he said to him, 'Thou shalt love the Lord thy God with all thy heart, and with all thy soul, and with all thy mind.' This is the great and first commandment. There is a second like it: 'Thou shalt love thy neighbour as thyself.' On these two commandments hang all the law and the prophets.

Then Jesus spoke to the multitudes, and to his disciples, saying, The scribes and the Pharisees sit in the seat of Moses. They say, and do not. They bind heavy burdens, and lay them on men's shoulders, and will not themselves move them with a finger. And all their works they do to be observed by men. They make broad their phylacteries, and enlarge their fringes, and love the first place at feasts, and the chief seats in the synagogues, and salutations in the markets, and to be called by men, Rabbi. But be not ye called Rabbi; for one is your teacher: and ye are all brothers. And call no one your Father on the earth; for one is your Father, he who is in heaven. Nor be ye called leaders: for one is your leader, the Christ. The greatest among you will be your servant. And whoever shall exalt himself will be humbled; and whoever shall humble himself will be exalted.

But woe to you, scribes and Pharisees, hypocrites! because ye shut up the kingdom of heaven against men; for ye go not in yourselves, nor suffer those who are entering to go in. Woe to you, scribes and Pharisees, hypocrites! for ye compass sea and land to make one proselyte; and when he is made, ye make him twofold more a son of hell than yourselves.

Woe to you, scribes and Pharisees, hypocrites! for ye pay tithes of the mint, and the dill, and the cummin, and have omitted the weightier matters of the law, justice, and mercy and faith. Blind guides! who strain out a gnat, and swallow a camel.

Woe to you, scribes and Pharisees, hypocrites! for ye make clean the outside of the cup and the platter, but within they are full of robbery and licentiousness.

Ye are like whited sepulchres, which outwardly indeed appear beautiful, but within are full of dead men's bones, and of all uncleanness. Even so ye also outwardly appear righteous to men, but within ye are full of hypocrisy and iniquity.

Woe to you, scribes and Pharisees, hypocrites ! because ye build the sepulchres of the prophets, and adorn the tombs of the righteous, and say, If we had been in the days of our fathers, we would not have been partakers with them in the blood of the prophets. Ye bear witness against yourselves, that ye are the sons of those who killed the prophets. Fill ye up then the measure of your fathers!

I send to you prophets, and wise men, and scribes; some of them ye will kill and crucify, and some of them ye will scourge in your synagogues, and persecute from city to city ; that on you may come all the righteous blood shed upon the earth, from the blood of righteous Abel to the blood of Zechariah, son of Barachiah, whom ye slew between the temple and the altar. Truly do I say to you, all these things will come upon this generation.

Jerusalem, Jerusalem! that killest the prophets, and stonest those who are sent to thee ! How often would I have gathered thy children together, as a hen gathereth her chickens under her wings, and ye would not! Lo, your house is left to you desolate ! For I say to you, ye will not see me henceforth, till ye shall say, Blessed is he that cometh in the name of the Lord !

And Jesus went out, and was going from the temple ; and his disciples came to him, to show him the buildings of the temple. And he answering said to them, See ye not all these? Truly do I say to you, there will not be left here one stone upon another, that shall not be thrown down!

CCXXI.
The Established Church.

And when he had come into the temple, the chief priests and the elders of the people came to him as he was teaching, and said, By what authority doest thou these things? and who gave thee this authority? And Jesus answering said to them, I also will ask you one question; which if ye answer me, I too will tell you by what authority I do these things. The baptism of John, whence was it? From heaven, or from men? And they reasoned among themselves, saying, If we say, from heaven, he will say to us, Why then did ye not believe him? But if we say, from men, we fear the multitude; for all regard John as a prophet. And they answered Jesus and said, We do not know. And he said to them, Neither do I tell you by what authority I do these things. Christian. Matt.

But what think ye? A man had two sons: he came to the first, and said, Son, go, work to-day in the vineyard. And he answered and said, I will not. Afterward he repented, and went. And he came to the other and said the same. And he answered and said, I will, sir; and went not. Which of the two did the will of his father? They say, the first. Jesus saith to them, Truly do I say to you, that the publicans and the harlots go into the kingdom of God before you. For John came to you as a preacher of righteousness, and ye did not believe him; but the publicans and the harlots believed him ; and ye, when ye had seen it, did not afterward repent, that ye might believe him.

CCXXII.
The Kingdom Within.

<small>Christian.
Luke.</small>
And being asked by the Pharisees when the kingdom of God was coming, he answered, The kingdom of God cometh not in such a manner as to be watched for ; nor will they say, Lo here ! or Lo there ! for behold, the kingdom of God is within you.

CCXXIII.
Hypocrisy.

<small>Christian.
Luke.</small>
And in the hearing of all the people he said to his disciples, Beware of the scribes, who like to walk about in long robes, and love salutations in the markets, and the chief seats in the synagogues, and the first places at feasts ; who devour widows' houses, and for a pretence make long prayers. These will receive a far greater condemnation.

CCXXIV.
Tradition.

<small>Christian.
John.
comp.</small>
On the last day, which is the great day, of the feast, Jesus stood and cried aloud, saying, If any one thirst, let him come to me, and drink. He that believeth in me, from within him shall flow rivers of living water. Some of the multitude therefore, when they heard these words, said, This is in truth the prophet. Others said, This is the Christ. Others said, Doth the Christ then come from Galilee ? Hath not the Scripture said, that the Christ cometh from the seed of David, and from Bethlehem, the town where David was ? So

there was a division among the multitude because of him. And some of them wished to seize him; but no one laid hands on him.

The officers came to the chief priests and Pharisees, who said to them, Why did ye not bring him? The officers answered, Never man spake like this man. The Pharisees answered them, Have ye also been deceived? Hath any one of the rulers believed in him? or of the Pharisees? but this multitude that know not the Law are accursed. Nicodemus saith to them, being one of them, Doth our law judge a man, unless it first hear from him, and know what he doeth? They answered and said to him, Art thou too from Galilee? Search and see that no prophet ariseth from Galilee.

Jesus said to the Jews, If ye continue in my word, ye are truly my disciples; and ye will know the truth, and the truth will make you free. They answered him, We are Abraham's offspring, and have never been in bondage to any one; how sayest thou, Ye will be made free? Jesus answered them, Truly, truly do I say to you, every one that committeth sin is a bond-servant of sin. If ye were Abraham's children, ye would do the works of Abraham. But now ye seek to kill me, a man that hath spoken to you the truth, which I received from God; this did not Abraham.

CCXXV.

Superstition and Silver.

Many of those who had practised magical arts brought their books together, and burned them before all men; and they counted the price of them, and found it fifty thousand pieces of silver. Christian. Acts. comp.

And about that time there arose no small tumult concerning the faith. For a certain man named Demetrius, a silversmith, made silver shrines of Diana, and brought no small gain to the craftsmen. And having called them together, with the workmen of like occupation, he said, Sirs, ye know that by this craft we have our wealth; and ye see and hear that this Paul hath persuaded and turned away much people, not only of Ephesus, but of almost all Asia, saying, that those are not gods which are made with hands. And there is not only danger that this branch of our business will come into disrepute, but also that the temple of the great goddess Diana will be despised, and her magnificence destroyed, whom all Asia and the world worship.

And hearing this, they became full of wrath, and kept crying out, Great is Diana of the Ephesians! And the city was filled with confusion; and they rushed with one accord into the theatre, having seized Gaius and Aristarchus, men of Macedonia, Paul's companions in travel. And when Paul wished to go into the people, the disciples would not suffer him. And some also of the Asiarchs, who were his friends, sent to him, and entreated him not to venture into the theatre. Some therefore were crying one thing, and some another; for the assembly was in confusion, and the greater part knew not wherefore they had come together. And they brought forward Alexander out of the multitude, the Jews putting him forward; and Alexander beckoned with his hand, desiring to make his defence to the people. But when they knew that he was a Jew, all with one voice for about two hours cried out, Great is Diana of the Ephesians!

CCXXVI.
Liberation.

When ye knew not God, ye were in slavery to those who in their nature are not gods; but now, after having known God, or rather having been known by God, how is it that ye are turning back to the weak and beggarly rudiments to which ye wish to be again in bondage? Do ye observe days, and months, and times and years? Christian. Gal. comp.

Stand firm in the liberty with which Christ made us free, and be not again bound fast to the yoke of bondage. Only use not your liberty for an occasion to the flesh, but by your love serve one another. For the whole Law is fulfilled in one commandment, even in this : 'Thou shalt love thy neighbour as thyself.'

Let no one then call you to account about food or drink, or a feast-day, or a new moon, or sabbaths. Col. comp.

Let no one defraud you of the prize, desiring to do it in humiliation and worshipping of the angels, intruding into those things which he hath not seen.

If ye died with Christ to the rudiments of the world, why, as though still living in them, do ye subject yourselves to ordinances, such as, Handle not, Taste not, Touch not (which all are to perish with the using), after the commandments and teachings of men; which things have indeed a show of wisdom, in will-worship and humiliation and severity to the body, not in any honour for the satisfying of the flesh.

Lie not one to another, seeing that ye have put off the old man with his deeds, and have put on the new man, who is renewed unto knowledge after the image of him that created him.

Clothe yourselves, therefore, as the chosen of God, holy and beloved, with compassionate affections, kindness, lowliness of mind, humility, long-suffering; bearing with each other, and forgiving each other.

CCXXVII.

Faithless Churches.

<small>Christian.
Rev.
comp.</small>

To the angel of the church in Ephesus write : I know thy works, and thy labour, and thy endurance, and that thou canst not bear evil men ; and thou didst try those who say they are apostles, and are not, and didst find them deceivers ; and thou hast endurance, and hast borne on account of my name, and hast not become weary. But I have this against thee, that thou hast left thy first love. Remember therefore whence thou hast fallen, and repent, and do the first works; or else I will remove thy light out of its place.

To the angel of the church in Sardes write : I know thy works, that hast a name that thou livest, and art dead.

And to the angel of the church in Laodicea write : I know thy works, that thou art neither cold nor hot ; I would thou wert cold or hot. So then, because thou art lukewarm, and neither hot nor cold, I will spew thee out of my mouth. Because thou sayest, I am rich, and have gotten wealth, and have need of nothing, and knowest not that thou art the wretched and the pitiable one, and poor, and blind, and naked : I advise thee to buy of me gold refined by fire, that thou mayest be rich ; and white garments, that thou mayest be clothed, and that the shame of thy nakedness may not be made manifest; and eye-salve to anoint thine eyes, that thou mayest see.

He that hath an ear, let him hear what the Spirit saith to the Churches.

CCXXVIII.
Formalism.

Sányásis acquaint themselves with particular words and vests; they wear a brick-red garb, and shaven pates; in these they pride themselves: their heads look very pure, but are their hearts so? <small>Hindu. Vémana. 12th cent. comp.</small>

Religion which consists in postures of the limbs, is just a little inferior to the exercises of the wrestler.

In the absence of inward vision boast not of oral divinity.

All acts performed under a false guise are paths leading to death.

False is the creed of those who hold that it is profitable to renounce the present life: cannot ye see that eternal existence commences in this life?

No man in the world considers truly who he is; alas! he cannot know his whole nature. How shall man learn to know himself?

The man that has attained perfection draws no distinctions between day and night, the mind and universal nature, or himself and another man.

He among the sons of men merits the title of Yogí (saint) who knows the god in his heart: know thyself, and thou shalt become the deity.

Ignorant that the living principle exists in your own body, why do ye search, imagining that it is to be found elsewhere? Ye are like one who while the sun shines shall search with a lamp.

CCXXIX.
Formalism.

<small>Heb.
Isa.</small>   Forasmuch as this people draw near me with their mouth, and honour me with their lips, but have removed their heart far from me, and their fear towards me is but a precept taught of men; therefore the wisdom of their wise men shall perish, and the discernment of their discerning men shall be hid.

CCXXX.

<small>Heb.
Isa.
comp.</small>

Give ear unto the law of our God, ye people!
To what purpose is the multitude of your sacrifices unto me?
Bring no more vain oblations;
Incense is an abomination unto me,
New moons, sabbaths, and the calling of assemblies:
I cannot endure injustice with solemn meetings:
Yea, when ye make many prayers I will not hear.
Wash you, make you clean;
Put away the evil of your actions from before mine eyes:
Cease to do evil, learn to do well;
Defend the fatherless, plead for the widow!
Sion shall be redeemed by justice,
And her converts by righteousness.

CCXXXI.
Hypocrisy.

<small>Heb.
Isa.
comp.</small>

Cry aloud, spare not;
Lift up thy voice like a trumpet,
And show my people their transgressions,
And the house of Jacob their sins:

For they seek me daily, and are eager to know
    my ways,
And forsook not the ordinance of their God :
They ask from me ordinances of justice ;
They are eager for the approach of God :
' Wherefore have we fasted,' say they, ' and thou seest
    not ?
Wherefore have we afflicted our soul,
And thou takest no knowledge ? '
Is it such a fast as I have chosen—
A day for a man to afflict his soul ?
Is it to bow down his head as a bulrush,
And to spread sackcloth and ashes under him ?
Wilt thou call this a fast, and an acceptable day to
    Jehovah ?
Is not this the fast that I have chosen,—
To loose the bands of wickedness,
To strike off the fastenings of the yoke,
And to let the oppressed go free,
And that ye break every yoke ?
Is it not to deal thy bread to the hungry,
And that thou bring the poor that are cast out to
    thy house ?
When thou seest the naked, that thou cover him ;
And that thou hide not thyself from thine own
    flesh ?
If thou take away from the midst of thee the
    yoke,
The putting-forth of the finger, and speaking vanity ;
And if thou bring out thy food to the hungry,
And satisfy the afflicted soul ;
Then shall thy light rise in obscurity,
And thy darkness be as the noon-day.

CCXXXII.

Priestcraft.

Heb.
Ezek.

And the word of God came unto me, saying, Son of man, prophesy against the shepherds of Israel prophesy, and say unto them, Thus saith the Lord unto the shepherds :

Woe to the shepherds of Israel who feed themselves Should not the shepherds feed the flocks ?

Ye eat the fat, and ye clothe you with the wool ; Ye kill the stall-fed, but ye feed not the flock.

The weak ye have not strengthened,

Neither have ye healed that which was sick,

And that which was wounded ye have not bound up,

And that which was driven away ye have not brought back,

And that which was lost ye have not sought ;

But with force and cruelty have ye ruled them :

And they were scattered, because there was no shepherd ;

And they became food for all the beasts of the field when they were scattered.

My sheep wandered through all the mountains, and upon every high hill ;

Yea, my flock was scattered over all the face of the land,

And none did search or seek after them.

Thus saith the Lord :

Behold, I am against the shepherds,

And I will require my flock at their hand,

And cause them to cease from feeding the flock ;

Neither shall the shepherds feed themselves any more ;

For I will deliver my flock from their mouth,
That they may not be food for them.
For ye, my flock, are men,
And I am your God.

CCXXXIII.
Hypocrisy.

The elements of his body will laugh within him at the feigned conduct of a deceitful man. Hindu.
Cural II.

The assumed appearance of power by a man who has no power, is like a cow feeding on grass covered with a tiger's skin.

There is no need of a shaven crown, nor of tangled hair, if a man abstain from deeds which the wise have condemned.

As the straight arrow has a crooked use, and the curved lute in effect is straight, so by their deeds, and not semblances, let men be estimated.

A man's deed is the touchstone of his greatness or littleness.

CCXXXIV.
Superstition.

The Duke Gae asked about the altars of the gods of the land. Tsae-Wo replied, 'The Hea sovereign used the pine-tree, the man of the Yin used the cypress, and the man of the Chow used the chestnut, —to cause the people to be in awe.' Chinese.
Confucius.
Analects.
comp.

Confucius, hearing this, said, 'Things that are done, it is needless to speak about; things that have had their course, it is needless to remonstrate with; things that are past, it is needless to blame.'

Kee-Loo asked about serving the gods. The

Master said, 'While you are not able to serve men, how can you serve the gods?'

Kee-Loo said, 'I venture to ask about death.' The Master said, 'While you do not comprehend life, how can you comprehend death?

'If a man in the morning hear of the right way, he may in the evening die without regret.

'Yew, shall I teach you what knowledge is? When you know a thing, consider that you know it; and when you do not know a thing, understand that you do not know it. This is knowledge.

'For a man to worship a deity not his own is mere flattery.

'To give one's-self earnestly to the duties due to men, and, while respecting the gods, to respect also their distance, may be called Wisdom.'

. CCXXXV.

Hypocrisy.

Persian.
Sádi.
Gul.

O thou whose inward parts are void of piety, and whose outside beareth the garb of hypocrisy! hang not a gorgeous curtain before the door of a house constructed of reeds.

CCXXXVI.

Self and Sect.

Sádi.
Gul.

Every one thinks his own wisdom perfect, and his own child beautiful. A Jew and a Mussulman were disputing in a manner that made me laugh. The Mussulman said in wrath, 'If this deed of con-

veyance is not authentic, may God cause me to die a
Jew!' The Jew said, 'I make oath on the Pentateuch,
and if I swear falsely, I am a Mohammedan like you.'
If wisdom was to cease throughout the world, no one
would suspect himself of ignorance.

KNOWLEDGE.

CCXXXVII.
Books.

Egypt.
Inscription on the Library at Alexandria:— 'Treasury of Remedies for the Mind.'

CCXXXVIII.
Knowledge.

Turkish. (Albitis.) comp.
Collect as precious pearls the words of those who are as an ocean of knowledge and virtue.

Many are ignorant through want of knowing how to listen.

Man is man's mirror.

Ignorance is perpetual childhood : it implies idleness, which engenders every vice.

It is not by living long, but by seeing much, that one learns much.

It is by experience that one becomes clever.

It is by degrees one gets to the top of the staircase.

Let us open our eyes, lest they be painfully opened for us.

CCXXXIX.
Reciprocity.

Hindu. (Albitis.)
Educate thy children ; then wilt thou know how much thou owest thy father and mother.

CCXL.
Science.

Believe in the law, and trust not the man who passes the night in watching the progress of the planets (for purposes of superstition). <small>Arabic. (El Wardi.) comp.</small>

Study the law with all thy mind, and be not drawn away from it by the search after worldly goods, or by domestic cares.

Curtail thy sleep, and increase thy knowledge. He who knows the value of his object despises the pains it cost him.

Say not the possessors of science have passed away and are forgotten; every one who has walked in the path of science has reached the goal.

Increase of knowledge is a victory over idleness; and the beauty of knowledge is rectitude of conduct.

CCXLI.
Learning.

Learning to a man is a name superior to treasures. Learning is better than hidden treasures. Learning is a companion on a journey to a strange country. <small>Hindu. Vishnu Sarma. comp.</small> Learning is strength inexhaustible. Learning is the source of renown, and the fountain of victory in the assembly. Learning is a superior sight. Learning is a livelihood. A man without learning is a beast of the field. Men are the same as other animals in eating, sleeping, fearing, and propagation: reason alone is a man's superior distinction. Deprived of reason, he is upon an equality with the brutes.

The Code of Yájnáválkya says, 'Through piety of mind comes knowledge.'

Truth.

Heb.
Apoc.
Esdras.
About 30 B.C.
Ab.

When Darius reigned, he made a great feast unto all his subjects. And when they had eaten and drunken, and being satisfied, were gone home, then Darius the king went into his bed-chamber and slept. Then three young men that were of the guard that kept the king's body spoke one to another, 'Let every one of us speak a sentence; he whose sentence shall be wiser than the others, unto him shall the king give great gifts in token of victory.'

Then every one wrote his sentence, sealed it, and laid it under King Darius's pillow.

The first wrote, Wine is the strongest.

The second wrote, The king is strongest.

The third wrote, Women are strongest; but above all things, Truth beareth away the victory.

Now when the king was risen up, he called together all the princes and chief officers, and the writings were read before them.

Then the king and the princes looked one upon another; and the king began to speak thus of truth—

'Great is truth, and stronger than all things. All the earth calleth upon the truth, and the heaven blesseth it: all works shake and tremble at it, and with it is no unrighteous thing: it endureth, and is always strong; it liveth and conquereth for evermore. With her is no accepting of persons or rewards; but she doeth the things that are just, and refraineth from all unjust and wicked things. Neither in her judgment is any unrighteousness; and she is the strength, kingdom, power, and majesty of all ages.'

CCXLIII.

Angels.

O my prophet, ever near me! I have given thee an exalted angel named Intelligence. Persian. Desátír. comp.
I am never out of thy heart,
And I am nearer unto thee than thou art to thyself.
Thou didst ask who are the angels :
The sentient principles of all bodies that act aright are angels.
Thy knowledge is a ray of the knowledge of God.
In dreams and in waking thy soul reacheth me.
Whatever is on the earth is the resemblance and shadow of something that is in the sphere.
While that resplendent thing remaineth in good condition, it is well also with its shadow.
When that resplendent object removeth far from its shadow, life removeth to a distance.
Again, that light is the shadow of something more resplendent than itself;
And so on up to the Light of lights.
Look therefore to God, who causeth the shadow to fall.

CCXLIV.

The Heart.

The wise in heart shall be called intelligent;
And sweetness of voice addeth learning. Heb. Proverbs.

CCXLV.
Grey Hairs.

The hoary head is a crown of beauty
When it is found in the way of righteousness.

<small>Heb.
Proverbs.</small>

CCXLVI.
Liberation.

That is active duty which is not for our bondage; that is knowledge which is for our liberation: all other duty is good only unto weariness; all other knowledge is only the cleverness of an artist.

<small>Hindu.
Vishnu.
Purána.</small>

CCXLVII.
Learning.

Letters and numbers are the two eyes of man.

The learned are said to have eyes; the ignorant have merely two spots in their face.

Let a man learn thoroughly whatever he may learn, and let his conduct be worthy of his learning.

It is the part of the learned to give joy to those whom they meet, so that they shall think, 'When shall we meet them again?'

The unlearned are as beggars before the learned.

Water will flow from a well in proportion to its depth, and influence from a man in proportion to his learning.

How is it that any one can remain until death without learning, which would make every country his own country, and every town his own town?

Learning is the excellent, imperishable riches; all other treasures are not riches.

<small>Hindu.
Cural II.
9th cent.</small>

The excellence of the unlearned is to keep silence before the learned.

The learned man's poverty is better than the ignorant man's wealth. The low caste of the learned is exalted above the high caste of the ignorant.

CCXLVIII.
Knowledge.

Heaven is nearer than earth to those men of purified minds who are freed from doubt. Hindu.
Cural II.

Even those who have all the knowledge that can be obtained by the five senses will derive no benefit from it if they are without a knowledge of the true nature of things.

True knowledge is the perception concerning everything of whatever kind, that in that thing is the true thing.

Let it not be thought that there is another birth for the mind that, having thoroughly considered all it has learned, has recognised essential Being.

They who have this knowledge enter a road which returns not.

CCXLIX.
Ignorance.

Ignorance is a sorry jade, which causes every one who mounts it to stumble, and each who leads it to be laughed at. Persian.
(Albitis.)
comp.

The porter to a fool can always say there is no one at home.

A man may be thought clever while he is seeking for wisdom ; but if he imagines he has found it, he is a fool.

CCL.
Knowledge.

Tartary.
(Albitis.)

The knowledge of the parents ought to be the inheritance of the children.

CCLI.
Prudence.

Russian.
(Albitis.)

Silence, prudence: prudence, science.

A fool throws a stone into the sea; a hundred sages cannot recover it.

CCLII.
Instruction.

Hindu.
Cural II.
9th cent.

That ear which instruction has not entered is deaf though it hears.

When there is no food for the ear, give some to the stomach.

The words of the good are like a staff in a slippery place.

It is a rare thing to find reverence with those who have not received careful instruction.

What does it matter whether they live or die who know tastes only in the mouth, and not by the ear?

If a man listen, never so little even, to good instruction, it will bring him dignity.

CCLIII.
Knowledge.

Hindu.
Manu.
comp.

A knowledge of right is a sufficient incentive for men unattached to wealth or to sensuality.

The senses, being strongly attached to sensual

delight, cannot be so effectually restrained by avoiding incentives to pleasure, as by a constant pursuit of divine knowledge.

A man is not therefore aged because his hair is grey : him surely the gods consider aged who, though young in years, has read and understands the sacred books (Vedas).

He whose discourse and heart are pure, and ever perfectly guarded, attains all the fruit arising from a complete course of studying the Vedas.

CCLIV.
Daughters.

If you neglect the education of your daughters, you are preparing shame for your own family and unhappiness for the houses in which they may enter. China. (Albitis.)

CCLV.
Teaching.

Good instruction must be given without pain to those receiving it ; and sweet, gentle speech must be used by a preceptor who would cherish virtue. Let him say what is true, but let him say what is pleasing; let him speak no offensive truth, nor yet agreeable falsehood : this is a primæval rule ; a maxim, says a Purána,[1] requiring wisdom for its use. Hindu. Manu. comp.
[1] Agui Pur.

Let not a sensible teacher tell any other what he is not asked, nor what he is asked improperly ; let him, however intelligent, act among the tumultuous as if he were dumb. Where virtue or diligent attention are not found, in that soil divine instruction would perish, like fine seed in a barren land.

CCLVI.

Knowing and being Known.

How can a man be concealed?

<small>Confucius. Analects.</small> Confucius said, 'The superior man is distressed by his want of ability. He is not distressed by men's not knowing him; he is afflicted that he does not know men. I am a happy man: if I have a fault, men observe it.'

CCLVII.

Ascent of Intelligence.

<small>Sufi. By Prof. Palmer. comp.</small> When the heart of man has been revivified and illumined by the Primal Spirit, he has arrived at intelligence; for intelligence is a light in the heart distinguishing between truth and vanity. Until he has been so revivified and illumined, it is impossible for him to attain to intelligence at all. But having attained to intelligence, then, and not till then, is the time for the attainment of knowledge, for becoming wise. Intelligence is a primal element, and knowledge the attribute thereof. When from knowledge he has successively proceeded to the attainment of divine light, and acquaintance with the mysteries of nature, his last step will be perfection, with which his upward progress concludes.

'Arise and look around, for every atom that has birth
Shines forth a lustrous beacon to illumine all the earth.'

The instinctive spirit should feed and supply the spirit of humanity, as the oil feeds and supplies the flame in a lamp. The traveller must aim at completing this lamp, so that his heart may be illumined, and he may see things as they really are.

CCLVIII.

Inspiration.

The companion of my loneliness is my genius.

The knowledge which men call certainty I deem the faintest dawn of thought.

Persian.
Faizi.
10th cent.
comp.

What the wild call revelation I deem drunken madness.

Did I bring forth what is in my mind, could the age bear it?

In my regulated reason I see the system of the universe, and in heaven and earth my motion and my rest.

• My own blood is the basis of the wine of my enthusiasm.

Expect in my arena the victory of both worlds.

Although I have buried my head in my hood, 1 can see both worlds; it may be that love has woven my garment from the threads of my contemplation.

My eye is open and waits for the manifestation of truth: the Spirit of the universe flees before the insignia of my ecstasy.

O cup-bearer Time! bring me a cup of wine;

Not wine that drives away wisdom,

But that unmixed wine whose hidden power vanquishes Fate,

That clear wine with which the worshipper sanctifies the garb of the heart,

That illuminating wine which shows lovers of the world the true path,

That impearling wine which cleanses the meditative mind of fanciful thoughts.

My heart is pearl, ocean, and diver.

I am myself hell, purgatory, and paradise.

These verses bear witness to a free-thinker who belongs to a thousand sects.

I have become dust, but from the odour of my grave people shall know that man rises from such dust.

CCLIX.

Progression.

<small>Chinese.
Budh.
Catena.</small>

From earliest dawn till setting sun
Each living soul might tend to self-advance,
Reflecting thus: My foot, firm planted on the earth,
Should make me think, 'Am I
Advancing on my road to heaven?'

CCLX.

Wavering.

<small>Chinese.
Budh.
Catena.</small>

The man who, travelling along a precipitous road,
Doubts whether he can proceed or not,
Is like the man who, living in the midst of the realities of life (religious virtues),
Doubts of their truth.

Because he wavers, he cannot diligently inquire
After the true marks of that which is.

There will be doubts as long as we reside in the world;

Yet, pursuing with joy the road of virtue,
We ought, like the man who observes the rugged path along the precipice,
Gladly and profitably to follow it.

CCLXI.
Knowledge.

A philosopher was thus exhorting his sons—' My dear children, acquire knowledge, for on worldly riches and possessions no reliance can be placed : rank will be of no use out of your own country, and on a journey, money is in danger of being lost ; for either the thief may carry it off all at once, or the possessor may consume it by degrees. But knowledge is a perennial spring of wealth, and if a man of education ceases to be opulent, yet he need not be sorrowful, for knowledge of itself is riches. There once happened an insurrection in Damascus, where every one deserted his habitation. The wise sons of a peasant became the king's ministers, and the stupid sons of the Vizier were reduced to ask charity in the village. If you want a paternal inheritance, acquire from your father knowledge, for his wealth may be spent in ten days.' [Persian. Sádi. Gul.]

They asked Iman Mûrsheed Mohammed Ben Mohammed Ghezaly (on whom be the mercy of God !) by what means he had attained to such a degree of knowledge ? He replied, ' In this manner,—whatever I did not know, I was not ashamed to inquire about.' There will be reasonable hopes of recovery when you get a skilful physician to feel your pulse. Inquire about everything that you do not know ; since, for the small trouble of asking, you will be guided in the respectable road of knowledge.

CCLXII.
Gentleness.

Oppose kindness to perverseness ; the sharp sword will not cut soft silk.

By using sweet words and gentleness you may lead an elephant with a hair.

He who quickly lays hold of the sword in his anger, will gnaw the back of his hand through sorrow.

Forgiveness is better than vengeance.

Whosoever is sensible of his own faults carps not at another's failing.

CCLXIII.
Fruitless Toil.

Two persons took trouble in vain, and used fruitless endeavours,—he who acquired wealth without enjoying it, and he who taught wisdom but did not practise it. How much soever you may study science, when you do not act wisely, you are ignorant. The beast whom they load with books is not profoundly learned and wise: what knoweth his empty skull whether he carrieth firewood or books?

CCLXIV.
Knowledge.

It is with knowledge as with water: this runs not to high summits; that reaches not the proud. Both seek the lowly places.

A wise man knows an ignorant one, because he has been ignorant himself; but the ignorant cannot recognise the wise, because he has never been wise.

CCLXV.
Temperance.

They tell a story of a certain religious man, who in one night would eat ten pounds of food, and who before the morning would have completely finished the Koran in his devotions. A holy man hearing this, said, 'If he had eaten half a loaf, and slept, it would have been much more meritorious.' Keep your belly unencumbered with food, in order that you may be able to discern the light of divine knowledge. You are void of wisdom, because you are crammed up to your nose with food.

CCLXVI.

Difficult Things.

Buddha said, 'There are difficult things in the world—Being poor, to be charitable; being rich and great, to be religious; to escape destiny; to repress lust and famish desire; to see an agreeable object and not seek to obtain it; to be strong without being rash; to bear insult without anger; to move in the world (to touch things) without setting the heart on it; to investigate a matter to the very bottom; not to contemn the ignorant; thoroughly to extirpate self-esteem; to be good, and at the same time to be learned and clever; to see the hidden principle in the profession of religion; to attain one's end without exultation; to exhibit in a right way the doctrine of expediency; to save men by converting them; to be the same in heart and life; to avoid controversy.' Chinese. Budh.

CCLXVII.

Mystery.

I said, 'My heart shall understand all science.' There was but little I did not comprehend; yet when I looked with maturer eye at all I knew, my life had passed and I comprehended nothing! Persian. Omar. Khèyam.

ETHICS OF INTELLECT.

CCLXVIII.
Compliance.

<small>Confucius.
Analects.</small> To worship in a temple that does not belong to you is mere compliment.

To see what is right, and not to do it, is want of courage.

Hold faithfulness and sincerity as first principles.

The commander of the forces of a large state may be carried off, but the will of even a common man cannot be taken from him.

CCLXIX.
Temptation.

<small>Siam.
Budh.</small> As the Grand Being went forth by night from his father's palace to become a devotee, the Prince of Evil, Mara, trembled, and determined to prevent him. Descending from his abode, he cried, 'Lord, that art capable of such vast endurance, go not forth to adopt a religious life, but return to thy kingdom, and in seven days thou shalt become an emperor of the world, riding over the four great continents.'

'Take heed, O Mara,' replied the Grand Being; 'I also know that in seven days I might gain universal empire, but I desire not such possessions. I know that the pursuit of religion is better than the empire of the world. You, thinking only of evil lusts, would force me to leave all beings without guide into your power. Avaunt! Get thou away far from me!'

The Lord rode onwards, intent on his purpose. The skies rained flowers, and delicious odours pervaded the air.

CCLXX.
Martyrdom.

King Olaf's men, who had secretly followed Harek (on his visit to his friend Eyvind), came up and took Eyvind prisoner. Then Eyvind was brought to a conference with King Olaf, who asked him to allow himself to be baptized like other people; but Eyvind decidedly answered he would not. The king still with persuasive words urged him to accept Christianity, and both he and the bishop used many suitable arguments; but Eyvind would not allow himself to be moved. The king offered him gifts and great fiefs, but Eyvind refused all. Then the king threatened him with tortures and death, but Eyvind was steadfast. Then the king ordered a pan of glowing coals to be placed upon Eyvind's belly, which burst asunder. The king said, 'Wilt thou now, Eyvind, believe in Christ?' 'No,' said Eyvind. With that died Eyvind.

<small>Iceland. Heims-kringla. Olaf Trygg-vesson's Saga. 10th cent. comp.</small>

Bishop Sigurd took all his mass-robes, and went forward to the bow of the king's ship; ordered tapers to be lighted and incense to be brought out. Then he set the crucifix upon the stem of the vessel, read the Evangelist and many prayers, and besprinkled the whole ship with holy water. Then they reached Godö Isle, where dwelt Rand the Strong, who while sleeping was taken prisoner. King Olaf ordered Rand t be brought before him, and offered him baptism, saying, 'I will not take thy property from thee, but rather be thy friend, if thou wilt make thyself worthy to be so.' Rand exclaimed that he would never be a Christian. Then the king was wroth, and ordered Rand to be bound to a beam of wood with his face uppermost, and a round pin of wood to be set between his teeth. Then the king ordered an adder to be stuck into the mouth of him; but the serpent shrunk back when Rand breathed against it. The king put his horn into his mouth, and forced the adder to go in by holding a red-hot iron before the opening. So the serpent crept into the mouth of Rand, and gnawed its way out of his side; and thus Rand perished.

CCLXXI.
The Good Mind.

Zoroaster.
Zendavesta.
Gatha.
Ahunavaiti.
comp.

I will now tell you who are assembled here the wise sayings of the Most Wise, the praises of the living God, and the songs of the good Spirit, the sublime truth which I see arising out of these sacred flames.

You shall therefore hearken to the soul of Nature.

Let us be such as help the life of the future. The wise living spirits are the greatest supporters of it. The prudent man wishes only to be there where wisdom is at home.

Wisdom is the shelter from lies. All perfect things are garnered up in the splendid residence of the good mind, the wise, and the true.

Thou wise, the Father of the good mind !

Thou wise, hast created the sacred visions !

The wicked perish through the wisdom and holiness of the living wise Spirit.

Who are opposed in their thoughts, words, and actions to the wicked, and think of the welfare of creation, their efforts will be crowned by success through the mercy of God.

CCLXXII.
Prayer.

A low-minded man must he be who can lift up his hand in prayer to God's throne for terrestrial goods. <small>Persian. Miyán Káli. 10th cent.</small>

O friend, whose tongue speaks of knowledge divine, and whose heart ever draws the veil from the light of truth!

Never cherish a thought of which thou oughtest to be ashamed; never utter a word for which thou wouldst have to ask God's pardon!

CCLXXIII.
Transition.

Our ability is from God; who also gave us ability to be ministers of a new covenant, not of the letter, but of the Spirit; for the letter killeth, but the Spirit giveth life. But if the ministration of death, engraven in letters on stones, was so glorious that the children of Israel could not look steadfastly on the face of Moses by reason of the glory of his countenance, which glory was to be done away, shall not the ministration of the Spirit be much more glorious? For if the ministration of condemnation had glory, much greater is the glory of the ministration of righteousness. For even that which was made glorious hath ceased to be glorious in this respect, by reason of the glory by <small>Christian. 2 Cor.</small>

which it is exceeded. For if that which was to be done away was glorious, much more glorious is that which endureth.

Having therefore such hope, we use great plainness of speech; and do not as Moses did, who put a veil over his face that the children of Israel might not steadfastly look on the end of that which was to be done away. But their understandings were blinded; for until this day, when the old covenant is read, the same veil remaineth, since it is not unveiled to them that it is done away in Christ; but even till this day, when Moses is read, there lieth a veil upon their heart; but whenever it turneth to the Lord, the veil is taken away. Now the Lord is the Spirit; and where the Spirit of the Lord is, there is liberty. But we all with unveiled face beholding in a mirror the glory of the Lord, are changed into the same image from glory to glory, as by the Lord, the Spirit.

Therefore, having this ministry through the mercy we received, we are not faint-hearted; but have renounced the hidden things of shame; not walking in craftiness, nor handling the word of God deceitfully, but by the manifestation of the truth commending ourselves to every man's conscience in the sight of God.

CCLXXIV.
The Timid Thinker.

<small>Hindu.
Hitopadesa.
comp.</small>

A man eminent in learning has not even a little virtue if he fears to practise it. What precious things can be shown to a blind man by a lamp which he holds in his hand? The patient is healed by careful thought, not by knowing his name.

CCLXXV.

The Prophet.

The Nûrâkh sages ask, 'What use is there for a prophet in this world?' A prophet is necessary on this account, that men are connected with each other in the concerns of life; therefore rules and laws are indispensable, that all may act in concert; that there may be no injustice in giving or taking, or partnership; but that the order of the world may endure. And it is necessary that these rules should all proceed from God, that all men may obey them. _{Persian. Desatír.}

He will ask thee, 'How can we know a prophet?' By his giving you information regarding your own heart.

CCLXXVI.

Truthfulness.

He whose mind and life are free from deceit has a dwelling in the hearts of all men. _{Hindu. Cural II.}

Is it asked, 'What is truth?' It is the speaking of words that are without the least degree of evil to others.

He who speaks the truth with all his heart is superior to those who make gifts and practise austerities.

If a man abstain from falsehood, though he practise no other virtue, it shall be well with him. Truth will lead to every virtue.

Purity of body comes by water; purity of mind by truthfulness.

The lamp of truth is a lamp of the wise.

CCLXXVII.
Moral Courage.

Heb.
Isa.
comp.

Hearken unto me, ye that know righteousness,
The people in whose heart is my law ;
Fear ye not the reproach of men,
Neither be dismayed at their revilings.
For the moth shall devour them like a garment,
Yea, the moth shall devour them like wool :
But my righteousness shall be for ever,
And my salvation from generation to generation.
Who art thou that fearest man that shall die,
And forgettest thy God ?
I will put my words in thy mouth,
And cover thee in the shadow of my hand,
To plant the heavens, and lay the foundations of the earth !

CCLXXVIII.
The Bringer of Glad Tidings.

Heb.
Isa.
comp.

How beautiful upon the mountains
Are the feet of him that bringeth good tidings,
That publisheth peace !
That bringeth glad tidings of good,
That publisheth salvation ;
That saith unto Zion, thy God reigneth !
The voice of thy watchmen,
They lift up the voice together ; they shout aloud ;
For face to face they see God appearing.
Break forth into singing together, ye waste places !
For God hath comforted his people ;
And all the ends of the earth
Shall see the salvation of our God.

CCLXXIX.

The Rejected Prophet.

Behold, my servant shall act prudently;
He shall be exalted and sustained very high. Heb.
Isa.
comp.
But who hath believed our report?
And to whom hath the arm of God been revealed?
For he hath grown as a root out of dry ground;
He had no form nor comeliness that we should desire him;
Despised and rejected of men,
A man of sorrows, and acquainted with grief:
Surely he hath borne our griefs, and carried our sorrows,
And with his stripes we are healed.

CCLXXX.

Silence and Sufferance.

He was oppressed and he was afflicted,
Yet he opened not his mouth; Heb.
Isa.
comp.
He is brought as a lamb to the slaughter,
And as a sheep before her shearers is dumb
So he openeth not his mouth.
The pleasure of God shall prosper in his hands;
He shall see of the travail of his soul and be satisfied.
By his knowledge the righteous servant shall make many righteous.
His portion shall be with the great.

CCLXXXI.

The False Prophet and the True.

Produce your cause, bring forth your strong reasons!
Declare the former things, what they were,

> Heb.
> Isa.
> comp.

That we may consider them, and know their issue;
Or let us hear of things to come,
That we may know that ye are gods!
I beheld and there was no man;
Even among them, and there was no counsellor
That when I asked could answer a word.
Behold, they are all vanity, their works nothing,
Their idols wind and emptiness:
Behold my servant whom I uphold,
My chosen one, in whom my soul delighteth:
I have put my Spirit upon him;
He shall publish right among the nations.
He shall not cry, nor lift up his voice,
Nor cause it to be heard in the street.
A bruised reed shall he not break,
And the smoking flax shall he not quench.
He shall publish right in truth.
He shall not grow feeble nor be discouraged,
Till he have established right in the earth;
And the isles shall wait for his law.
I have called thee for deliverance,
A light of the nations,
To open blind eyes,
To set at liberty them that are bound,
Even them that sit in the prison of darkness.

CCLXXXII.
The Prophet.

> Persian.
> Zendavesta.
> Spenta-
> Mainyno-
> Gátha.

Zoroaster is the prophet who through his wisdom and truth utters in words the sacred thoughts.

Through his tongue he makes known to the world the laws given by my intellect, the mysteries hidden in my mind.

Kava obtained through the possession of the spiritual power, and through the verses which the Good Mind had revealed, that knowledge which the living Wise himself, as the cause of truth, has invented.

Cry aloud that they must aspire after truth!

CCLXXXIII.
Fidelity to Truth.

Ye are the salt of the earth. But if the salt have lost its savour, wherewith shall itself be salted? It is thenceforth good for nothing, but to be cast out, and to be trodden under foot by men. <small>Christian. Matt. comp.</small>

Ye are the light of the world. A city that is set on a hill cannot be hid; nor do men light a lamp, and put it under the bushel, but on the lampstand; and it giveth light to all that are in the house. In like manner let your light so shine before men that they may see your good works and glorify your heavenly Father.

CCLXXXIV.
Fidelity to Truth.

The divine law is as the salt; for as the world cannot exist without salt, so it cannot exist without the divine law. <small>Talmud. Sopherim.</small>

Whoso undertaketh to instruct mankind without the necessary qualifications, of him it is said, 'Many are the victims he has slain;' but he who, though fully qualified, abstains from promoting knowledge and instructing mankind, of him it is likewise said, 'Many are also his victims.' <small>Ethics.</small>

CCLXXXV.
Reproof.

Heb.
Prov.

Reprove a wise man, and he will love thee. Teach a wise man, and he will be yet wiser.

Citrons of gold in figured work of silver is a word spoken in season. An ornament of fine gold is a wise reprover upon a listening ear. As the coolness of snow in a day of harvest is the faithful messenger; for he refresheth the soul. But a cloud without rain is the man that boasteth a delusive gift.

CCLXXXVI.
Kindness and Truth.

Heb.
Prov.

Let not kindness and truth forsake thee;
Bind them about thy neck,
Write them upon the tablet of thy heart.
Then shalt thou find favour and good esteem
In the sight of God and man.

CCLXXXVII.
The Sower.

Christian.
Matt.

The same day Jesus went out of the house, and sat by the shore of the lake; and great multitudes were gathered together to him, so that he went into a boat, and sat down; and all the multitude stood on the beach. And he spoke many things to them in parables; he said, Behold, a sower went forth to sow. And as he sowed, some seeds fell by the wayside; and the birds came and devoured them. And others fell upon rocky places, where they had not much earth; and they sprung up immediately, because they had no depth of earth. But when the sun was up, they were scorched; and because they had no root, they withered away. And others fell among thorns; and the thorns grew up and choked them. And others fell upon good ground, and yielded fruit, some a hundred-fold, some sixty, some thirty-fold. He that hath ears, let him hear.

CCLXXXVIII.

Prophet and People.

And seeing the multitudes, he was moved with compassion for them, because they were harassed and scattered about, as sheep having no shepherd. Then he saith to his disciples, The harvest indeed is great, but the labourers are few.

Christian. Matt. comp.

These twelve Jesus sent forth, when he had charged them, saying, Go not away to Gentiles, and enter not any city of the Samaritans; but go rather to the lost sheep of the house of Israel. And as ye go, proclaim, saying, The kingdom of heaven is at hand.

Lo! I send you forth as sheep into the midst of wolves. Be therefore wise as serpents, and harmless as doves. They will deliver you up to the councils, and they will scourge you in their synagogues; and ye will be brought before governors and kings for my sake, that ye may bear testimony to them and to the Gentiles.

But when they deliver you up, be not anxious as to how or what ye shall speak; for it will be given you in that hour what ye shall speak. For it is not ye that speak, but the breath of your Father that speaketh in you.

And brother will deliver up brother to death, and

the father his child; and children will rise up against their parents, and put them to death; and ye will be hated by all on account of my name. But he that endureth to the end will be saved.

Fear them not, therefore. For there is nothing covered that will not be revealed; and hid, that will not be known. What I say to you in darkness, speak ye in the light; and what ye hear in the ear, proclaim ye upon the housetops. And fear not those who kill the body, but are not able to kill the soul.

Are not two sparrows sold for a penny? and not one of them shall fall to the ground without your Father. But even the hairs of your head are all numbered. Fear not, therefore; ye are of more value than many sparrows.

Think not that I came to send peace on earth: I came not to send peace, but a sword. For I came to set a man at variance with his father, and a daughter with her mother, and a bride with her mother-in-law; and they of a man's own household will be his foes. He that loveth father or mother more than me is not worthy of me; and he that loveth son or daughter more than me is not worthy of me; and he that doth not take his cross, and follow me, is not worthy of me. He that findeth his life will lose it; and he that loseth his life for my sake will find it.

He that receiveth you, receiveth me; and he that receiveth me, receiveth him that sent me. He that receiveth a prophet because he is a prophet, will receive a prophet's reward; and he that receiveth a righteous man because he is a righteous man, will receive a righteous man's reward. And whoever shall give to drink only a cup of cold water to one of these little ones because he is a disciple, truly do I say to you, he will by no means lose his reward.

But to what shall I liken this generation? It is like children sitting in the markets, who call to their fellows, and say, We piped to you, and ye did not dance; we sung a dirge, and ye did not lament. For John came neither eating nor drinking; and they say, He hath a demon. The Son of man came eating and drinking; and they say, Behold, a glutton and a winebibber, a friend of publicans and sinners! But wisdom is justified by her works.

At that time Jesus answered and said, I thank thee, O Father, Lord of heaven and earth, that, though thou didst hide these things from the wise and discerning, thou didst reveal them to babes. Yea, Father, for so it seemed good in thy sight.

Come to me, all ye that labour and are heavy laden, and I will give you rest. Take my yoke upon you, and learn from me; for I am meek and lowly in heart, and ye shall find rest for your souls. For my yoke is easy, and my burden is light.

CCLXXXIX.

The Unrecognised Prophet.

Having come into his own country, Jesus taught them in their synagogue, so that they were astonished, and said, Whence hath this man this wisdom, and these powers? Is not this the builder's son? Is not his mother called Mary, and his brothers, James, and Joseph, and Simon, and Judas? And his sisters, are they not all with us? Whence then hath this man all these things? And they took offence at him.

Christian. Matt. comp.

But Jesus said to them, A prophet is not without honour, except in his own country, and in his own house.

CCXC.
Demand of a Cause.

<small>Christian.
Matt.</small>

A young man came to Jesus and said, Teacher, what good thing shall I do, that I may have everlasting life? And he said to him, Why dost thou ask me concerning what is good? There is but one who is good. But if thou wilt enter into life, keep the commandments. Which? saith he. And Jesus said, These— 'Thou shalt not kill; Thou shalt not commit adultery; Thou shalt not steal; Thou shalt not bear false-witness; Honour thy father and thy mother;' and, 'Thou shalt love thy neighbour as thyself.' The young man saith to him, All these things have I kept; in what am I still wanting? Jesus said to him, If thou wilt be perfect, go, sell what thou hast, and give to the poor, and thou shalt have treasure in heaven; and come, follow me. But the young man, on hearing this, went away sorrowful; for he had great possessions.

CCXCI.
Self-surrender.

<small>Christian.
John.
comp.</small>

Jesus said, Of myself I do nothing. As I hear I judge; and my judgment is just, because I seek not my own will, but the will of him that sent me. If I bear witness of myself, my witness is not true.

My teaching is not mine, but his that sent me. If any one is desirous to do his will, he will know concerning the teaching, whether it be from God, or whether I speak from myself. He that speaketh from himself seeketh his own glory; but he that seeketh the glory of him that sent him, he is true, and in him is no unrighteousness.

CCXCII.
Fear and Boldness.

Of the rulers many believed in him; but on account of the Pharisees they did not acknowledge him, lest they should be put out of the synagogue; for they loved the glory that is of men more than the glory that is of God. Christian.
John.
comp.

But Jesus cried aloud, and said, He that believeth in me believeth not in me, but in him that sent me; and he that beholdeth me, beholdeth him that sent me. I have come a light into the world, that whoever believeth in me may not remain in the darkness. And if any one hear my words, and keep them not, I do not judge him; for I came not to judge the world, but to save the world. He that rejecteth me, and receiveth not my words, hath one that judgeth him; the word that I have spoken, that will judge him in the last day. Because I have not spoken from myself; but the Father who sent me hath himself committed to me what I should say, and what I should speak; and I know that what he hath committed to me is eternal life.

CCXCIII.
Scepticism.

Philip findeth Nathanael, and saith to him, We have found him of whom Moses in the Law and the Prophets wrote, Jesus, the son of Joseph, who is of Nazareth. And Nathanael said to him, Can any good Christian.
John.

thing come out of Nazareth? Philip saith to him, Come and see. Jesus saw Nathanael coming to him, and saith of him, Behold an Israelite indeed, in whom is no guile.

CCXCIV.

Ordeal.

<small>Christian. Mark. comp.</small> And having sung a hymn, they went out to the Mount of Olives. And Jesus saith to them, Ye will all fall away from me; for it is written, 'I will smite the shepherd, and the sheep will be scattered.' But Peter said to him, Even if all shall fall away, yet will not I. And Jesus saith to him, Truly do I say to thee, that even thou, to-day, on this night, before a cock crow twice, wilt thrice deny me. But Peter spoke the more vehemently: If I must die with thee, I will not deny thee. And so also said they all.

And they come to a place called Gethsemane; and he saith to his disciples, Sit here, while I pray. And he taketh with him Peter and James and John; and began to be in great consternation and anguish. And he saith to them, My soul is exceedingly sorrowful, even to death; remain here and watch. And going on a little farther, he fell on the ground, and implored that, if it was possible, the hour might pass from him. And he said, Abba, Father, all things are possible to thee! take away this cup from me. But not what I will, but what thou wilt.

And he cometh and findeth them sleeping; and he saith to Peter, Simon, sleepest thou? Couldst not thou watch one hour?

And again he went away and prayed, saying the same words. And returning, he found them again sleeping, for their eyes were heavy.

And he cometh the third time, and saith to them, Sleep on, and take your rest ! It is enough ! the hour is come.

And immediately, while he was yet speaking, cometh Judas Iscariot, one of the twelve, and with him a multitude with swords and clubs, from the chief priests and the scribes and elders. And his betrayer had given them a signal, saying, Whomsoever I shall kiss, he is the man ; seize him, and lead him away securely. And on coming, he immediately went up to Jesus, and said, Rabbi ! and kissed him. And they laid hands on Jesus and seized him. And his disciples all forsook him and fled.

CCXCV.

Trial.

And they led Jesus away to the high priest; and all the chief priests and the elders and the scribes came together. And Peter followed him afar off, even into the court of the palace of the high priest, and was sitting with the officers, and warming himself at the fire.

Christian. Mark. comp.

And the chief priests and the whole council sought for testimony against Jesus in order to put him to death ; and they found none. For many bore false-witness against him, but their testimonies did not agree together. And some stood up and bore false-witness against him, saying, We heard him say, I will destroy this temple that is made with hands, and in three days I will build another not made with hands. And not even so did their testimony agree. And the high priest stood up in the midst, and asked Jesus, saying, Dost thou make no answer to what these men testify against thee? But he was silent, and answered nothing.

CCXCVI.
Timidity.

<small>Christian. Mark.</small> And as Peter was below in the court, there cometh one of the maid-servants of the high priest; and seeing Peter warming himself, she looked at him and said, Thou too wast with the Nazarene, Jesus. But he denied, saying, I do not know nor understand what thou sayest. And he went out into the forecourt; and a cock crew. And the maid-servant, seeing him, began again to say to those who were standing by, This is one of them. And he denied it again. And shortly after, those who were standing by said again to Peter, Surely thou art one of them; for thou art a Galilæan. But he began to curse and to swear, saying, I know not this man of whom ye speak. And immediately a cock crew a second time. And Peter called to mind the word that Jesus had said to him, Before a cock crows twice, thou wilt thrice deny me. And when he thought thereon, he wept.

CCXCVII.
Sufferance.

<small>Christian. Mark. comp.</small> And some began to spit on him, and to cover his face and buffet him, and say to him, Prophesy! And the officers, with blows, took him in charge.

And as soon as it was morning, the chief priests, having held a consultation with the elders and the scribes, and the whole council, bound Jesus, and carried him away, and delivered him up to Pilate.

And Pilate asked him, Art thou the king of the Jews? And he answering saith to him, I am. And the chief priests brought many charges against him. And Pilate asked him again, Dost thou make no answer? See what things they are testifying against thee! But Jesus made no further answer; so that Pilate marvelled.

CCXCVIII.

The Majority.

Now at the feast he was wont to release to them one prisoner, whom they might ask. And there was one named Barabbas, who lay bound with insurgents who had committed murder in the insurrection. And the multitude coming up, began to ask him to do as he had been wont to do for them. And Pilate answered them, saying, Will ye that I release to you the king of the Jews? For he knew that for envy the chief priests had delivered him up. But the chief priests stirred up the multitude that he should rather release to them Barabbas. And Pilate answering again said to them, What then would ye have me do with him whom ye call the king of the Jews? And they cried out again, Crucify him! Then Pilate said to them, Why, what evil hath he done? And they cried out the more, Crucify him! And Pilate, wishing to satisfy the multitude, released to them Barabbas, and when he had scourged Jesus, delivered him up to be crucified.

Christian. Mark.

CCXCIX.

Martyrdom.

And the soldiers led him away into the court, which is the Prætorium; and they called together the whole band. And they clothe him with purple, and having platted a crown of thorns, they put it on him. And they began to salute him, Hail, king of the Jews! And they struck him on the head with a reed, and spit upon him, and kneeling down, did him homage. And after they had made sport of him, they stripped him of the purple robe, and put his own garments on him.

Christian. Mark.

And they lead him out to crucify him. And they compel one Simon a Cyrenæan, who was passing by, coming from the country, the father of Alexander and Rufus, to carry his cross. And they bring him to the place Golgotha, which is, when interpreted, Place of a skull. And they gave him wine mingled with myrrh; but he did not take it. And they crucify him, and divide his garments, casting lots for them, what each should take. And it was the third hour when they crucified him. And on the cross the inscription of the charge against him was written: 'The king of the Jews.' And with him they crucify two robbers; one on his right hand, and one on his left. And they that passed by reviled him, wagging their heads, and saying, Ha! thou that destroyest the temple, and buildest it up in three days, save thyself, and come down from the cross. In like manner also the chief priests, with the scribes, making sport among themselves, said, He saved others, cannot he save himself? And Jesus, having uttered a loud cry, expired.

CCC.

Devotion of Women.

There were women looking on from a distance; among whom was Mary the Magdalene, and Mary the mother of James the less and of Joses, and Salome; who, when he was in Galilee, followed him, and rendered him their services; and many other women who came up with him to Jerusalem.

<small>Christian. Mark.</small>

And when the sabbath was past, Mary the Magdalene, and Mary the mother of James, and Salome, bought spices, that they might come and anoint him. And very early on the first day of the week they came to the tomb at the rising of the sun.

CCCI.

Piety of the Intellect.

By devoting the illumined Intellect to piety thou shalt preserve the changing forms of piety.

Your only saviour is your deeds.

<small>Persian. Avestá. Zoroaster. comp.</small>

The aspirations of the holy shall be fulfilled.

Give me, O God! the two desires,—to see and to self-question.

Under the protection of God's great wisdom man acquires wisdom. In virtuous thoughts, words, deeds, God is manifested.

With these are past all the days of a perfect man.

Wicked spirits are of dull reason.

I invoke the angels that reach us; the angels of good conscience, exalted piety, love of excellence, high and perfect thought; the angels of comfort and of joy!

CCCII.

The Rejected.

Set forth the instance of the people of the city when the Sent Ones came to it.

They said, 'Of a truth we augur ill from you: if

<small>Koran, s. 36, 'The Sent Ones.'</small>

ye desist not, we will surely stone you, and a grievous punishment will befall you from us!'

Then from the end of the city a man came running: he said, 'O my people! follow the Sent Ones;

'Follow those who ask not of you a recompense, and who are rightly guided.'

Oh, the misery that rests upon my servants! No apostle cometh to them but they laugh him to scorn.

<small>S. 39, 'The Troops.'</small> See they not how many generations we have destroyed before them?

Not to false gods is it that they shall be brought back;

But all, gathered together, shall be set before us.

Never before thy time did we send a warrior to any city but its wealthy ones said, 'Verily we found our fathers with a religion, and in their tracks we tread.'

<small>S. 43, 'Ornaments of Gold.'</small> Say, 'What! even if I bring you a religion more right than that ye found your fathers following?'

Bear in mind when Abram said to his father and to his people, 'Verily I am clear of what ye worship, save him who hath created me; for he will vouchsafe me guidance.'

Whoso shall withdraw from the warning of the God of mercy, we will chain a Satan to him, and he shall be his fast companion.

He who is God in the heavens is God in the earth also; and he is the Wise, the Knowing.

And blessed is he whose is the kingdom of the heavens, and of the earth, and of all that is between them; for with him is the knowledge of the hour, and to him shall ye be brought back.

Put thou then thy trust in God; for thou hast clear truth on thy side.
And thou shalt see the mountains, which thou thinkest so firm, pass away with the passing of a cloud! S. 27, 'The Ant.'

CCCIII.

Religion.

Though permitted to receive presents, let the Brahman avoid a habit of taking them, since by taking many gifts his divine light soon fades. Hindu. Manu.

By falsehood, the sacrifice becomes vain; by pride, the merit of devotion is lost; and by proclaiming a largess, the fruit of life is destroyed.

Giving no pain to any creature, let a man collect virtue by degrees, as the white ant builds his nest by degrees, that he may acquire a companion to the next world. His virtue alone will adhere to him. With virtue for his guide he will traverse a gloom, how hard to be traversed!

All things have their sense ascertained by speech. In speech they have their basis, and from speech they proceed; consequently, a falsifier of speech falsifies everything.

Alone in some solitary place, let him meditate on the divine nature of the soul; by such meditation he will attain happiness.

Neither by explaining omens and prodigies, nor by skill in astrology and palmistry, nor by casuistry and expositions of holy texts, let the Brahman gain his daily support.

No man who is ignorant of the Supreme Spirit can gather the fruit of mere ceremonial acts.

The soul itself is its own witness; the soul itself is its own refuge : offend not thy conscious soul, the supreme internal witness of men!

CCCIV.

Indifference.

Christian.
Acts.

And when Gallio was proconsul of Achaia, the Jews rose up with one accord against Paul, and brought him before the judgment-seat, saying, This man persuadeth people to worship God contrary to the law. And as Paul was about to open his mouth, Gallio said to the Jews, If it were some act of injustice or wicked misdeed, O Jews, with reason I should bear with you ; but if it be questions of doctrine, and names, and your law, look to it yourselves ; I will not be a judge of these matters. And he drove them from the judgment-seat. But they all laid hold of Sosthenes, the ruler of the synagogue, and beat him before the judgment-seat ; and Gallio cared for none of these things.

CCCV.

The True Word.

Christian.
Heb.

The word of God is living, and powerful, and sharper than any two-edged sword, piercing even to the dividing asunder of soul and spirit, both the joints and marrow, and is a discerner of the thoughts and intents of the heart : and there is no creature that is not manifest in his sight ; but all things are naked and laid open to the eyes of him with whom we have to do.

CCCVI.

Martyrdom.

At that time Herod the Tetrarch heard of the fame of Jesus, and said to his servants, This is John the Baptist; he hath risen from the dead, and therefore do these powers work in him. For Herod had seized John, and bound him, and put him in prison, on account of Herodias, his brother Philip's wife. For John said to him, It is not lawful for thee to have her. And wishing to put him to death, he feared the multitude, because they regarded him as a prophet. But when Herod's birthday was kept, the daughter of Herodias danced before them, and pleased Herod; whereupon he promised with an oath to give her whatever she might ask. And she, being set on by her mother, saith, Give me here on a platter the head of John the Baptist. And the king was sorry; but on account of his oath, and of those at table with him, he ordered it to be given, and sent and beheaded John in the prison. And his head was brought on a platter, and given to the damsel; and she brought it to her mother. And his disciples came and took up the body, and buried it, and went and told Jesus.

Christian.
Matt.

When Jesus heard of it, he withdrew thence in a boat into a desert place apart; and the multitudes hearing of it, followed him on foot from the cities.

And when he came forth, he saw a great multitude; and he was moved with compassion for them.

CCCVII.

Inward Strength.

Christian.
John.
comp.

Because I have spoken these things to you, sorrow hath filled your hearts. But I tell you the truth; it is expedient for you that I depart. For if I do not depart, the Comforter will not come to you.

I have yet many things to say to you, but ye cannot bear them now. But when he, the Spirit of Truth, is come, he will guide you into all the truth. Ye will weep and lament, but the world will rejoice; ye will be sorrowful, but your sorrow will be turned into joy. A woman, when she is in travail, hath sorrow, because her hour is come; but as soon as she is delivered of the child, she remembereth no more the anguish, through joy that a man is born into the world. So ye also now have sorrow; but I shall see you again, and your heart will rejoice, and your joy no one taketh from you.

I do not tell you that I will pray the Father for you; for the Father himself loveth you.

Behold, the hour is coming, yea, is now come, when ye will be scattered, every one to his own, and will leave me alone; and yet I am not alone, because the Father is with me.

CCCVIII.

The Crown of Truth.

Christian.
John.
comp.

Pilate therefore said to him, Art thou a king then? Jesus answered, Thou sayest what is true; for I am a king. For this end have I been born, and for this cause have I come into the world, that I may bear witness to the truth. Every one that is of the truth listeneth to my voice. Pilate saith to him, What is truth ? And having said this, he went out again to the Jews, and saith to them, I find nothing criminal in him. But ye have a custom that I should release to you one at the passover : do ye desire, therefore, that I release to you the king of the Jews? Then they cried out again, saying, Not this man, but Barabbas. Now Barabbas was a robber.

Then therefore Pilate took Jesus and scourged him. And the soldiers platted a crown of thorns, and put it on his head, and put on him a purple robe, and approached him and said, Hail, king of the Jews! and they gave him blows on the face.

Again Pilate went forth, and saith to them, Behold, I bring him forth to you, that ye may know that I find nothing criminal in him. Jesus therefore came forth, wearing the crown of thorns and the purple robe. And [Pilate] saith to them, Behold the man ! The chief priests and the officers cried out, Crucify ! crucify ! Pilate saith to them, Take him yourselves, and crucify him ; for I find nothing criminal in him. The Jews answered him, We have a law, and according to the law he ought to die, because he made himself the Son of God.

When Pilate therefore heard this, he was the more afraid ; and went again into the palace, and saith to Jesus, Whence art thou ? But Jesus gave him no answer. Pilate saith to him, Dost thou not speak to me ? Dost thou not know that I have power to release thee, and have power to crucify thee ? Jesus answered, Thou wouldst have no power against me unless it had been given thee from above.

From this time Pilate sought to release him. But

the Jews cried out, saying, If thou release this man, thou art not a friend of Cæsar. Every one that maketh himself a king setteth himself against Cæsar. When therefore Pilate heard these words, he brought Jesus forth, and sat down on the judgment-seat, in a place called the Pavement, but in Hebrew, Gabbatha. Now it was the preparation of the passover. It was about the sixth hour. And he saith to the Jews, Behold your king! Upon this they cried out, Away with him! Away with him! Crucify him! Pilate saith to them, Shall I crucify your king? The chief priests answered, We have no king but Cæsar. Then therefore he delivered him up to them to be crucified.

They therefore took Jesus; and bearing his own cross, he went forth into the place called Place of a Skull; in Hebrew, Golgotha; where they crucified him, and with him two others, one on each side, and Jesus in the midst. And Pilate wrote an inscription also, and put it on the cross. And the writing was, 'Jesus the Nazarene, the king of the Jews.' This inscription therefore was read by many of the Jews; for the place where Jesus was crucified was near the city; and it was written in Hebrew, Latin, and Greek. Therefore the chief priests of the Jews said to Pilate, Write not, The king of the Jews; but that he said, I am king of the Jews. Pilate answered, What I have written, I have written.

Now there stood by the cross of Jesus his mother and his mother's sister, Mary the wife of Clopas, and Mary the Magdalene. Jesus therefore, when he saw his mother, and the disciple whom he loved standing by, saith to his mother, Woman, behold thy son!

Then he saith to the disciple, Behold thy mother! And from that hour the disciple took her to his own home.

After this, Jesus saith, I thirst. A vessel was brought full of vinegar; and putting a sponge filled with vinegar upon a stalk of hyssop, they raised it to his mouth. When therefore he had received the vinegar, he said, It is finished! and he bowed his head, and died.

CCCIX.

Martyrdom.

Some of those who belonged to the so-called synagogue of the Freedmen, and of the Cyrenæans and Alexandrians, and of those from Cilicia and Asia, arose and disputed with Stephen; and they were not able to resist the wisdom and the influence with which he spoke. Then they suborned men, who said, We have heard him speak blasphemous words against Moses and God. *(Christian. Acts.)*

And they stirred up the people, and the elders, and the scribes, and came upon him, and seized him, and brought him to the council, and set up false witnesses, who said, This man ceaseth not to speak words against the holy place and the Law. For we have heard him say, this Jesus the Nazarene will destroy this place, and change the customs which Moses delivered to us. And all that sat in the council, looking steadily upon him, saw his face like the face of an angel.

Their hearts were filled with rage, and they gnashed their teeth at him. But, being full of the Holy Spirit, he looked up earnestly into heaven, and saw the glory of God, and Jesus standing on the right hand of God, and said, Lo, I behold the heavens opened, and the Son of Man standing on the right hand of God. And they cried out with a loud voice, and stopped their ears, and rushed upon him with one accord; and having cast him out of the city, they stoned him. And the witnesses laid down their garments at the feet of a young man named Saul; and they stoned Stephen, making supplication, and saying, Lord Jesus, receive my spirit. And kneeling down, he cried with a loud voice, Lord, lay not this sin to their charge. And saying this, he fell asleep.

CCCX.
Higher Law.

Christian.
Acts.

The high priest questioned them, saying, We strictly commanded you not to teach in this name, and lo ! ye have filled Jerusalem with your teaching, and mean to bring this man's blood upon us.

But Peter and the apostles answered and said, We ought to obey God rather than men. The God of our fathers raised up Jesus, whom ye slew by hanging him on a cross; him hath God exalted by his right hand as a leader and saviour, to give reformation to Israel, and liberation from error. And we are his witnesses of these things, as also is the sacred spirit which God hath given to those who obey him.

But when they heard this, they were filled with rage, and were resolving to kill them. But there stood up one in the council, a Pharisee, named Gamaliel, a doctor of the law, in high esteem with all the people, and commanded to put the men forth a little while, and said to them [of the council], Men of Israel, take heed to yourselves as to what ye are about to do in respect to these men. For before these days arose Theudas, boasting himself to be somebody ; to whom a number of men, about four hundred, joined themselves : who was slain, and all, as many as obeyed him, were scattered, and came to nought. After this man arose Judas the Galilæan, in the days of the registering, and drew people away after him; he also perished, and all, as many as obeyed him, were dispersed. And now I say to you, Refrain from these men, and let them alone ; for if this design or this work be of men, it will come to nought ; but if it be of God, ye will not be able to overthrow it ; lest haply ye be found also fighting against God.

And they were persuaded by him ; and having called the apostles, they beat them, and commanded them not to speak in the name of Jesus, and released them. They therefore went away from the presence of the council, rejoicing that they were counted worthy to suffer shame in behalf of that name ; and every day, in the temple, and in houses, they ceased not to teach, and to publish the glad tidings concerning Christ.

CCCXI.

The Voice of Conscience.

On the morrow Agrippa and Bernice came with great pomp, and entered into the place of hearing, with the chief captains and principal men of the city, and at the order of Festus, Paul was brought forward. <small>Christian. Acts. comp.</small>

And Agrippa said to Paul, Thou art permitted to speak for thyself. Then Paul stretched forth his hand, and made his defence—

I think myself happy, King Agrippa, that I am to make my defence this day before thee concerning all things of which I am accused by the Jews; especially as thou art acquainted with all the customs and questions among the Jews. Wherefore I beseech thee to hear me patiently.

My manner of life, then, from my youth, which was from the beginning among my own nation and at Jerusalem, all Jews know : and they know, if they are willing to testify, that from the first, according to the strictest sect of our religion, I lived a Pharisee. And now I stand on trial for the hope of the promise made by God to the fathers, which our twelve tribes, earnestly serving God day and night, hope to obtain ; concerning which hope, O king, I am accused by Jews.

Why is it judged incredible with you, when God is arousing the most inanimate ?

I indeed thought with myself that I ought to do many things in opposition to the name of Jesus the Nazarene. Which I also did in Jerusalem ; and many of the saints did I myself shut up in prisons, having received authority from the chief priests ; and when they were put to death, I gave my voice against them. And I punished them often in all the synagogues, and compelled them to blaspheme ; and being exceedingly mad against them, I pursued them even to foreign cities.

And as I was going to Damascus on this business, with authority and a commission from the chief priests, at midday, on the road, O king, I saw a light from heaven above the brightness of the sun, shining around me and those who were journeying with me. And when we had all fallen to the earth, I heard a voice speaking to me, and saying in the Hebrew tongue, Saul, Saul, why persecutest thou me? It is hard for thee to kick against the goad. And I said, Who art thou, Lord? And the Lord said, I am Jesus, whom thou persecutest. But arise and stand upon thy feet; for I have appeared to thee for this purpose, to prepare thee as a minister and a witness both of the things which thou sawest, and of those on account of which I will appear to thee; delivering thee from the people, and from the nations, to whom I send thee, to open their eyes that they may turn from darkness to light.

Wherefore, O King Agrippa, I was not disobedient to the heavenly vision; but first to those in Damascus, and Jerusalem, and to all the country of Judea, and then to the peoples, I proclaimed that they should repent and turn to God, doing works worthy of repentance. For these causes the Jews seized me in the temple, and attempted to kill me.

And as he was thus speaking in his defence, Festus said with a loud voice, Paul, thou art beside thyself; much learning is making thee mad. But he saith, I am not mad, most noble Festus, but utter words of truth and soberness. For the king knoweth about these things well; to whom also I speak boldly; for I am persuaded that none of these things is hidden from him: for this was not done in a corner. King Agrippa, believest thou the Prophets? I know that thou believest. Then Agrippa said to Paul, With little effort thou thinkest to persuade me to become a Christian. And Paul said, I would to God, that with little effort or with great, not only thou, but also all that hear me this day, might be made such as I am, except these bonds.

And the king rose up, and the governor and Bernice, and those who sat with them; and going aside they talked with each other, saying, This man is doing nothing deserving death or bonds.

CCCXII.
Ministry.

Christian.
Acts.
comp.

And now behold, I go, bound in my spirit, to Jerusalem, not knowing the things that will befall me there, save that the sacred spirit testifies in every city, saying that bonds and afflictions await me. But I count life of no value to me, so that I may finish my course, and the ministry which I received from the Lord Jesus, to testify the glad tidings of the good-will of God.

And now, behold, I know that ye all, among whom I went about preaching the kingdom, will see my face no more. Wherefore I testify to you this day, that I am pure from the blood of all men; for I have not shunned to declare to you the whole counsel of God. Grievous wolves will enter in among you, not sparing the flock. And from among yourselves will men arise speaking perverse things, to draw away the disciples after them. Therefore be watchful, and remember that for the space of three years, night and day, I ceased not to warn every one with tears.

And now I commend you to God, and to the promise of his love, who is able to build you up, and to give you an inheritance among all the perfect. I have coveted no man's silver, or gold, or apparel. Ye yourselves know, that these hands ministered to my necessities, and to those that were with me. In all ways I showed you that so labouring ye ought to support the weak, and to remember the words of the Lord Jesus, that he himself said, It is more blessed to give than to receive.

And having thus spoken, Paul kneeled down, and prayed with them all. And they all wept sorely, and fell on Paul's neck, and kissed him, sorrowing most of all for the word which he had spoken, that they were to see his face no more. And they accompanied him to the ship.

CCCXIII.

Charge to a Minister.

Now the end of the commandment is love, out of a pure heart and a good conscience and faith unfeigned; from which some swerving, turned aside to vain babbling, desiring to be teachers of the Law, understanding neither what they say, nor whereof they affirm. Christian.
1 Tim.
2 Tim.
comp.

Exercise thyself unto godliness. For bodily exercise is profitable for little; but godliness is profitable for all things, having promise of the life that now is, and of that which is to come.

Neglect not the gift that is in thee.

Meditate on these things; give thyself wholly to them, that thy progress may be manifest to all. Give heed to thyself, and to thy teaching; continue in them; for in doing this thou shalt save both thyself and them that hear thee.

Do not sharply rebuke an aged man, but exhort him as a father; the younger men, as brethren; the elder women, as mothers; the younger, as sisters, with all purity. She that giveth herself up to pleasure is dead while she liveth.

If any provideth not for his own, especially for those of his own house, he has denied the faith, and is worse than an unbeliever.

Some men's sins are openly manifest, going before them to judgment; and some men they follow after. In like manner also the good works of some are openly manifest; and those that are otherwise cannot be hid.

Godliness with contentment is great gain. For we brought nothing into the world; and it is certain we can carry nothing out. If we have, then, food and raiment, we will be therewith content. But they who desire to be rich fall into temptation and a snare, and into many foolish and hurtful lusts, which drown men in destruction and perdition. For the love of money is a root of all evils; which some coveting, have strayed away from the faith, and have pierced themselves through with many pangs.

But do thou, O man of God, flee these things; and follow after righteousness, godliness, faith, love, patience, meekness. Fight the good fight of faith, lay hold on everlasting life.

Charge those who are rich in this world that they be not high-minded, nor place their hope in uncertain riches, but in God, who giveth us richly all things to enjoy; that they do good, that they be rich in good works, liberal in imparting, willing to communicate, laying up in store for themselves a good foundation against the time to come, that they may lay hold on the true life.

O Timothy! keep that which is committed to thy trust.

God gave us not the spirit of cowardice, but of power, and of love, and of admonition.

No one serving as a soldier entangleth himself with the affairs of life, that he may please him who chose him to be a soldier. And if a man contendeth in the games, he is not crowned unless he contendeth lawfully. The husbandman that laboureth must be the first partaker of the fruits.

Study to present thyself approved unto God, a workman not ashamed, rightly dividing the word of truth.

Flee youthful lusts, and follow righteousness, faith, love, peace.

Foolish and ignorant questionings avoid, knowing that they gender quarrels ; and a servant of the Lord must not quarrel, but be gentle to all, apt in teaching, patient of wrong, in meekness admonishing those that oppose themselves.

Know this, that in the last days grievous times will come. For men will be lovers of themselves, lovers of money, boasters, proud, blasphemers, disobedient to parents, unthankful, unholy, without natural affection, implacable, slanderers, incontinent, fierce, without love for what is good, betrayers, headstrong, puffed up, lovers of pleasure rather than lovers of God ; having a form of godliness, but denying the power thereof. And from these turn away. For of these are they who creep into houses, and lead captive silly women laden with sins, led away by divers lusts, ever learning, and never able to come to the full knowledge of the truth.

But do thou continue in the things which thou didst learn and wast assured of.

Every Scripture inspired by God is profitable for teaching, for reproof, for correction, for discipline in righteousness ; that the man of God may be perfect, thoroughly furnished unto every good work.

Be urgent in season, out of season, confute, rebuke, exhort with all long-suffering and teaching. For the time will come when they will not endure sound doctrine, but after their own desires will they heap to themselves teachers; because they have itching ears; and they will turn away their ears from the truth, and turn aside to fables. But be thou watchful in all things; endure hardship; do the work of an evangelist; fully accomplish thy ministry.

For myself, I am already about to be offered as a sacrifice, and the time of my departure is at hand. I have fought the good fight, I have finished my course, I have kept the faith; henceforth there is laid up for me the crown of righteousness.

CCCXIV.

Size and Substance.

Persian. (Maximes Orientaux.)

The philosophers of India once possessed a book so large that it required a thousand camels to bear it. A king desired to have it abridged; it was reduced so that it could be carried by a hundred camels. Others demanded that it should be diminished still more; until at last the volume was reduced to four maxims. The first bade kings be just; the second prescribed obedience to the people; the third recommended mankind not to eat except when they were hungry; the fourth advised women to be modest.

CCCXV.

Knowledge without Character.

Sin, by whomsoever committed, is detestable, but most so in a learned man. An ignorant plebeian of dissolute manners is better than a learned man without temperance; for that through blindness lost the road, and this, who had two eyes, fell into the well. Persian. Sádi. Gul.

CCCXVI.
Nature.
Have patience! All things are difficult before they become easy.

In the land of Baelkán, relates Sádi, I visited a religious man, to whom I said, 'Cleanse me from ignorance by your doctrine.' He replied, 'Go and suffer with patience, like the earth, O learned in the law, or else bury in the earth all that you have studied.' Persian.

CCCXVII.
The Faithful Prophet.
Thou, O Prophet! by the grace of thy Lord art not
. possessed;
And truly a boundless recompense doth await thee,
For thou art of a noble nature.
Thou shalt see and they shall see
Which of you is the demented.
They desire thee to deal smoothly with them: then
 would they be smooth as oil with thee.
Have ye a scripture wherein ye can search out
That ye shall have the things ye choose? Koran, s. 68, 'The Pen.' comp.

CCCXVIII.
Fidelity.
God said, O Sásán! thou art my friend; hide not the
 right road.
There is no one who seeketh me and findeth me not; Persian. Desátír. Sásán.

All know me according to the capacity of their understanding.
Instead of sensible words, men are answered with weapons of war.
O Sásán! evils await thee. Thou art my prophet: If mankind follow thee not, for them it is evil, not for thee.
The good will come into thy path.
Lay not affliction to heart; God will give it an end.

CCCXIX.
The Prophet.

Koran. comp.
S. 6,
'The Cow.'

Whatever scripture we cancel or cause thee to forget, we bring a better or its like.
Nearer of kin to the faithful is the prophet than they are to their own selves.
O prophet! we have sent thee to be a witness, and a warner, and a herald of glad tidings;

S. 33,
'The Confederates.'

And one who, through his own permission, summoneth to God, and a light-giving torch.
Of the mercy of God thou hast spoken to them in gentle tones. Hadst thou been severe and harsh-hearted, they would have broken away from thee.

S. 3,
'The Family of Imran.'

Traverse the earth, and see what hath been the end of those who treat prophets as liars!

S. 17, 77.

Did angels walk the earth, God had sent them an angel-apostle out of heaven. God is witness enough between you and me.

S. 7,
'Al Araf.'

O children of Adam! there shall come to you apostles from among yourselves rehearsing my signs to you; and whoso shall fear God and do good works, no fear shall be upon them, neither shall they be put to grief.

Every nation hath its set time; and when their time is come, they shall not retard it an hour, and they shall not advance it.

Truth is come, and falsehood is vanished. Verily falsehood is a thing that vanisheth. S. 17.

Assert not your own purity.

Nothing shall be reckoned to a man but that for which he hath made efforts; S. 53. 'The Star.'

And his efforts shall at last be seen in their true light.

CCCXX.

Sufferance.

Patience is the column which sustains Prudence. It is not the human force which hurls a man to the ground, but that which restrains the power that might do so. The only way to answer a fool is to answer nothing. Each word of reply can only recoil from the insensate to thyself. To return insult to the insulter is to increase his disrespect, as fuel feeds flame; but he who meets an accuser with calmness has already confuted him. Persian.

Mahomet and Ali were walking together when they were met by a man who, on account of some fancied injury, began abusing and insulting Ali. Mussulman Tradition.

The venerable man bore this for some time in silence, but at length his patience gave way, and he returned railing for railing. Upon this Mahomet passed on, leaving the two to settle their quarrel as they could. When next the friends met, Ali, deeply offended, said, 'Why didst thou leave me alone to bear the abuse of that insolent fellow?' Mahomet said, 'O Ali! while that man was denouncing you so outrageously, and thou wert silent, I saw ten angels around thee who replied to him. But when thou didst begin to return his insults, the angels one by one left thee, and I also departed.'

CCCXXI.

Speaking the Truth.

Persian.
(Alger.)

Otáye, from his earliest youth,
Was consecrated unto truth;
And if the universe must die
Unless Otáye told a lie,
He would defy the fate's last crash,
And let all sink in one pale ash,
Or e'er by any means was wrung
One drop of falsehood from his tongue.

CHARITY.

CCCXXII.
Charity.

Though I speak with the tongues of men and of angels and have not charity, I am become as sounding brass, or a tinkling cymbal. And though I have the gift of prophecy, and understand all mysteries and all knowledge, and though I have all faith, so as to remove mountains, and have not charity, I am nothing. And though I bestow all my goods to feed the poor, and though I give up my body that I may be burned, and have not charity, it profiteth me nothing. Charity suffereth long, is kind; charity envieth not; charity vaunteth not herself, is not puffed up, doth not behave herself unseemly, seeketh not her own, is not easily provoked, maketh no account of an injury; rejoiceth not at iniquity, but rejoiceth in the truth, beareth all things, believeth all things, hopeth all things, endureth all things. Charity never faileth; but whether there are prophesyings, they will come to an end; whether tongues, they will cease; whether knowledge, it will vanish away. For we know in part, and we prophesy in part; but when that which is perfect is come, that which is in part will be done away. When I was a child, I spoke as a Christian.
1 Cor.

child, I had the feelings of a child, I thought as a child ; since I have become a man, I have put away childish things. For now we see in a mirror, obscurely ; but then face to face ; now I know in part, but then I shall fully know, even as I also am fully known. And now there abide faith, hope, charity, these three ; but the greatest of these is charity.

CCCXXIII.
Charity.

<small>Mishkát.
Mahomet.
Traditional.</small>

Every good act is charity. Giving water to the thirsty is charity. Removing stones and thorns from the road is charity. Exhorting your fellow-men to virtuous deeds is charity. Putting a wanderer in the right path is charity. Smiling in your brother's face is charity. A man's true wealth is the good he does in this world. When he dies, mortals will ask what property has he left behind him ; but angels will inquire, ' What good deeds hast thou sent before thee ? '

CCCXXIV.
Compassion, Economy, Humility.

<small>Chinese.
Lao-Tsze.
B.C. 604.</small>

I have three precious things, which I hold fast and prize—Compassion, Economy, Humility. Being compassionate, I can therefore be brave. Being economical, I can therefore be liberal. Not daring to take precedence of the world, I can therefore become chief among the perfect ones. In the present day men give up compassion, and cultivate only courage. They give up economy, and aim only at liberality. They give up the last place, and seek only the first. It is their death. Compassion is that which is victorious in attack and secure in defence. When Heaven would save a man, it encircles him with compassion.

CCCXXV.

The Covered Sins.

In a dream of resurrection one saw a vast multitude of the wicked driven forth in terror, and heard their cries; but from among these one was placed under a cool shade, and a heavenly jewel suspended about his neck. 'Who art thou,' he asked, 'thus adorned; and why art thou helped out of woe?' He replied, 'I trained a vine around my door, and once a venerable man rested sweetly beneath it.' Persian.
Sádi.
Bóstán.
comp.

CCCXXVI.

Bountifulness.

The prophet Moses (upon whom be peace!) thus admonished Karoon—'Do thou good, in the same manner that God hath done good unto thee.' The Arabs say, 'Be bountiful without accounting it an obligation, when most certainly the benefit will return to you.' Whenever the tree of beneficence takes root, it sends forth branches beyond the sky. Persian.
Sádi.
Gul.

CCCXXVII.

Compassion.

An old man having embraced the religion of Sugata, his son reviled him. 'Why do you abuse me?' said the father. The son replied, 'You have abandoned the law of the Vedas, and followed a new law, which is no law.' Hindu.
Buddhist.
Somadeva.
comp.

The father answered, 'There are different forms

of religion : one looks to another world, the other is intended for the people. You should not abuse my religion, which grants protection to all beings. For surely there is no doubt that to be kind cannot be unlawful, and I know no other kindness than to give protection to all living beings. Therefore, if I am too much attached to my religion, whose chief object is love, and whose end is deliverance, what sin is there in me, O child ? '

But the son continued his abuse, and the father laid the matter before the king, who ordered the son to be executed. When the day for his execution arrived, the youth was brought before the king, who asked why he had grown so pale and thin. The youth replied, 'Seeing the day of death approaching, I could not eat.' The monarch said, ' Live then, and learn to respect a religion which enforces compassion for all beings.'

CCCXXVIII.

Kindness to Animals.

Hindu.
Manu.

He who injures animals that are not injurious, from a wish to give himself pleasure, adds nothing to his own happiness, living or dead ; while he who gives no creature willingly the pain of confinement or death, but seeks the good of all sentient beings, enjoys bliss without end.

CCCXXIX.

Love.

The sweet current of primæval love still flows throughout the veins of all Nature. The nightingale mourns for the perished rose, and the winds are laden with the sighings of sympathy. *Von Hammer.*

Whoso would carelessly tread one worm that crawls on earth, that heartless one is darkly alienate from God; but he that, living, embraceth all things with his love, to dwell with him God bursts all bounds above, below.

CCCXXX.

Candour and Detraction.

In the market-place lay a dead dog. Of the group gathered around it, one said, 'This carcase is disgusting;' another, 'The sight of it is a torment.' Every man spoke in this strain. But Jesus drew near and said, 'Pearls are not equal in whiteness to his teeth.' Look not on the failures of others and the merits of thyself: cast thine eye on thine own fault. *Persian. Nizámi. 12th cent.*

CCCXXXI.

Charity.

Charity is the free gift of anything not injurious. If no benefit is intended, or the gift is harmful, it is not charity. There must be also the desire to assist, or to show gratitude. It is not charity when gifts are given from other considerations, as when animals are fed that they may be used, or presents given by lovers to bind affection, or to slaves to stimulate labour. It is found where man, seeking to diffuse happiness among all men—those he loves, and those he loves not—digs canals and pools, makes roads, bridges, and seats, and plants trees for shade. It is found where, from compassion for the miserable and the poor, who have none to help them, a man erects resting-places *Siamese. Buddhist. Kathá Chari.*

for wanderers, and drinking-fountains, or provides food, raiment, medicine for the needy, not selecting one more than another. This is true charity, and bears much fruit.

CCCXXXII.

Character (Domestic).

Propriety of conduct is true greatness of birth.

<small>Hindu. Cural.</small> Call him not a man who parades empty words; call him the chaff of men. The wise will not even forgetfully speak that which cannot profit.

Humility and sweetness of speech are the ornaments of man.

He will be called the true householder who is a firm support to the virtuous.

He will be said to flourish in domestic virtue who aids the forsaken.

What will he who lives virtuously in the domestic state gain by becoming an ascetic? Among those who labour for future happiness, he is greatest who lives well in his household.

They only live who live without disgrace.

The ground which supports an ignoble body but diminishes its blameless produce.

CCCXXXIII.

Benevolence.

<small>Cural.</small> Benevolence seeks not a return. What does the world give back to the clouds?

To exercise benevolence is the whole design of acquiring property.

He truly lives who knows and discharges the

duties of benevolence. He who knows them not may be reckoned among the dead.

The man of great knowledge who desires the good of the world is as the full waters of a city tank.

The wealth of a benevolent man is as the ripening of a fruitful tree in the midst of a town.

The wise will know how to be benevolent even when they are without wealth.

Such loss as results from benevolence is worth being procured by the sale of one's self.

CCCXXXIV.
Brotherhood.

And it came to pass, as he was reclining at table in the house, lo! many publicans and sinners came and reclined with Jesus and his disciples. And when the Pharisees saw it, they said to his disciples, Why doth your teacher eat with the publicans and sinners? But when he heard that, he said, They who are well do not need a physician, but they who are sick. But go ye and learn what this meaneth,' I desire mercy and not sacrifice.' _{Christian. Matt.}

CCCXXXV.
Forgiveness.

Then came Peter, and said to him, Lord, how often shall my brother sin against me, and I forgive him? Until seven times? Jesus saith to him, I say not to thee, until seven times, but until seventy times seven. _{Matt.}

Therefore the kingdom of heaven is likened to a king who would settle accounts with his servants. And when he had begun to reckon, there was brought to him one who owed him ten thousand talents. But as he was unable to pay, his lord ordered him to be sold, and his wife and children, and all that he had, and payment to be made. Then that servant fell down and did obeisance to him, saying, Have patience with me, and I will pay thee all. And the lord of that servant, being moved with compassion, released him, and forgave him the debt. But that servant went out, and found one of his fellow-servants who owed him a hundred denāries; and he laid hold of him, and took him by the throat, saying, Pay what thou owest. His fellow-servant then fell down and besought him, saying, Have patience with me, and I will pay thee. And he would not; but went away and cast him into prison, till he should pay the debt. Then his fellow-servants, seeing what was done, were greatly grieved, and went and told their lord all that had been done. Then his lord, having called him, saith to him, Thou wicked servant, all that debt I forgave thee because thou didst beseech me; shouldst not thou also have had pity on thy fellow-servant, even as I had pity on thee?

CCCXXXVI.

Humanity the Christ.

Christian.
Matt.

And when the son of Man shall come in his glory, and all the angels with him, then will he sit on the throne of his glory, and before him will be gathered all the nations; and he will separate men one from another, as a shepherd separateth the sheep from the goats; and he will set the sheep on his right hand, and the goats on the left. Then will the king say to those on his right hand, Come, ye blessed by my

Father, inherit the kingdom prepared for you from the foundation of the world. For I was hungry, and ye gave me food; I was thirsty, and ye gave me drink; I was a stranger, and ye took me in; naked, and ye clothed me; I was sick, and ye visited me; I was in prison, and ye came to me.

Then will the righteous answer him, saying, Lord, when saw we thee hungry, and fed thee? or thirsty, and gave thee drink? and when saw we thee a stranger, and took thee in? or naked, and clothed thee? or when did we see thee sick, or in prison, and come to thee? And the king will answer and say to them, Truly do I say to you, inasmuch as ye did it to one of the least of these my brethren, ye did it to me.

Then will he say also to those on the left hand, Depart from me! For I was hungry, and ye gave me no food; I was thirsty, and ye gave me no drink; I was a stranger, and ye took me not in; naked, and ye clothed me not; sick, and in prison, and ye visited me not.

Then will they also answer, saying, Lord, when saw we thee hungry, or thirsty, or a stranger, or naked, or sick, or in prison, and did not minister to thee? Then will he answer them, saying, Truly do I say to you, inasmuch as ye did it not to one of the least of these, ye did it not to me.

CCCXXXVII.
Compassionateness.

A certain lawyer, to try Jesus, said, Teacher, what shall I do to inherit everlasting life? Jesus said, How readest thou in the law? And he answered, 'Thou shalt love the Lord thy God with all thy heart, and with all
<small>Christian. Luke.</small>

thy soul, and with all thy strength, and with all thy mind, and thy neighbour as thyself.' And he said to him, Thou hast answered rightly; do this, and thou shalt live. But he, wishing to justify himself, said to Jesus, And who is my neighbour? Jesus answering said, A certain man was going down from Jerusalem to Jericho, and fell among robbers; who, after stripping him of his raiment, and wounding him, departed, leaving him half dead. And by chance a certain priest was going down on that road; and when he saw him, he passed by on the other side. And in like manner also a Levite, having arrived at the place, came and saw, and passed by on the other side. But a certain Samaritan, as he was journeying, came where he was, and when he saw him, had compassion, and went to him, and bound up his wounds, pouring on oil and wine, and setting him on his own beast, brought him to an inn, and took care of him. And the next day, he took out two denāries and gave them to the host, and said, Take care of him; and whatever thou spendest more, I, when I come back, will repay thee. Which of these three, dost thou think, was neighbour to him that fell among the robbers? And he said, He that took pity on him. Then said Jesus to him, Go and do thou likewise.

CCCXXXVIII.

Values.

Christian.
Luke.

And he looked up and saw the rich men casting their gifts into the treasury. And he saw also a certain poor widow casting in thither two mites. And he said, In truth I say to you, that this poor widow hath cast in more than they all. For all these out of their abundance cast into the offerings; but she out of her penury cast in all the living that she had.

CCCXXXIX.
Altruism.

Setting out with hope on thy soul's pilgrimage, unite to thee what hearts thou canst. When thou reachest the sacred Presence, bind to thee a true friend: know well that a hundred holy temples of Mecca have not the value of a heart. Leave there thy Kaaba with its holy stone from paradise, and go thou rather to find a heart! Persian.
Omar
Khèyam.
11th cent.

The entire world shall be populous with thy benefits of that action of thine which saves one soul from despair. A thousand chains broken by thee are less than to have chained to thee by sweetness the heart of a free man.

The dogmas admit only what is obliging to the deity. But refuse not that bit of bread in thy possession to another. Guard thy tongue from speaking evil, and seek not injury for any being; and then I undertake on my own account to promise thee paradise.

CCCXL.
Love of Enemies.

Abou-Hanifah died in prison at Bagdad, wherein he was cast by the Calif Almansor for refusing to subscribe to the doctrine Cadha (absolute predestination). This famous teacher having once received a severe blow, said to the man who struck him, 'I am able to return injury for injury, but this will I not do: I am Persian.
7th cent.
(D'Herb.)

able to complain of thee to the Calif, but will not complain: I am able to utter in my prayers to God the outrage you have inflicted, but from that I shall guard myself most carefully. Finally, in the day of judgment I shall be able to demand upon thee divine vengeance; but if that day should arrive this moment, and my intercession should avail, I would not enter paradise unless in thy company.' On this story a poet wrote, 'Think not that the valour of a man consists only in courage and force: if you can rise above wrath and forgive, you are of a value inestimable.'

CCCXLI.

Good for Evil.

<small>Mussulman.
Egyptian.
Zamakshrí.
Kassháf.</small>

Gabriel said to Mahomet, 'Seek again him who drives you away; give to him who takes away from you; pardon him who injures you; for God loveth that you should cast into the depths of your souls the roots of his perfections.'

The Prophet said, 'Think only of what is good for each, and consider not the wrong that has been done thee: pardon others readily, and do good only unto all; but avoid the society of the ignorant, the opinionated, and the quarrelsome. Fair is the dwelling-place of those who have bridled anger and forgiven their adversaries. Return good for evil.'

The Mathnévi says, 'Let us be like trees, that yield their fruits to those who throw stones at them.'

Ali said, 'To pardon the conquered is a tithe of the victory.'

Tamám said, 'If the great punish those who offend them, how shall they be distinguished from the vulgar?'

To one who had followed him with much abuse Ahnaf said, 'If there remains anything for you to say against me, say it before we enter this town, lest others should observe, and return you injury for injury.'

CCCXLII.
Varied Gifts.

There are diversities of gifts, but the same Spirit; and there are diversities of services, but the same Lord; and there are diversities of operations, but it is the same God who worketh all things in all. But the manifestation of the Spirit is given to each one for the good of others. For to one is given by the Spirit the word of wisdom; to another, the word of knowledge; to another, faith; to another, the gifts of healing; all these worketh the one and self-same Spirit, allotting to each one severally as it will.

Christian. 1 Cor. comp.

The body is not one member, but many. If the foot say, Because I am not a hand, I am not of the body, is it for this reason not of the body? And if the ear say, Because I am not an eye, I am not of the body, is it for this reason not of the body? If the whole body were an eye, where would be the hearing? If the whole were hearing, where would be the smelling? But as it is, God set the members every one of them in the body, as it pleased him. And if they were all one member, where would be the body? But now there are indeed many members, but one body. And the eye cannot say to the hand, I have no need of thee; nor, again, the head to the feet, I have no need of you. And so if one member suffereth, all the members suffer with it; or if one member is honoured, all the members rejoice with it.

CCCXLIII.

Loving Service.

<small>Christian.
John.</small>
Now before the feast of the passover, Jesus, knowing that his hour had come that he should depart out of this world to the Father, having loved his own who were in the world, loved them unto the end. And supper being served—the accuser having already put it into the heart of Judas Iscariot, the son of Simon, to betray him—he, knowing that the Father had given all things into his hands, and that he came forth from God, and was going to God, riseth from the supper, and layeth aside his garments, and took a towel, and girded himself. Then he poureth water into the basin, and began to wash the disciples' feet, and to wipe them with the towel wherewith he was girded. So he cometh to Simon Peter; who saith to him, Lord, dost thou wash my feet? Jesus answered, What I do thou shalt know presently. Peter saith, Thou shalt never wash my feet. Jesus answered, If I wash thee not thou hast no part with me. Simon Peter saith to him, Lord, not my feet only, but also my hands and my head.

So after he had washed their feet, and had taken his garments, and placed himself again at the table, he said to them, Know ye what I have done to you? Ye call me the Teacher and the Lord. If I then, the Lord and the Teacher, have washed your feet, ye also ought to wash one another's feet.

A new commandment I give you, that ye love one another; as I have loved you, that ye also love one another. By this will all men know that ye are my disciples, if ye have love one for another.

CCCXLIV.
Liberality.

But as ye abound in everything, in faith, and utterance, and knowledge, and all earnestness, and in your love to us, see that ye abound in this exercise of liberality also. I speak not by way of command, but by reason of the earnestness of others, and to prove the genuineness of your love. For ye know the grace of our Lord Jesus Christ, that though he was rich, yet for your sakes he became poor, that ye through his poverty might be rich. _{Christian. 1 Cor. comp.}

If there be first the willing mind, it is accepted according to what a man hath, not according to what he hath not.

He that soweth sparingly shall reap also sparingly, and he that soweth bountifully shall reap also bountifully. Each one, as he purposeth in his heart, so let him give; not grudgingly, or of necessity; for God loveth a cheerful giver.

CCCXLV.
Fraternity.

Christ hath broken down the dividing wall between us. He brought the glad tidings of peace to you who were afar off, and to those that were near. Ye are no longer strangers and foreigners, but fellow-citizens with the devout, and members of God's household, and are built on the foundation of the prophets and apostles. _{Christian. Eph. comp.}

I exhort you, therefore, I, the prisoner in the Lord, to walk worthily of the calling with which ye were called, with all humility and meekness, with long-suffering; bearing with one another in love, endeavouring to keep unity of spirit in the bond of peace. There is one body, and one soul, even as ye were called in one hope of your calling.

That we may no longer be children, tossed to and fro and borne about by every wind of doctrine, through the dishonest tricks of men, and their cunning in the wily arts of error, but cleaving to truth in love, may grow up in all things unto him who is the head.

Be renewed in the spirit of your mind, and put on the new man, which was created according to God in justice, and the holiness of truth.

Having put away falsehood, speak every man truth with his neighbour; we are members one of another.

Let not the sun go down on your wrath. Let no foul language proceed out of your mouth. Let all bitterness, anger, clamour, evil-speaking be put away from you with all malice; and be kind to one another, tender-hearted, forgiving. Be imitators of God as dear children.

CCCXLVI.

Fraternity.

Christian.
1 Thess.
comp.

But concerning brotherly love there is no need of writing to you; for ye yourselves are taught of God to love one another; for indeed ye do it toward all our brothers who are in Macedonia. But we exhort you, brothers, to abound in love still more; and to study to be quiet, and to do your own business, and to work with your own hands, as we commanded you; that ye may walk becomingly towards those without, and may have need of nothing.

Be at peace among yourselves. Admonish the unruly, comfort the feeble-minded, support the weak, be forbearing to all. See that none render evil for evil to any one ; but ever follow that which is good, both toward one another and toward all.

Be always joyful. In everything give thanks. Quench not the Spirit ; despise not prophesyings, but prove all things ; hold fast that which is good ; abstain from every form of evil.

CCCXLVII.
Morals.

Let brotherly love continue.

Be not forgetful to entertain strangers ; thereby some have entertained angels unawares. <small>Christian. Heb. comp.</small>

Remember those in bonds as bound with them.

Let marriage be honoured in all respects.

Follow peace with all men.

Let your disposition be without covetousness.

Works of kindness and liberality forget not.

CCCXLVIII.
Liberality.

Be like the ant during the summer days.

If in prosperity you do no good, in misfortune you must suffer. <small>Arabic. (Albitis. comp.</small>

Light thy candle before the darkness comes on.

To avoid sin is better than repentance.

The liberality of the poor is best.

There is no rest for the envious.

Be persuaded that there is no offence too great to be pardoned.

The worst of men is he who does not employ his talents for the good of others.

Riches and the world will pass away : good actions will remain.

CCCXLIX.

Charity.

Persian.
(Albitis.)
comp.

Charity is the salt of riches ; without this preservative they would corrupt themselves.

A generous man's gift is a true present ; an interested man's gift is a demand.

O thou to whom is granted the enjoyment of tranquil slumber ! think of him whom sorrow does not permit sleep.

O thou who canst walk expeditiously ! have pity on thy companion who cannot follow thee.

O thou who art rich ! think of those who are oppressed by poverty.

Enjoy the benefits of Providence—that is wisdom : make others enjoy them—that is virtue.

CCCL.

Bountifulness.

Turkish.
(Albitis.)

Do good, and throw it into the sea : though the fishes may not know it, God will.

All that thou givest thou wilt carry away with thee.

CCCLI.

Charity.

Singhalese.
Buddhist.

Where shall charity be found ? In the footprint of one bound on works of charity and faith ; in the merciful spirit ; in lips that dwell lovingly on that which the great Teacher hath taught us to adore.

CCCLII.

Mercifulness.

It is the determination of the spotless not to give sorrow to others, although they could obtain by it the right powers which confer greatness. _{Hindu. Cural II.}

It is the determination of the spotless not to do evil in return to those who have done evil to them.

If a man inflict suffering, even on those who without cause hate him, it will in the end give him irremovable sorrow.

The punishment of those who have done you evil, is to put them to shame by showing great kindness to them.

What benefit has he derived from his knowledge who does not endeavour to keep off pain from another as much as from himself?

Why does a man inflict on others that which were grievous to himself?

If a man in the morning seek sorrow for another, in the evening sorrow will visit him unsought.

CCCLIII.

Sympathy.

Never will I seek, nor receive, private individual salvation—never enter into final peace alone; but for ever, and everywhere, will I live and strive for the universal redemption of every creature throughout all worlds. Until all are delivered, never will I leave the world of sin, sorrow, and struggle, but will remain where I am. _{Chinese. Kwan-yin. A Fo prophetess.}

CCCLIV.

The Heart of Actions.

Burmese.
Para Taken.

It is the heart of love and faith accompanying good actions which spreads, as it were, a beneficent shade from the world of men to the world of angels.

CCCLV.

Kindness.

Hindu.
Cural II.
9th cent.

What is the value of eyes in which there is no kindness?

Kindness is the real wealth. Property is owned alike by best and basest.

Stand in the right path, consider, and be kind; though you may study perfectly the rules of many sects, kindness must gain your heaven.

They will enter no region of darkness or grief whose mind is the abode of kindness.

No evil that the soul dreads can come upon him who is kind and protects all creatures.

This great, rich earth, with all its generations of men, is vigilant that sorrow shall not come upon kind hearts.

Those who are without wealth may one day be prosperous; for the unkind there is no change, they are utterly destitute.

Our world is not for those without wealth; another is not for those without kindness.

The virtue of one without kindness is like the worship of one without wisdom.

CCCLVI.

Enough.

Thou sayest, 'When I have enough I will relieve the distressed.' How I pity thee! Thou wilt never relieve them. _{Chinese. (Albitis.)}

CCCLVII.

Charity.

A good work performed with a pure heart, though small, is not trifling. How large is the seed of the banyan-tree? _{Hindu. Vémana.}

Look closely at musk; its hue is dark, but it perfumes all things. Thus hidden are the virtues of men of weight.

Those who look after the faults of others are often ignorant of their own.

If you consider your possessions as your own, fools will agree with you.

That alone belongs to you which you have bestowed.

From buried wealth what is derived? Anxiety alone.

Be a man evil-doer or unlettered, charity regards only his destitution.

To what end is liberality without love?

Injure not others, O men, and live for ever!

CCCLVIII.

Charity.

In the name of God the Compassionate, the Merciful.

What thinkest thou of him who treateth our religion as a lie?

<small>Koran.
S. 107,
'Religion.'
comp.</small>

He it is who thrusteth away the orphan,
And stirreth not up others to feed the poor.
Woe to those who pray,
And in their prayers are careless;
Who make a show of devotion,
But refuse to help the needy.

CCCLIX.
The Destitute.

<small>Hindu.
Cural.</small>
To give to the destitute is true charity. Other gifts may be returned. This is the characteristic of the inherently noble.

The power of those who perform penance is that of enduring hunger. It is inferior to the power of those who remove hunger from others.

The benevolent lay up their wealth in the place from which they have removed the hunger of the poor.

Do the hard-hearted who lay up only the possessions to be lost know the happiness which springs from giving? The solitary feast and unshared wealth are more joyless than begging.

Even death is joyful when charity cannot be exercised.

By giving live with praise. The world contains but one thing imperishable,—the good fame which rises in grandeur from the earth it has blessed with charity.

CCCLX.
Kindness.

Whenever you speak, watch yourself: repentance follows every word which gladdens no heart.

Let every thorn which people sow in thy road bloom in the lustre of thy smiles.

Sádi says, 'He that plants thorns will not gather roses.'

Persian.
Hayáti.
10th cent.
Ab.

CCCLXI.
Servants.

The duty of a servant is extremely hard, and not performable even by saints. If he be silent, he is called a fool; if eloquent, a prattler; at hand, an artful fellow; at a distance, a bad attendant; if patient, a coward; if he endure not, a rascal. What sort of master is that who does not honour his servants while they discharge their duty? To secure service or the discharge of duty there is no need of dragging by violence. He is truly wise who knows the word or deed suited to the occasion. By taking up the whole time of a servant, by increasing expectation, by denying reward, the ill-disposed master is recognised. Favourable discourse to a servant; presents that denote affection; even in blaming faults, taking notice of virtues; these are the manners of a kind master. He who knows how to consider his servants abounds with good ones.

Hindu.
Hitopadesa.
comp.

CCCLXII.
Hospitality.

To the guest who comes of his own accord, let a seat be offered, and water, with such food as can be prepared, after the due rites of courtesy.

Hindu.
Manu.
comp.

Grass and earth to sit on, water to wash the feet, and affectionate speech, are at no time wanting in the mansions of the good, though they be indigent.

CCCLXIII.

Hospitality.

<small>Hindu.
Hitopadesa.
'Amicable
Instruction.'
comp.</small>

Even to an enemy entering our house, hospitality must not be withheld. The tree does not withhold its shade even from the wood-cutter. Straw, earth, water and kind speech: these four are never absent from the houses of good men. The stranger who departs from the house for want of kind reception, leaves behind to the owner his faults, and bears away all his merits.

The good will not withhold kindness from the ignorant, as the moon sends her light into the hovel. The best friend is that which remains with us even after death,—a good heart.

Who is a foreigner to those who speak civilly?

Is this one of us, or is he a stranger? is the reckoning of the base: to the generous, all men are of one family.

CCCLXIV.

Hospitality.

<small>Scand.
Sæmund's
Edda.
Havamál.</small>

Liberal and brave men live best; they seldom cherish sorrow: but a base-minded man dreads everything; the niggardly are uneasy even under benefits.

Givers hail! a guest has come in. Where shall he sit? Fire is needful to him who has entered: he is cold. Food and raiment are required: he has wandered over the fell. Water he needs, who craves refreshment; a towel; hospitable invitation, a good reception. If he can obtain it, discourse and answer, and wit.

Never with insult or derision treat thou a guest or wayfarer : men often little know who sits within.

For the hated oft is spared what for the dear was destined.

CCCLXV.

Hospitality.

It is not fit that one should wish his guests to be outside, even though he were eating the food of im- Hindu. Cural. mortality.

The Goddess of Prosperity (Lakshmi), with joyous mind shall dwell in the house of that man who with cheerful countenance entertains the good as guests.

Those who know not how to act agreeably, though they may have learnt many things, are still ignorant.

The inhospitable shall at length lament, saying—

'We have laboured and laid up wealth, and are now without support.' Such is the property of the stupid. It is poverty in the midst of wealth.

As the Anicham flower fades in smelling, so fades the feast from which faces are turned away.

CCCLXVI.

Sweet Speech.

Why does he use harsh words who sees the plea- Cural. sure which sweet speech yields ? It is like eating unripe fruit when ripe is at hand.

Sweet speech flows from love, is free from deceit, and is the right word of the mouth of virtue.

Sweet speech with a cheerful countenance surpasses the gift of the more prosperous.

Sorrow shall not increase on those who increase pleasure by constant kindness.

That speech which unites usefulness with sweetness diminishes evil and increases virtue.

That speech which, while imparting benefits, ceases not to please, bears earthly, bears celestial fruit.

CCCLXVII.

Good for Evil.

<small>Chinese. Buddhist. Catena.</small>

Buddha said, 'A man who foolishly does me wrong (or regards me as being, or doing, wrong), I will return to him the protection of my ungrudging love; the more evil comes from him, the more good shall go from me; the fragrance of these good actions always redounding to me, the harm of the slanderer's words returning to him.' There was a foolish man once heard Buddha, whilst preaching, defend this great principle of returning good for evil, and therefore he came and abused Buddha. Buddha was silent, and would not answer him, pitying his mad folly. The man having finished his abuse, Buddha asked him, saying, 'Son, when a man forgets the rules of politeness in making a present to another, the custom is to say, "Keep your present." Son, you have now railed at me; I decline to entertain your abuse, and request you to keep it—a source of misery to yourself. For as sound belongs to the drum, and shadow to the substance, so in the end misery will certainly overtake the evil-doer.' Buddha said, 'A wicked man who reproaches a virtuous one, is like one who looks up and spits at heaven; his action soils not heaven.'

CCCLXVIII.

The Highest Love.

Abou Ben Adhem—may his tribe increase!—
Awoke one night from a deep dream of peace
And saw, within the moonlight in the room,
Making it rich, and like a lily in bloom,
An angel writing in a book of gold.
Exceeding peace had made Ben Adhem bold,
And to the presence in the room he said,
'What writest thou?' The vision raised its head,
And, with a look made of all sweet accord,
Answered, 'The names of those who love the Lord.'
'And is mine one?' said Abou. 'Nay, not so,'
Replied the angel. Adhem spoke more low,
But cheerly still, and said, 'I pray thee, then,
Write me as one that loves his fellow-men.'
The angel wrote, and vanished. The next night
He came again, with a great wakening light,
And showed their names whom love of God had
 blessed—
And, lo! Ben Adhem's name led all the rest!

<small>Sufi.
Abou Ben Adhem, of Khorassan.
d. A.C. 782.
(Leigh Hunt. Version from D'Herb.)</small>

CCCLXIX.

Charity.

Mahomet stood beneath a palm-tree, and taught his followers, saying, 'He who clothes the naked shall be clothed by God with the green robes of paradise. If a good man give with his right hand and conceal it from his left, he overcomes all things.' 'O Prophet!' said one, 'my mother Umm Sâd is dead; what is the best alms I can give away for her soul?' Mahomet

<small>Mahomet. Mishkát. comp.</small>

bethought him of the panting heats of the desert, and said, 'Dig a well for her, and give water to the thirsty.' The man dug a well, and said, 'This is for my mother.'

CCCLXX.

Mercifulness.

Arabic.
Mishkât.

The Prophet was sleeping alone at the foot of a tree, at a distance from his camp, when he was awakened by a noise, and beheld Durther, a hostile warrior, standing over him with a drawn sword. 'Mohammed,' cried he, 'who is there now to save thee?' 'God!' replied the Prophet. Struck with awe, Durther let fall his sword, which was instantly seized upon by Mohammed. Brandishing the weapon, he exclaimed in turn, 'Who is there now to save thee, O Durther?' 'Alas! no one!' replied the soldier. 'Then learn from me to be merciful.' So saying, Mohammed returned the sword. And thenceforth these two were friends.

CCCLXXI.

Liberality.

Persian.
Sádi.
Gul.

They asked a wise man which was preferable, fortitude or liberality? He replied, 'He who possesseth liberality hath no need of fortitude. It is inscribed on the tomb of Bahram-Goar, that a liberal hand is preferable to a strong arm.' Hátim Tái no longer exists; but his exalted name will remain famous for virtue to eternity. Distribute the tithes of your wealth in alms, for when the husbandman lops off the exuberant branches from the vine, it produces an increase of grapes.

CCCLXXII.
Considerateness.

One can live well without much, but not without consideratencss. <small>Persian. (Maximes Orientaux.)</small>

The character of a wise man consists in three things: to do himself what he tells others to do; to act on no occasion contrary to justice; and to bear with the weaknesses of those around him.

Treat inferiors as if you might one day be in the hands of a master.

I recollect, says Sádi, the verse which the elephant-driver rehearsed on the banks of the river Nile—'If you are ignorant of the state of the ant under your foot, know that it resembles your own condition under the foot of the elephant.'

LOVE AND FRIENDSHIP.

CCCLXXIII.
Love.

<small>Persian.
The Moolah
of Rúm.
13th cent.
comp.</small>

'Tell me, gentle traveller, who hast wandered through the world, and seen the sweetest roses blow, and brightest gliding rivers,—of all thine eyes have seen, which is the fairest land?'

'Child, shall I tell thee where Nature is most blest and fair? It is where those we love abide. Though that space be small, ample is it above kingdoms; though it be a desert, through it runs the river of paradise, and there are the enchanted bowers.'

CCCLXXIV.
Grades of Love.

<small>Persian.
Mohammed
Ben Ahmed
Attar.</small>

Because love is the soul of this sphere, it, too, is celestial; a pendulum vibrating in accord with the universe. Many paths hath love, each with its own finger-post. The first is right intention, whither good fortune leads; then reach we the longing of affection, leading to the source of friendship; thence open desire and benevolence, guiding the heart aright to faith and sincerity, which lead straight to love. But this love? It is another road; at its end is the shining palace where dwells the Lord of love.

CCCLXXV.
Love.

Is there any bolt that can shut in love ? A tear will publish it. _{Hindu. Cural.}

Those destitute of love appropriate all they have to themselves : those who possess love consider even their bones to belong to others.

The domestic state of that man who is without love is like the flourishing of a withered tree in a desert. Divine virtue will burn up the soul that has no love. The ignorant say love is an ally to virtue only, but it is also the one help of vice, consuming it.

That body which enshrines a heart came by the path of love ; when life leaves those without love it leaves—dust.

Love begets desire, and desire the immeasurable excellence of friendship. They say that the union of soul and body in man is the fruit of the union of Love and Virtue.

They say that the felicity of heaven and the happiness of earth is the fruit of the union of Love and Virtue.

CCCLXXVI.
The Wife.

Every wise woman buildeth her home ; but a foolish woman overthroweth her home with her own hands. _{Heb. Prov. comp.}

A virtuous wife who can find ?
For her price is above pearls.
The heart of her husband trusteth in her.
She worketh with the delight of her hands.

She openeth wide her hand to the afflicted ;
And she reacheth forth her hands to the needy.
Strength and honour are her clothing ;
And she laugheth at the future day.
Her mouth she openeth with wisdom ;
And on her tongue is the law of kindness.
She watcheth the goings of her household ;
And the bread of sloth she eateth not.
Her children rise up and call her blessed ;
Her husband riseth up and praiseth her :
' Many daughters have done excellently,
But thou excellest them all ! '

CCCLXXVII.
The Wife.

Ecclesiasticus. Apoc. Ab.

In three things I (Wisdom) was adorned, and stood up beautiful before God and men: the unity of brethren, the love of neighbours, a man and a wife that agree together.

Blessed is the man that hath a virtuous wife, for the number of his days shall be double. He shall fulfil the years of his life in peace. A silent and loving woman is a gift of God ; and there is nothing so much worth as a mind well instructed. A modest and faithful woman hath double grace, and her pure mind cannot be valued. As the sun when it riseth is the beauty of a good wife in the ordering of her house.

My son, keep the flower of thine age sound, and give not thy strength to strangers. When thou hast gotten a fruitful field, sow it with thine own seed, trusting in the goodness of thy stock. So shall thy race which thou leavest be magnified, having the confidence of their good descent.

CCCLXXVIII.
Gentleness.

The wise tongue maketh knowledge pleasant. A healing tongue is a tree of life. A soft answer turneth away wrath, but grievous words stir up anger.

<small>Heb. Prov. comp.</small>

CCCLXXIX.
Faithfulness.

Naomi, bereaved of her two sons and her husband, arose with her daughters-in-law to return from Moab (there being famine in the land) into Judah. And Naomi said to her daughters-in-law, 'Return each of you to her mother's house; and the Lord deal kindly with you, as ye have dealt by the dead and by me!' Orphah kissed her mother-in-law: Ruth clave unto her. And Ruth said, 'Entreat me not to leave thee, nor to return from following thee; for whither thou goest I will go, and where thou dwellest I will dwell; thy people shall be my people, and thy God my God. Where thou diest will I die, and there will I be buried. Nought but death shall part thee and me!'

<small>Heb. Book of Ruth. Ab.</small>

CCCLXXX.
Good Company.

One day as I was in the bath, a friend of mine put into my hand a piece of scented clay. I took it, and said to it, 'Art thou of heaven or earth? for I am charmed with thy delightful scent.' It answered, 'I was a despicable piece of clay; but I was some time in company of the rose: the sweet quality of my companion was communicated to me; otherwise I should have remained only what I appear to be,—a bit of earth.

<small>Persian. Sádi. b. A.C. 1176.</small>

CCCLXXXI.
Low Society.

Singhalese. Budh.

Better the desert brake for a home, herbs for food, foliage for raiment, grass for a couch, and wild creatures for companions, than to herd with the base and mean.

CCCLXXXII.
Satisfactions.

Hindu. Hitopadesa. comp.

How great a delight is good health to all creatures! How great a satisfaction is friendship! How high a gratification to the wise is the completion of works well begun! The tree of the world hath its poisons, but beareth two fruits of exquisite flavour,—poetry sweet as nectar, and the society of the good.

CCCLXXXIII.
Friendship.

Persian. Ghazáli. 10th cent. Blochmann.

I shun a friend who pronounces my actions to be good though they are bad. I like a simple friend, who holds my faults like a looking-glass before my face.

CCCLXXXIV.
The Friend.

Singh. Budh. Wáda Gogerly. comp.

The flatterer may be known, though professing friendship: he approves your virtues, and he approves your vices.

The true friend restrains you from vice, and encourages you in virtue.

He is a friend who renders assistance, who is faithful in prosperity and adversity, who gives judicious advice, and shows kindness of feeling.

The wise man, knowing his friends, cleaves to them constantly, as a child clings to its mother.

The virtuous wise man shines as a resplendent light. If he partake of the bounty of others, it is as a bee gathers honey, without injuring the beauty or fragrance of the flower.

CCCLXXXV.

Friends.

The worst country is that in which you have no friends. Tartary. (Albitis.)

CCCLXXXVI.

Friendship.

The preserver from grief, from enmity, from fear,— the seat of affection and confidence,—is friendship,— a little word of two syllables. By whom was this precious gem created? Such friends as in prosperity make a bustle for their own ends, are everywhere to be found; but a union of true affection, the delight of both eye and heart,—this precious vase in which to deposit both pleasure and pain, is hard to be acquired. Hindu. Hitopadesa.

CCCLXXXVII.

Friendship.

If thou hast a friend whom thou dost fully trust, and from whom thou wouldst receive good, blend thy mind with his. Scand. Sæmund's Edda. Havamál.

There is a mingling of affection when one can tell another all his mind.

The paths to a true friend lie direct, though he be far away.

Visit thy friend : the way is overgrown with brushwood that no one treads.

I was journeying alone, and lost my way : rich I thought myself when I met another.

Man is the joy of man.

CCCLXXXVIII.
Friendship.

Have no friend unlike yourself.

A man's fault partakes the nature of his company.

There are some with whom we may study in common, but we shall find them unable to go along with us to principles.

The superior man on literary grounds meets his friends, and by their friendship helps his virtue.

Gau-Ping knew well how to maintain friendly intercourse. The acquaintance might be long, but he showed the same respect as at first.

Confucius.
Analects.

CCCLXXXIX.
Friendship.

By melting, metals are united ; for mutual benefit animals herd together ; for safety or gain ignorant men join together ; but the virtuous are attached at first sight.

If the friendship of the good be interrupted, their minds admit of no long change. When the lotos stem is broken the filaments are more visibly connected.

Piety, charity, forbearance, participation in pains and pleasures, goodness of heart, reputation, and truth,—these are the sciences of friendship. By these arts what higher advantage can I acquire ?

Hindu.
Hitopadesa.
comp.

CCCXC.
Slander.

The affection of the righteous is the same in presence as in absence; not like those who censure you behind your back, but before your face are ready to die for you; when you are present, meek as a lamb, but when absent, like the wolf, a devourer of mankind. Whosoever recounts to you the faults of your neighbour will doubtless expose your defects to others.

<small>Persian.
Sádi.
Gul.</small>

CCCXCI.
Filial Affection.

One day, through the ignorance of youth, I spoke sharply to my mother, which vexing her to the heart, she sat down in a corner and wept, saying, 'Have you forgotten all the trouble that you gave me in your infancy, that you thus treat me with unkindness?' What a good saying was that of an old woman to her son, when she saw him able to subdue a tiger, having the strength of an elephant!—'If you had but recollected your time of childhood, when you lay helpless in my arms, you would not treat me with violence now that you have the strength of a lion, whilst I am an old woman.'

<small>Sádi.
Gul.</small>

CCCXCII.
Considerateness.

When you have anything to communicate that will distress the heart of the person whom it concerns, be silent, in order that he may hear from some one else. O nightingale! bring thou the glad tidings of spring, and leave bad news to the owl!

<small>Sádi.
Gul.</small>

CCCXCIII.
Gratitude.

Hindu. Cural.

A benefit finds its only measure in the worth of those who have received it.

Heaven and earth are not an equivalent for a benefit conferred where none has been received.

Though the benefit be small as a millet-seed, they who know its advantage will see it large as a palmyra-tree.

It is not good to forget a benefit: it is good to forget an injury, even on the moment. He who has forgotten every virtue may escape; there is no escape for him who forgets a benefit.

Forget not the benevolence of the blameless: forsake not the friendship of those who have been your staff in adversity.

The wise will remember through sevenfold births the love of those who have wiped away their falling tears.

CCCXCIV.
Reverence for Parents.

Confucius. Analects.

Tsze-Yew asked what filial piety was. Confucius said, 'The filial piety of now-a-days means the support of one's parents. But dogs and horses likewise are able to do something in the way of support. Without reverence, what is there to distinguish the one support given from the other?

'What does the Shoo-King say of filial piety? "You are filial, you are fraternal. These qualities are displayed in government."

'In serving his parents a son may remonstrate with

them, but gently; when he sees that they do not incline to follow his advice, he shows an increased degree of reverence, but does not abandon his purpose.'

CCCXCV.
Children.

Good children are the jewels of the good wife. Hindu. Cural.

Men call their sons their wealth.

Sweet is the lute to those who have not heard the prattle of their own children.

The mother who hears her son called ' a full man,' rejoices more than at his birth. It is pleasant to the greatest that their children should be greater.

So to act that it may be said, ' By what great favour did his father obtain him,' is the benefit which a son should render to his father.

CCCXCVI.
Parents.

We have enjoined on man to show kindness to his parents. With pain his mother beareth him. Arabic. Koran, s. 46.

The Lord hath ordained that ye worship none but him; and kindness to your parents, whether one or both of them, attain to old age with thee: and say not to them 'Fie!' neither reproach them; but speak to them both with respectful speech; s. 17, 'The Night-Journey.' comp.

And defer humbly to them out of tenderness; and say, ' Lord, have compassion on them both, even as they reared me when I was little.'

CCCXCVII.
Filial Duty.

<small>Chinese.
(Albitis.)
comp.</small>

The portrait of a father is to strangers but a picture; but for a son it is a book which teaches him his duties.

Every rogue has begun by being a bad son.

He who remembers the benefits bestowed by his parents is too grateful to remember their faults.

They are happy who can return to their father and mother the care they received from them in infancy; still more happy they who can return them their smiles and caresses, and feel the same love. Old age is sometimes a second childhood; why may not filial piety repeat parental love?

CCCXCVIII.
Gentleness.

<small>Hindu.
(Albitis.)</small>

The edge of the sword is less penetrating than gentleness.

<small>Hindu.
Cural.</small>

Is there a greater enemy than anger, which kills both laughter and joy?

This flame will burn up the pleasant barge of friendship.

Chain anger, lest it chain thee.

CCCXCIX.
Loving much.

<small>Christian.
Luke.
comp.</small>

And one of the Pharisees asked him to eat with him; and he went into the Pharisee's house, and reclined at the table. And lo! a woman who was in the city, a sinner, learning that he was at table in the Pharisee's house, brought an alabaster bottle of ointment, and standing behind at his feet, weeping, began to wet his feet with tears, and wiped them with the hair of her head, and kissed his feet, and anointed them with the ointment. And the Pharisee who had invited him, when he saw this, said within himself, This man, if he were a prophet, would know who and what sort of woman this is that toucheth him; for she is a sinner. And Jesus answering said to him, Simon, I have somewhat to say to thee. And he saith, Teacher, say on. A certain money-lender had two debtors; one owed five hundred denāries, and the other fifty. When they had nothing to pay, he freely remitted the debt of both. Which of them, now, will love him the most? Simon answering said, He, I suppose, to whom he remitted the most. And he said to him, Thou hast judged rightly. And turning to the woman, he said to Simon, Seest thou this woman? I entered thy house, no water didst thou give me for my feet; but she wet my feet with tears, and wiped them with her hair. No kiss didst thou give me; but she, from the time I came in, did not cease to kiss my feet. My head with oil thou didst not anoint; but she anointed my feet with costly ointment. Her many sins have been forgiven; for she loved much.

CCCC.
The Power of Love.

Moshi says, 'Benevolence is the heart of man; righteousness is the path of man. How lamentable a thing is it to leave the path and go astray, to cast away the heart and not to know where to seek for it! If a man lose a fowl or a dog, he knows how to reclaim it. If he lose his soul, he knows not how to reclaim it. The

Japanese.
Kit-ô.
From Mitford.
comp.

true path of learning has no other function than to teach us how to reclaim lost souls.'

Upon which text Kito relates this story. In a certain part of the country there was a well-to-do farmer, who had a son whom he indulged beyond all measure. So the child grew to be sly, selfish, and undutiful. From an undutiful boyhood he grew to a reckless youth. He would fight and quarrel for a trifle, and spent his time in debauchery and riotous living. If his parents remonstrated with him, he would ask insolently, ' Who asked you to bring me into this world ? ' At length this young man became so great a scandal in the neighbourhood, that the relatives and friends of the family urged his parents to disown and disinherit him. They threatened to do so, but he was an only child, and they postponed this last resort from time to time, until at last the relatives and friends declared that they must break off all intercourse with the parents unless this wicked son were disinherited. The parents reflecting that to be so separated from their relatives would be a dishonour to their ancestors, agreed to disinherit the prodigal, and on a certain day all the relatives were gathered to their house that the act might be formally completed.

At that time the undutiful son was drinking and gaming with his evil associates, and one came and told him that his relatives and parents were convened to formally disown and disinherit him. 'What do I care?' said he. 'I am able to take care of myself; and if I choose to go to China or India, who is to prevent me ? But I will swagger to this meeting, and make them all give me seventy ounces of silver to get rid of me.'

So, taking a dagger, he went to the place where his parents and friends had assembled. But he resolved at first to listen from the verandah, and enjoy hearing their abuse of him. Peeping through a chink, he beheld his relatives one after another affixing their names to the petition of disinheritance, and this at last handed to his father. The father took a seal from a bag, and was about to affix it as the final act. 'Now is my time for leaping in among them,' thought the vagabond; but for a moment he held his breath. As the old man was about to seal the document, his wife clutched his hand and said, 'Pray wait a little. During fifty years that we have lived together, this has been the only favour I have ever asked of you,—put a stop to this act of disinheritance. Though my son should beggar me, I cannot feel resentment against him.' So speaking she sobbed aloud, and the old man, pushing the petition back to the relatives, said, 'Though we lose your countenance, and are renounced, we will not disown our son. He may indeed run through our means, but we shall not ask you for charity: we have but one life to lose, and we will die by the roadside seeking our one beloved child.'

The son hearing this, lay down on the ground in silence : this love had burnt away the self-will and baseness from him. In another moment he was kneeling before his parents, and said to his relatives, 'Entreat my parents for me that they shall delay from disowning me for thirty days, and find if in that time I do not give proofs of repentance.' From that hour he became a loving and tender son, and an honour to his family. When at last, years afterwards, the venerable mother came to die, she said to her son, 'Had you not

B

repented, I should have gone to hell, because of my foolish conduct towards you. But now I go to paradise.'

She spake truly. The troubled heart is hell, the heart at rest is paradise. The trouble or peace of parents depends upon their children. Let the young remember this, that they are daily consigning their parents to heaven or hell ; and if they have lost their hearts, let them seek and find them, and bring them back again, that all may have joy.

NATURE.

CCCCI.
Day and Night.

By the brightness of the Sun when he shineth,
By the Moon when she followeth him !
By the Day when it revealeth his glory,
By the Night when it enshroudeth him !
By the Heaven and him who builded it,
By the Earth and him who spread it forth !
By a Soul and him who balanced it,
And breathed into it the evil and the good,—
Blessed now is he who hath kept it pure,
And undone is he who hath corrupted it!

Arabic.
Korân,
s. 91,
'The Sun.'

CCCCII.
Temple of Nature.

The temple I frequent is the turkis-vaulted dome of the sky. I sell my rosary, and all the holy names around it, for that wine which fills creation's cup. I have turned the prayers of the pious to happy songs. The earth is all enchanted ground. Thine it is, Wisdom Supreme, with its light and shadow, its ebb and flow ! Whither leads the path of destiny ? He knows it—he knows it—he knows it !

Persian.
Omar
Khèyam.
12th cent.
comp. &
par.

CCCCIII.
Nature's Voice.

Heb.
Ps.
comp.

The heavens declare the glory of God ;
Day uttereth speech unto day,
And night showeth knowledge unto night.
There is no speech, and no words ;
Their voice is not heard :
Yet through all the earth their sound goeth forth,
And their words to the end of the world.
The law of the Lord is perfect, refreshing the soul ;
The precepts of the Lord are true, making wise the simple ;
The statutes of the Lord are right, rejoicing the heart ;
The commandments of the Lord are clear, enlightening the eyes ;
The fear of the Lord is pure, enduring for ever ;
The laws of the Lord are true, and righteous altogether ;
More to be desired than gold, yea, than much fine gold ;
Sweeter also than honey, and the droppings of the honeycomb.
Moreover, by them is thy servant admonished :
In keeping them is great reward.
Who can discern his errors ?
Cleanse me from hidden faults ;
Restrain thy servant also from presumptuous sins ;
Let them not have dominion over me :
Then shall I be blameless, and innocent of great transgression.
May the words of my mouth be acceptable,
And the meditations of my heart, before thee,
O Lord ! my rock and my deliverer !

CCCCIV.

The Genius of Nature.

I am the father and mother of the world. I am the journey of the good; generation and dissolution; the inexhaustible seed of all nature. I am sunshine, and I am rain. I now draw in, and now let forth. I am death and immortality, entity and non-entity.

I am the same to all mankind. They who serve other gods with a firm belief, in doing so involuntarily worship me. I am he who partaketh of all worship, and I am their reward. I am in them, and they in me. Recollect, O son of Kŏŏntēē, that my servant doth not perish!

<small>Hindu. Bhágavat. Gita. comp.</small>

CCCCV.

The Earth.

Truth which is mighty, righteousness which is strong, consecration and dedication to holiness, sustain the world : may the world, the mistress of the past and future, give us free room!

<small>Hindu. Atharva Veda. (Bruce. Jour. of R.A.S.) comp.</small>

May the earth, the place of habitation, which containeth all things, which holdeth all treasure, which suffereth every creature that hath life to repose on its golden breast; may earth, which holdeth fire whose presence is in all men, grant us the object of our desires!

The earth is our mother.

May thy hills and thy snow-clad mountains,— may thy waste and thy woodland, O world, be pleasant! Unwearied may I dwell on the many-coloured world.

And thou, O earth, do thou give me sweetness of speech!

With the odour of thee which exists in humanity —loveliness and beauty in men and women, in the horse and in the elephant—which is the glory of the maiden—fill us, too, with that : may no one hate us!

I praise the world which is continually renewed.

May clean waters flow for our body : I wash me thoroughly and am clean.

All the range of thee, O earth, which I look over by the help of the sun—may the sight of my eye lose none of it, till the latest years which are to come!

May thy summer, O earth, thy rains, thine autumn, thine early and late winter, thy spring—may thine appointed seasons, thy years, thy day and night, O world, yield us blessings as it were milk !

Thou hast many paths on which men go, a highway for the chariot and for the cart, paths on which the proud and the humble travel. The world which endureth the burden of the oppressor beareth up the abode of the lofty and of the lowly, suffereth the hog, and giveth entrance to the wild-boar.

May fire, sun, and water give me wisdom. May I be a lord on the earth.

May I be full of force, pressing forward : may I scatter all them that are violent.

May the peaceful earth, whose fragrance is excellent, whose breasts contain the heavenly drink, bless me with her milk !

Thou art the capacious vessel of humanity, bestowing all desires, and art not exhausted ; that which thou lackest may the lord of creation fill up—the firstborn of righteousness !

Mother earth, do thou fix and establish me, that it may be well with me—thou that art the associate of heaven!

CCCCVI.
The Burning Bush.

Learn, O student, the true wisdom! See yon bush aflame with roses, like the burning-bush of Moses! Listen, and thou shalt hear if thy soul be not deaf, how from out it, soft and clear, speaks to thee the Lord Almighty! Háfiz.

CCCCVII.
Mediators.

Take example of the roses, that live direct on dew and sunshine. They never question after Moses; and why should you? Háfiz.

CCCCVIII.
The Earth.

The Earth is the sustainer and holder of all objects, superior to all things, containing every treasure. It is adorned with holiness, sacred and pure, related to the Supreme. It is the goddess of prosperity, and brings forth corn and food for all creatures, for it is the blessed womb of all. The Earth possesses a universal form. It is the best of mothers, fulfilling the desires of all her children. Of her milk have the serpent-like men drunk, and it has been to them venom; by it the powerful have been nourished, and it has been to them strength and heroism; to the devourers of men her milk became blood. Men of virtue and knowledge drew from the breast of the Earth a pure nectar, whereby they shared the happiness and immortality of gods. Padma Purána. Bhumi Khanda. comp.

CCCCIX.

Dawn.

<small>Sáma Veda.</small>

The footless Dawn is now advancing, overtaking all the tribes of men with her silver tongue (of awakened song).

The daughter of heaven, subduing with her brilliant eye the mighty power of Darkness, unites with bands of illustrious men, causing the day to shine.

The pure, all-sustaining, divine rays of light remain ever without fault.

The resplendent rays proceed forward with freedom. All intelligences awake with the morning.

The radiant sun rises (in heaven), and the fire is lighted up on earth.

CCCCX.

Hymn to the Sun.

<small>Persian. Desátír. Shet Tahmúrás. comp.</small>

Praise be on thee, amplest of stars!
Revolving in the abundant love and greatness of God,
Abiding in the midst of perfect order,
Author of the powers of the senses,
Cause of whatever is produced anew, and creator of
    the seasons!
In the circle of thy sphere, which is without rent, which
    neither assumeth a new shape nor putteth off a
    new one, nor taketh a straight course,
Thou, maker of the Day, art most near to the lustre of
    God.
Thou art a symbol of his grandeur,
A beam of his glory;
Thou art as a proof of him upon his servants,
Clothing the stars with the garment of thy splendour.

Through the medium of thy active soul, which beam-
eth with glory,
I seek him whose shadow thou art,—
The Lord that giveth harmony to worlds,
The Limit and Establisher of all,
Light of lights !
That he may illuminate my soul with pure light,
adorable knowledge, lofty excellence :
And make me one of those who are nigh unto him,
who are filled with his love !

CCCCXI.
Nature.

They who invent a lie of God shall not prosper.
Is any more wicked than he who deviseth a lie of God, or saith, 'I have had a revelation' when nothing was revealed to him ? <small>Koran.
S. 16.
S. 6,
'Cattle.
comp.</small>

Clear have we made our signs for men of insight.

God causeth the grain and the date-stone to put forth ; he bringeth forth the living from the dead and the dead from the living !

Look ye on their fruits when they ripen. Truly herein are signs unto people who believe.

He causeth the dawn to appear, and hath ordained the night for rest, and the sun and moon for comput-
ing time.

And it is he who hath ordained the stars for you, that ye may be guided thereby in the darknesses of the land and of the sea.

Clear have we made our signs to men of knowledge !

Whoso seeth them, the advantage will be his own ; and whoso is blind to them, his own will be the loss.

God is not ashamed to set forth the parable of a gnat as well as any nobler thing :

The believers will know it to be the truth from their Lord.

He hath placed on the earth the firm mountains which tower above it; and he hath blessed it, and distributed food throughout it for the cravings of all alike.

S. 49.

We have divided you into peoples and tribes, that ye might have knowledge of one another. Only the faithful are brothers.

S. 41,
'The Truth made Plain.'

We will show them our signs in different countries and among themselves, until it become plain to them that it is the truth. Is it not enough for thee that thy Lord is witness of all things ?

Men are in doubt as to the meeting with their Lord. But doth he not encompass all things ?

CCCCXII.

The Artist.

Persian.
Desátír.
Jemshíd.
comp.

In the name of the Almighty God, Jemshíd is my prophet ; him have I chosen for arts, and I will show him the excellencies of the world.

In the name of the art-creating God,

O Jemshíd, I have taught thee all manner of arts, and adorned the world by them :

My light is on thy countenance ;

My word is on thy tongue ;

Me thou seest, me thou hearest, me thou smellest, me thou tastest, me thou touchest :

Thou findest me in everything and in every place; thou perceivest the unity of Being by all its shadows.

What thou sayest that I say; and thy acts are my acts.
Adore the planet Venus (Star of Beauty),
Revolving in the love of her beloved,
Ornament of joy, friendship, and goodness,
That thou mayest attain unto the universal intelligence,
Whose light extendeth over all.
The perfect seeth unity in multiplicity, and multiplicity in unity.
The world is an idea of the self-existent.
The worlds invisible and visible are one in respect to the one Mind.
The roads tending to God are more in number than the breathings of created beings.
The world is a man, and man is a world.

CCCCXIII.
The World Divine.

Show kindness to those under you, that you may receive kindness from God. Persian.
Desátír.
Abad.

The superior and inferior beings are the gift of the Giver: they cannot be separated from him: they have been, are, and shall be.

The world, like a radiation, is not and cannot be separated from the sun of the substance of the mighty God.

The lower world is subject to the sway of the upper world.

There is a band who know and do good, without practising austerities, and who investigate the real nature of things by the guidance of reason.

They deem it not lawful to hurt anything having life.

By what shines on the heart in the worship of God, and by words consonant with reason, the pure-hearted are distinguished.

Stand in dread of guilt, and deem the smallest offence great.

CCCCXIV.
Idealism.

<small>Hindu. Manu.</small> Mind, with operations infinitely subtile, is the imperishable cause of all apparent forms.

This universe is compacted from divine and active principles ; a mutable universe from immutable ideas.

Among them, each succeeding element acquires the quality of the preceding; and in as many degrees as each of them is advanced, with so many properties is it endued.

Intellect repeats the work of creation.

CCCCXV.
Signs.

<small>Koran, s. 51, 'The Scattering.' comp.</small> They say, ' By no means will we believe on thee, till thou cause a fountain to gush forth for us from the earth, or till thou have a garden of palm-trees and grapes, and thou cause rivers to flow in its midst.'

On earth are signs for men of firm belief, and also in your own selves : will ye not then behold them ? The heaven hath sustenance for you, and that which you are promised.

<small>S. 15, 'Hedjr.'</small> We have set the signs of the zodiac in the heavens, and adorned and decked them forth for the beholders.

<small>S. 36, Y.S.</small> The dead earth is a sign to them : we quicken it and bring forth the grain from it, and they eat thereof :

And we make in it gardens of the date and vine ; and we cause springs to gush forth in it ;

That they may eat of its fruits and of the labour of their hands. Will they not therefore be thankful?

A sign to them also is the night. The sun hasteneth to its setting.[1] As for the moon, we have decreed stations for it, till it change like an old and crooked palm branch. . . . Each in its own sphere doth journey on.

[1] Lit. 'Place of rest.'

Behold they not the birds over their heads, outstretching and drawing in their wings? The Merciful regardeth all things.

S. 67, 'The Kingdom.'

And thy Lord hath taught the bee, saying, 'Provide thee houses in the mountains, and in the trees, and in the hives which men do build thee: Feed, moreover, on every kind of fruit, and walk the appointed[2] paths of thy Lord. From it cometh forth a fluid of varying hues, which yieldeth benefit to man. Verily in this is a sign for those who consider.

S. 16, 'The Bee.'

[2] Lit. 'Beaten.'

If ye would reckon up the favours of God, ye could not count them. Bear in mind the benefits of God, and lay not the earth waste with deeds of license.

S. 16, 7.

The heavens praise him, and the earth and all that are therein; neither is there aught that doth not celebrate his praise; but their utterances of praise ye understand not.

S. 17, 'The Night-Journey.'

Think within thine own self on God, with lowliness and fear and silence, at even and at morn; and be not one of the heedless.

S. 7.

To those only who lend an ear will he make answer.

S. 6.

It is he who hath sown you in the earth, and unto him shall ye be gathered.

S. 67.

CCCCXVI.

Optimism.

<small>Heb.
Ecclesiasticus.
Apoc.
Ab.</small>

Hearken unto me, ye holy children, and bud forth as a rose growing by the brook; give ye a savour sweet as frankincense, and flourish as a lily, and sing a song of praise to the Highest!

All the works of God are exceeding good, and whatsoever he ordereth shall be accomplished in due season.

And none may say, 'What is this? Wherefore is that?' for at time convenient they shall all be sought out.

He seeth from everlasting to everlasting, and there is nothing wonderful before him.

He hath made all things for their uses.

All the works of God are good : he will give every needful thing in due season. So that a man cannot say, 'This is worse than that.' In time they will all be well approved.

CCCCXVII.

Spiritual Evolution.

<small>Christian.
Rom.
comp.</small>

As many as are lead by the spirit of God, they are sons of God. For ye did not receive the spirit of bondage so as to be again in fear; but ye received the spirit of adopted children, whereby we cry, dear Father! The Divine Soul itself beareth witness with our soul that we are children of God; and if children, then heirs; heirs of God, and fellow-heirs with Christ; if indeed we are suffering with him, that we may also be glorified with him.

I esteem the sufferings of this present time as of

none account when compared with the glory which is about to be revealed to us. For the earnest expectation of the universe is waiting for the manifestation of the sons of God. The universe was subjected to immaturity not of its own will, but by reason of him who put it into subjection, in hope that even Nature itself will be liberated from the bondage of decay and brought into the freedom of the glory of the children of God. For we know that the whole creation is together groaning and suffering the pains of labour, up to this time ; and not only so, but even we ourselves also, though having the firstfruits of the Spirit, even we ourselves groan within ourselves, waiting for the adoption as sons, for the deliverance of our body. For we were saved only in hope. But hope which is seen is not hope ; how can a man hope for that which he seeth ? But if we hope for that which we do not see, then do we with patience wait for it. In like manner the spirit also helps our weakness; for we know not what to pray for as we ought, but the spirit itself pleads with groans which cannot be uttered in words. But he that searches hearts knows the mind of the spirit, because for the good it harmonises with the purpose of God.

If God be for us, who can be against us ? We know that all things work together for good to those who love God. I am persuaded that neither death nor life, nor angels nor principalities, nor things present nor things to come, nor powers, nor height nor depth, nor any other created thing, will be able to separate us from the love of God.

CCCCXVIII.

Oracles of Flowers.

Burmese.
Dhammapada.
Buddha.
comp.

Who shall find out the plainly shown path of virtue, as a clever man finds out the right flower?

Death carries off a man who is gathering flowers, and whose mind is distracted, before he is satiated in his pleasures.

As a bee collects nectar and departs without injuring the flower, its colour or scent, so let the wise man dwell on earth.

Not the failures of others, not their sins of omission and commission, but his own misdeeds and negligences should he take notice of.

Like a beautiful flower, full of colour but without scent, are the fine but fruitless words of him who does not act accordingly.

The fields are damaged by weeds; mankind by hatred. As the Vassiká-plant sheds its withered flowers, men should shed passion and hatred.

As many kinds of wreaths can be made from a heap of flowers, so many good things may be achieved by a mortal if once he is born.

The scent of flowers does not travel against the wind, nor that of sandal-wood; but the odour of good people travels even against the wind: a good man pervades every place.

Sandal-wood or Tagara, Vassiká, the lotus-flower, have a peerless fragrance; but the odour of excellent people rises up as the highest.

As from a heap of rubbish cast on the highway, the lily will grow full of sweet perfume and delight-

ful, even so the disciple of the truly enlightened
Teacher[1] will shine forth amid those who are like [1] Buddha.
rubbish, those who walk in darkness.

CCCCXIX.
Hymn to Saturn.
O thou who sittest aloft in dignity,
Obedient unto God,   Persian. Desátír.
High of purpose, the receptacle of reflection,   Gilshah. comp.
Revolving in the love of a most pure passion !
Through thee I seek the Intelligence that glorified
   thee with light ;
Asking by the splendour of thy soul, and of all the
   free and blazing lights that shine with intelligence,
To be made one of those who approach the band of
   his lights, and the secret of his essence, while the
   world endureth.

CCCCXX.
Nature.
To the eyes of the intelligent the foliage of the
grove displays, in every leaf, a volume of the Creator's   Sádi. Gul.
works. It is the vernal season ; for the heart is every   comp.
moment longing to walk in the garden, and every bird
of the grove is melodious in its carols as the nightingale. Thou wilt fancy it the dawning zephyr of an
early spring, or New Year's day morning ; but it is the
breath of Isa, or Jesus ; for in that fresh breath and
verdure the dead earth is reviving.

CCCCXXI.
The Present Paradise.
Of all those who have taken the long journey, who
has returned of whom I can ask tidings ? O friend !

Persian.
Khèyam.
11th cent.

take care to lose nothing in sight for hope of something in that close-barred seraglio,—for, rest assured, thou shalt not return here!

Since from the beginning of life to its end there is for thee only this earth, live at least as one who is on the earth, and not like one buried beneath it.

Wherever I cast my eyes I see the sward of paradise, and its crystal stream. One would say that this meadow, issuing from fires beneath, is transformed to a celestial abode. Repose thyself in this abode, close to the heavenly beauty!

Thou, man, who art the universe in little! cease for a moment from thy absorption in loss and gain: take one draught at the hand of him who presses creation's cup to thy lips, and so free thyself at once from the cares of this world, and those about another!

CCCCXXII.
Books.

Sâdi.
Gul.
Ab.

It was the season of spring; the air was temperate, and the rose in full bloom. The vestments of the trees resembled the festive garments of the fortunate. It was midspring, when the nightingales were chanting from the pulpits of the branches, the rose decked with pearly dew, like blushes on the cheek of a chiding mistress. It happened once that I was benighted in a garden, in company with one of my friends. The spot was delightful, the trees intertwined; you would have said that the earth was bedecked with glass spangles, and that the knot of the Pleiades was suspended from the branch of the vine. A garden with a running stream, and trees from whence birds were warbling melodious strains : that filled with tulips of various hues; these loaded with fruits of several kinds. Under the shade of its trees the zephyr had spread the variegated carpet. In the morning, when the desire to return home overcame our inclination for remaining, I saw in his lap a collection of roses, odoriferous herbs, and hyacinths, which he had intended to carry to town. I said, 'You are not ignorant that the flower of the garden soon fadeth, and that the enjoyment of the rosebush is but of a short continuance; and the sages have declared that the heart ought not to be set upon anything that is transitory.' He asked, 'What course is then to be pursued?' I replied, 'I am able to form a book of roses, which will delight the beholders, and gratify those who are present; whose leaves the tyrannic arm of the autumnal blasts can never affect, nor injure the blossoms of its spring.' As soon as I had uttered these words, he flung the flowers from his lap, and, laying hold on the skirt of my garment, exclaimed, 'When the beneficent promise, they faithfully discharge their engagements.' Whilst the rose was yet in bloom, the book entitled the Rose Garden was finished.

CCCCXXIII.

Human Nature.

All men have in themselves the feelings of mercy and pity, of shame and hatred of vice. It is for each one by culture to let these feelings grow or to let them wither. They are part of the organisation of men, as much as the limbs or senses, and may be trained as well. The mountain Nicon-chau naturally brings forth beautiful trees. Even when the trunks are cut down, young shoots will constantly rise up. If cattle Chinese. Mencius.

are allowed to feed there, the mountain looks bare: shall we say then that bareness is natural to the mountain? So the lower passions are let loose to eat down the nobler growths of reverence and love in the heart of man: shall we therefore say there are no such feelings in his heart at all? Under the quiet peaceful airs of morning and evening the shoots tend to grow again. Humanity is the heart of man; justice is the path of man. To know heaven is to develop the principle of our higher nature.

MAN.

CCCCXXIV.
Man and Animal.

God brought the animals to Gilshádeng, and made them subject to him, and he divided them into seven classes.

<small>Persian. Desátír. Zoroaster. (Apoc.) comp.</small>

And when seven sages were with the prince, there came seven kings from the animal kingdom, soliciting redress from the tyranny of mankind.

The wise camel said, 'O prophet of God! in what consists the superiority of man over us?'

The sage Huristeh said, 'There are many proofs of man's superiority over animals; one of them is speech.'

The camel answered, 'If the object of speech be to make the hearer understand, animals possess it.'

Huristeh said, 'The speech of man is alone intelligible.'

The camel replied, 'Because thou dost not understand the language of animals, dost thou imagine it unintelligible? The inhabitants of the West understand not them of the East.'

Huristeh said, 'You have been ordained for our service.'

The camel answered, 'And you also have been ordained to bring us water and grain and grass.'

The sage said nothing in answer.

Then the sage ant came forward, and said, 'O prophet! wherein consisteth the surpassing excellence of man above animals.'

The sage Shásar hastily answered, 'In the excellence of his shape and upright deportment.'

The ant replied, 'The intelligent do not pride themselves on shape, and yet we are all on a level in regard to the combinations of the members of our body. And even you, when you would praise any beautiful person, describe her as stag-eyed, as having the gait of a partridge, or a peacock's waist; whence it may be understood that the superiority is ours.'

To this Shasar returned no answer.

Next the knowing fox, taking up the speech, said, 'What superiority in arts doth man possess?'

The wise Jemshíd answered, 'The superiority of men consisteth in the good dress, and agreeable food and drink which they have always had.'

The wise fox said, 'In former times your clothes were of wool, and hair, and skins of animals, and still are so.. And your sweetest food is supplied by the bee. With animals, all that requireth to be covered is covered naturally.'

Jemshíd replied, 'It ill becometh you to join in this controversy, you who cruelly tear each other to pieces.'

The fox rejoined, 'We have learned this practice from you, for Jilmis slew Tilmis. Moreover ravenous animals live on flesh; but men slay each other without necessity.'

Jemshíd returned no answer.

Next the sagacious spider coming forward said, 'Wherein consisteth the superior excellence of man?'

The sage Simrâsh said, 'Men understand the arts.'

The spider answered, 'Animals exceed men in these: knowest thou not that crawling things and insects build triangular and square houses without wood or brick? Behold my work, how, without loom I weave fine cloth.'

Simrâsh replied, 'Man can write and express his thoughts on paper.'

The spider said, 'Animals do not transfer the secrets of God from a living heart to a lifeless body.'

Simrâsh hung down his head from shame.

The tortoise next advanced saying, 'What proof is there of the superiority of man?'

The sage Shalish-herta said, 'Kings and ministers, and generals, and physicians, and astronomers afford proofs of man's superiority.'

The tortoise said, 'Animals too possess the classes that you have mentioned. Observe the sovereignty of the bee and of the ant in their kind, and attend to the viziership of the fox; and recollect the generalship of the elephant; and the cock is an astronomer, who knoweth right well the time of the day and night.'

Shalish-herta remained silent.

Next the peacock, sailing in, said, 'What proof is there of man's superior dignity?'

The wise vizier, Vizlûr, said, 'Mankind possess the faculty of judgment and discrimination.'

The peacock answered, 'If during the darkness of a single night a hundred sheep have young, each knoweth its lamb, and each lamb knoweth its mother, and turns to its mother ; and this kind of instinct mankind do not possess.'

Vizlûr then said, 'Men are brave.'

The peacock answered, 'They are not bolder than the lion.'

Vizlûr had nothing to reply.

Next the hûmâ advancing said, 'Where is the sage who will afford me proof of man's superiority ? '

The sage Mezdam-hertaiendeh said, 'One superiority of man consisteth in knowledge, as by means of it he ascendeth from a low to an exalted station.'

The hûmâ replied, 'By knowledge animals distinguish good plants from poison.'

The sage said, 'Knowledge has a root and a branch ; you have the branch, but the root consisteth in the sayings of the prophets, which belong to man alone.'

The hûmâ said, 'Among animals each tribe hath its customs, and in like manner as among you prophets reveal their prophecies, among us there are counsellors, one of whom is the bee.'

The sage said, 'The heart of man attaineth self-possession, and effecteth an union with the soul, and by means of knowledge is elevated to the glorious nature of the angels.'

The hûmâ said, 'We animals likewise become tame.'

The sage replied, 'It is true ; yet your perfection consisteth in attaining only a single one of the qualities of man, while man's perfection consisteth in attaining the nature of disembodied spirits.'

The hûmâ said, 'True ; yet in spite of this, in his

putting to death of animals and similar acts, man resembleth the beasts of prey, and not angels.'

The Prophet of the World then said, 'We deem it sinful to kill harmless, but right to slay ravenous, animals. Were all ravenous animals to enter into a compact not to kill harmless animals, we would abstain from slaying them, and hold them dear as ourselves.'

Upon this the wolf made a treaty with the ram, and the lion became the friend of the stag. And no tyranny was left in the world; till man (Dèhak) broke the treaty, and began to kill animals.

In consequence of this, nobody observed the treaty except the harmless animals.

This is the dialogue that passed concerning the grand secret.

CCCCXXV.

Man.

O Man! thou coin bearing the double stamp of body and spirit, I do not know what thy nature is; for thou art higher than heaven and lower than earth. Persian. Faizí. 10th cent. comp.

Do not be cast down because thou art a mixture of the four elements; do not be self-complacent because thou art the mirror of the seven realms.

Those that veil their faces in heaven love thee; thou, misguiding the wise, art the fondly petted one of the solar system.

Be attentive; weigh thy coin, for thou art a correct balance; sift thy atoms well, for thou art the philosopher's stone; learn to understand thy value, for thy light is that with which planets shine.

Act not against thy reason; it is a sure guide: set not thy heart on illusions.

Why art thou an enemy to thyself, that, wanting

perfection, thou shouldst weary thy better nature and cherish thy tongue?

The heart of time sheds its blood on thy account: thy speech is balm, thy deed a lancet.

Priding thyself as the sum total, thou art but a marginal note.

Be not proud because thou art the centre of the body of the world.

If thou wishest to understand the secret meaning of the phrase 'to prefer the welfare of others to thy own,' treat thyself with poison and others with sugar.

Accept misfortune with a joyful look.

Place thy face low on the threshold of truth.

CCCCXXVI.

Man Aspiring.

[Persian. Hayátí. 10th cent. A.b.]

I am neither so high as the Pleiades, nor so low as the abyss; I neither cherish the old grief, nor do I possess a new thought.

If I am not the wailing nightingale, there is yet this excellence left, I am the moth and pledged to the flame.

I am the heart-grief of my dark nights, I am the misfortune of the day of my fate.

It is a long time that I have been waiting for myself.

CCCCXXVII.

Reason.

[Nizámi. A.C. 1180.]

The first stroke of the eternal pen was the first letter of the word, the first veil was the word, the first reflection was the word. Until the word resounded and echoed in the heart, soul and body did not unite.

CCCCXXVIII.

Qualities.

Men have their metal, as of gold and silver. Those of you who were the worthy ones in the state of igno- rance, will be the worthy ones in the state of faith, as soon as you embrace it.

<small>Mahometan Tradition.</small>

CCCCXXIX.

Joy.

Restrain thy desire for the things of this world, if thou wouldst be happy : break the fetters that bind thee to its good fortune or its ill : live content, for the heavens will continue to march through their periods, and this life does not last long.

<small>Persian. Khèyam. 11th cent.</small>

To drain the cup of joy is my condition of existence. To be indifferent to heresy or orthodoxy, that is my religion. I asked my fair bride—the World—what was her dower : she replied, 'My dower is in the joy of thy heart !'

CCCCXXX.

The Inner World.

Heaven and hell are virtue and vice.

What can be called constant ? The same object serves at one time for our happiness and at another for our distress. Hence happiness and sorrow are abstract ideas.

<small>Hindu. Vishnu Pur. (Wilson MS.) comp.</small>

Wisdom is identical with the Supreme Being, and at the same time the cause of our relation to the affairs of the world.

Thou art separated from all the members of the body : meditate on the question—who am I ?

CCCCXXXI.
Mankind.

Chinese.
Kang-Tsze
Chow.

On hearing of the slander of mankind, taste not its anger.

On hearing of the flattery of mankind, taste not its joy.

On hearing persons talk of man's wickedness, partake not their pleasure.

On hearing men speak of the virtues of mankind, approve, follow, and rejoice therein.

Rejoice on beholding the virtuous man.

Rejoice on hearing the record of virtuous actions.

Rejoice in the diffusion of correct principles.

Rejoice in the diffusion and doing of good.

On hearing of the wickedness of mankind, let it be to you as thorns penetrating the back.

On hearing of virtuous and benevolent acts, bind them about you as a garland of flowers.

Then the heart will never cease thinking thereon, and the feet never cease walking in the right path.

When man ceases not the exchange of civilities there is nothing he may not possess.

CCCCXXXII.
Seeking.

Persian.
Omar
Khèyam.
12th cent.
comp.

Ye who seek holy fame, who would leave a name wreathed in light, love your neighbour, harm none !

I follow not the guidance of men erring as myself; but appeal to thee, great Spirit, who ever unsealest the gates of Truth ! Men perish, but thou remainest : a little makes man base or great ; he bears in one hand that which exalts, in the other that which degrades him : God alone is great !

CCCCXXXIII.
Possibilities of Man.

Providence is divine order. All things in heaven do profit and advantage the things upon earth. The vision of Good is not like the beams of the sun, whose fiery brightness blindeth the eye by excess of light; rather enlighteneth, and so much increaseth the power of the eye, that any man is able to receive this intelligible clearness. For it is more swift and sharp to pierce, and harmless withal, and full of immortality; and they that are capable, and can draw any store of this spectacle and sight, do many times fall asleep from the body into this most fair and beauteous vision.

<small>Egyptian. Hermes Trismegistus. (Apoc.) comp.</small>

The knowledge of it is a divine silence, and the rest of all the senses.

Shining steadfastly on and round about the mind, it enlighteneth all the soul, and changeth it wholly into the essence of God.

For it is possible for the soul to be deified if it contemplate the beauty of the good.

He who can be truly called man is a divine being, and not to be confused with any brute man living in the earth.

Man is a mortal god.

He leaveth not the earth, and yet dwelleth above, so great is the greatness of his nature.

CHARACTER.

CCCCXXXIV.
Character.

<small>Chinese.
The She-King.</small>   The first requisite in the pursuit of virtue is, that the learner think of his own improvement, and do not act from a regard to (the admiration of) others.

<small>Confucius.
'The Meun.'</small>   What heaven has conferred is the Nature; an accordance with this nature is the Path. This path may not be left for an instant. On this account the superior man does not wait till he sees things, to be cautious, nor till he hears things, to be apprehensive.

There is nothing more visible than what is secret, and nothing more manifest than what is minute. Therefore, the superior man will watch over himself when he is alone. He examines his heart that there may be nothing wrong there, and that he may have no cause for dissatisfaction with himself. That wherein he excels is simply his work which other men cannot see.

Are you free from shame in your apartment, when you are exposed only to the light of heaven?

How abundantly do spiritual beings display their powers! We look for them, but do not see them; we listen, but hear them not: yet they enter into all things, and there is nothing without them.

Such is the manifestness of what is hidden! Such

is the impossibility of repressing the outgoings of sincerity!

CCCCXXXV.
Poets.

Poets strike out a road to the inaccessible realm of thought, and divine grace beams forth in their genius. <small>Persian. Abul Fazl.</small> He who unites word to word gives away a drop from the blood of his heart. I do not mean a mere external union. Truth and falsehood, wisdom and foolishness, pearls and common shells, though far distant from each other, have a superficial similarity.

CCCCXXXVI.
Essential Worth.

Though a gem be worn on the feet and glass on the head, yet glass is glass and a gem a gem. <small>Hindu. Hitopadesa.</small>

CCCCXXXVII.
Firmness.

A firm-hearted man, improperly repulsed, is not abased: though the fire fall down the flame will not descend. <small>Hindu. Hitopadesa.</small>

CCCCXXXVIII.
Least and Greatest.

Even though a speech be a thousand senseless words, one word of sense is better, which, if a man hear, he becomes quiet. <small>Burmese. Buddha. Dhammapada. comp. (Müller.)</small>

If one man conquer in battle a thousand times thousand men, and if another conquer himself, he is the greatest of conquerors.

One's own self conquered is better than all other people; not even a god, a Gandharva, not Mâra with

Brahmân could change into defeat the victory of a man who has vanquished himself, and lives under restraint.

If a man for a hundred years sacrifice month after month with a thousand, and if he but for one moment pay homage to a man whose soul is grounded (in true knowledge), better is that homage than a sacrifice for a hundred years.

If he has lived a hundred years vicious and unrestrained, a life of one day is better if a man is virtuous and reflecting.

CCCCXXXIX.
Counsels.

True art lies in the abandonment of artifice.

Arabic.
El Wardi.
comp.

Of an empire large as Cæsar's, how small a portion suffices for my wants! and though I have an ocean to quench my thirst, how small a draught allays it!

For thy part, never presume to say, 'My origin is such—my property is such;' the basis of a man is on his knowledge.

Avoid the things which concern thee not: none can prosper without doing so.

Excellence receives no hurt from the slight of the world, as the sun is unimpaired by the darkness of the evening.

Curtail thy hopes, that thou mayest prove happy, for the retrenchment of hope is the health of intellect.

CCCCXL.
Self-discipline.

Hindu.
Hitopadesa.

It is easy for all men to display learning in instructing others; but it is the part of one endued with a great mind to form himself by the rules of justice.

CCCCXLI.

Patience.

To bear with those who revile us, even as the earth bears with those who dig it, is the first of virtues. <small>Hindu. Cural I.</small>

Bear, even when you can retaliate; to forget is still better.

To neglect hospitality is poverty of poverty. To bear with the ignorant is might of might.

If you desire that greatness should never leave you, preserve patience.

The wise will not at all esteem the resentful. They will treasure the patient as fine gold.

The pleasure of the resentful is for a day; the praise of the patient lasts while the world lasts.

If others wrong you, compassion for their affliction should keep you from harming them.

No pious abstinence equals the abstinence of those who overcome injury by patience.

CCCCXLII.

The Just Man.

O Lord! who shall abide in thy tabernacle? <small>Heb. Ps.</small>
And who shall dwell on thy holy mountain?
He who walketh in integrity, and doeth righteousness,
And speaketh the truth from his heart;
Who slandereth not with his tongue,
Who injureth not his friend,
And who bringeth not a reproach against his neighbour.
And he taketh not a bribe against the innocent.
He that doeth these things shall never be removed.

T

CCCCXLIII.
Freedom.

Persian.
Sádi.
Gul.

They asked a wise man why, out of many trees which the Almighty hath created, lofty and fruit-bearing, the cypress alone is called *azad* or free, although it beareth not fruit? He replied, 'Every tree hath its appointed fruit and season, with which it is at one time flourishing, and at another time destitute and withering; to neither of which states is the cypress exposed, being always flourishing, as is the state of those who are free.' Place not your heart on that which is transitory; for the river Tigris will continue to flow through Bagdad after the Califs shall have ceased to reign. If you are able, imitate the date-tree in liberality; but if you have not the means of munificence, be an *azad* or free, like the cypress.

CCCCXLIV.
Rank.

Hindu.
Vémana.

Which is the chief caste among all the sects? He who has understanding is of the noblest tribe.

Consider not him a pariah who is so by birth: he who breaks his word is far viler. He who reproaches the pariah is baser than he. Of what caste is He who speaks in the pariah?

CCCCXLV.
Rare Qualities.

Hindu.
Hitopadesa.

Liberality attended with mild language; divine learning without pride; valour united with mercy; wealth accompanied with generosity: these four qualities are with difficulty acquired.

CCCCXLVI.
Passive Power.

He who may behold, as it were, inaction in action, and action in inaction, is wise amongst mankind. <small>Hindu. Bhágavat. Gita.</small>

He abandoneth the desire of a reward in his actions; he is always contented and independent; and although he may be engaged in a work, he as it were doeth nothing. He is unsolicitous, of a subdued mind and spirit.

He hath gotten the better of duplicity, and is free from envy. He is the same in prosperity and adversity; and although he acteth, he is not confined in the action.

CCCCXLVII.
Virtue.

Is virtue far off? I wish to be virtuous, and lo! it is at hand. Virtue runs swifter than the royal postilions. <small>Confucius. Analects.</small>

Is any one able for one day to apply his strength to virtue? I have not seen the case in which his strength would be insufficient.

Even a man's faults may reflect his virtues.

A man should not be concerned that he has no place: he should be concerned to fit himself for one.

Virtue is not left to stand alone. He who practises it will have neighbours.

Let every attainment in what is good be firmly grasped.

The man of perfect virtue is slow of speech; for when a man feels the difficulty of doing, can he be other than cautious and slow in speaking?

The firm, the enduring, the simple, and the modest, are near to virtue.

Let every man consider virtue as what devolves upon himself. He may not yield the performance of it to any teacher.

My friend Chang can do things hard to be done, but yet he is not perfectly virtuous.

The wise man never hastens, neither in his studies nor words; he is sometimes, as it were, mute, but when it concerns him to act and practise rectitude, he, as I may say, precipitates all.

The She-King says, 'Heaven created all men, having their duties and the means of performing them. It is the natural and constant disposition of men to love beautiful Virtue.' He who wrote this ode knew right principles.

CCCCXLVIII.
True Living.

<small>Hindu. Hitopadesa.</small> That course which men pursue for a short time but with lasting renown, never separated from learning, valour, and good fame, this the wise truly call living; not that of the crow or raven, who live indeed long, and—devour their food.

CCCCXLIX.
The Hid Treasure.

<small>Singh. Budh. Khuddaka Patha (or Lesser Readings). comp.</small> A man buries a treasure, saying within himself, 'When occasion arises, this treasure will be of use to me,—if I am accused, or robbed, or in debt, or in famine, or other misfortune.' Meanwhile his treasure lies in the pit, day by day, profiting him nothing. Perhaps it is stolen away.

There is a treasure that man or woman may possess, a treasure laid up in the heart,—charity, piety, temperance!

A treasure secure, impregnable, enduring; the one treasure that will follow man after death.

A treasure that none can take away,—health, a sweet voice, beauty and greatness, wisdom and calmness, the emancipation of the intellect, spiritual insight, and perfect enlightenment.

This is the treasure that can procure all others.

CCCCL.
Virtue.

I saw an Arab who said to his son, 'O my child! in the day of resurrection they will ask you what have you done in the world, and not from whom are you descended.' That is, they will inquire about your virtue, and not about your father. The cloth that covers the holy Kaaba, and which they kiss, is not famous from having been manufactured by the silkworm; it associated some days with one who is venerable, on which account it became venerable like himself.

<small>Persian. Sádi. Gul.</small>

CCCCLI.
Devotion.

All the bliss of deities and of men is declared by sages to have in devotion its cause, in devotion its continuance, in devotion its fulness.

<small>Hindu. Manu.</small>

Devotion is equal to the performance of all duties.

Perfect health, or unfailing medicine, and divine learning are acquired by devotion alone.

Whatever is hard to be traversed, whatever is hard

to be acquired, whatever is hard to be visited, whatever is hard to be performed ; all this may be accomplished by true devotion.

CCCCLII.

The Individual Conviction and Task.

Hindu.
Bhágavat.
Gita.
comp.

The wise man seeketh for that which is homogeneous to his own nature. All things act according to their nature; what then will restraint effect ?

A man's own religion is better than the faith of another, let it be ever so well followed. It is good to die in one's own faith, for another's faith beareth fear.

A man being contented with his own particular lot and duty, obtaineth perfection.

The duties of a man's own calling, though not free from faults, is far preferable to the duty of another. A man, by following the duties which are appointed by his birth, doeth no wrong. A man's own calling, with all its faults, ought not to be forsaken. Every undertaking is involved in its faults, as the fire in its smoke.

CCCCLIII.

Manhood.

Persian.
Sádi.
Gul.

Manhood is composed of liberality and benevolence ; do not imagine that it consists merely in the material form ; virtue also is requisite ; for a human figure may be painted on the gate of the palace with vermilion and verdigris. When a man hath not virtue and benevolence, what is the difference between him and the figure on the wall ? It is not wisdom to acquire worldly wealth, but to gain one single heart.

CCCCLIV.

Health.

Who is this natural beauty who advances with so much grace? The rose is on her cheeks, her breath is sweet as the morning dew, a joy tempered with modesty animates her countenance. It is Health, the daughter of Exercise and Temperance.

Hindu.
(Albitis.)

CCCCLV.

Current Qualities.

The presence of a wise man resembles pure gold, because whithersoever he goeth they know his intrinsic value and consequence. An ignorant son of a rich man is like leather money passing current in a particular city, but which in a foreign country no one will receive for anything. A little beauty is preferable to great wealth. I saw a peacock's feather in the leaves of a Koran. I said, 'I consider this an honour much greater than your quality deserves.' He replied, 'Be silent; for whosoever has beauty, wherever he puts his foot, doth not every one receive him with respect?'

Persian.
Sádi.
Gul.

A sweet singer, who with the throat of David arrests the waters in their course, and suspends the birds in their flight; consequently, by the power of this perfection, he captivates the hearts of mankind in general, and the religious are desirous of associating with him. A sweet voice is better than a beautiful face; for the one gives sensual delight, and the other invigorates the soul. According to the saying of the wise :—

'If a mechanic goes a journey from his own city,

he suffers not difficulty nor distress; but if the king of Neemroze should wander out of his kingdom, he would sleep hungry.'

CCCCLVI.

Self.

Burmese.
Budh.
Dhammapada.
comp.
(Müller.)

If a man hold himself dear, let him watch himself carefully.

Let each man make himself as he teaches others to be; he who is well subdued may subdue (others); one's own self is difficult to subdue.

Self is the lord of self. The evil done by one's self, self-begotten, self-bred, crushes the wicked, as a diamond breaks a stone.

By one's self the evil is done; by one's self one suffers; by one's self evil is left undone; by one's self one is purified.

Let no one forget his own duty for the sake of another's, however great.

CCCCLVII.

Courage.

Persian.
Sádi.
Gul.

He is the proper person to give advice to kings who neither dreads the loss of his head nor seeks for reward.

CCCCLVIII.

Individual Character.

Hindu.
Vémana.
comp.

If there be one dry tree in a forest, it may produce flame by friction, and sweep away all the rest; thus if a base wretch be born in a noble race, he will destroy it all.

If there be in a tribe one of excellence, the tribe becomes illustrious by reason of his virtues ; as a grove is distinguished for the sandal-tree therein.

CCCCLIX.
With the Majority.

In the grove of Gotama lived a Brahman, who, having bought a sheep in another village, and carrying it home on his shoulder to sacrifice, was seen by three rogues, who resolved to take the animal from him by the following stratagem. Having separated, they agreed to encounter the Brahman on his road as if coming from different parts. One of them called out, ' O Brahman ! why dost thou carry that dog on thy shoulder ? '   Hindu. Pilpay. (B.C.)

' It is not a dog,' replied the Brahman ; ' it is a sheep for sacrifice.' As he went on, the second knave met him, and put the same question ; whereupon the Brahman, throwing the sheep on the ground, looked at it again and again. Having replaced it on his shoulder, the good man went with mind waving like a string. But when the third rogue met him and said, ' Father, where art thou taking that dog ? ' the Brahman, believing his eyes bewitched, threw down the sheep and hurried home, leaving the thieves to feast on that which he had provided for the gods.

CCCCLX.
Simplicity in Life.

And it came to pass, as they journeyed, that he entered into a certain village ; and a certain woman, named Martha, received him into her house. And she had a sister called Mary, who sat down at the feet   Christian. Luke.

of the Lord, and listened to his word. But Martha was cumbered about serving much; and she came to him, and said, Lord, dost thou not care that my sister hath left me to serve alone? Tell her therefore to help me. But the Lord answering said to her, Martha, Martha, thou art anxious and troubled about many things. But one (dish) is needful. Mary hath chosen the good part which shall not be taken away from her.

CCCCLXI.

Independence.

Hindu.
Hitopadesa.

That life is good which is not sustained by another: if he who is dependent on others be truly alive, who is dead? He salutes for the sake of gain; for the sake of living he resigns the privileges of life; he is miserable for the sake of pleasure.

CCCCLXII.

Independence.

Hindu.
Manu.

Whatever act depends on another, that act let a man carefully shun; but what depends on himself, to that let him studiously attend. All that depends on another gives pain: all that depends on himself gives pleasure.

CCCCLXIII.

Servility.

Christian.
James.
comp.

If there come into your assembly a man with a gold ring, in splendid apparel, and there come in also a poor man in vile raiment, and ye have respect to him that weareth the splendid apparel, and say, Sit thou here in a good place, and say to the poor man, Stand thou there, or, Sit under my footstool; have ye not been partial among yourselves, and become judges with evil thoughts?

If indeed ye fulfil the royal law, according to the scriptures, 'Thou shalt love thy neighbour as thyself,' ye do well. But if ye have respect to persons, ye commit sin.

CCCCLXIV.
Reputation.

If you are ashamed of a thing, do not do it. Birds when they fly leave only a sound: man passes, and his reputation follows him.

Chinese. (Albitis.) comp.

CCCCLXV.
Rich and Poor.

The rich look forward to the year; the poor think only of the day.

Chinese. (Albitis.)

A house of straw and laughter is better than a palace and weeping.

CCCCLXVI.
Seasonable Aid.

To him who gives thee immediately a drop of water, thou wilt give in exchange a vast fortune.

Chinese. (Albitis.)

CCCCLXVII.
Riches.

If thirst of riches be abandoned, who is poor? While the satisfied man is rich in himself, the insatiable with a river of gold is still poor. As food is acquired by fowls in the air, and by beasts on earth, and fish in water, a man may in all places be rich. Mark the bounty of God! When the new-born babe falls from the mother, the breast streams for its sup-

Hindu. Hitopadesa. comp.

port. He by whom flamingoes, green parrots, and peacocks are brilliantly attired, hath made provision for thee also.

CCCCLXVIII.

Contentment.

<small>Persian. Sádi. Bóstán.</small>

Smile not at the legend as vain, that once in holy hands a worthless stone became a heap of silver. Let thy alchemist be Contentment, and stone or ore shall be equal to thee. The infant, with heart untroubled by avarice, fills its little hand with sand, and knows not that silver has more worth. A small coin makes the beggar rich; but Féridoun was not satisfied with a kingdom.

CCCCLXIX.

Prosperity.

<small>[1] Lacshmí. Hindu. Hitopadesa. comp.</small>

The goddess of Prosperity [1] hastens voluntarily to inhabit the mansion of that brave man who lives contented, despatches his business, knows the difference of actions, is able to bear misfortunes, and is firm in friendship.

The goddess of Prosperity desires not to dwell with a lazy unemployed man.

Gain all you can, and what you gain keep with care; what you keep increase, and what you increase bestow on good works. The man who neither gives nor enjoys the wealth that every day increases, breathes indeed, like the bellows of a smith, but cannot be said to live.

Let a man remark the quick increase of a white ant's nest, and suffer no day to pass unfruitful in charity, study, and work.

CONDUCT OF LIFE.

CCCCLXX.
Living with Others.

An ill-conditioned man sneers at everything : one thing he ought to know, and knows not—his own faults. _{Scand. Sæmund's Edda. Havamál.}

Vices and virtues the sons of mortals bear in their breasts mingled : no one is so good that no failing attends him, nor so bad as to be good for nothing.

The heart alone can buy the heart; the soul alone can discern the soul.

Happy is he whom others love ; for all that mortals undertake requires the helping hand.

No man lacks everything, although his health be bad : one in his sons is happy, one in his kindred ; one in his abundant wealth, another in his good works.

The halt can ride on horseback, the one-handed drive cattle, the deaf fight and be useful.

Little are the sand grains (that make the earth) ; little are human wits: men are everywhere by halves.

No disease is worse to a sensible man than not to be content with himself.

Home is still home, however homely, and sweet the crust shared with our kindred ; but he who feasts at others' boards shall often bite a writhing lip.

CCCCLXXI.

Happiness.

Burmese.
Budh.
Dhammapada.
comp.
(Müller.)

Men driven by fear go to many a refuge, to mountains and forest, to groves, and sacred trees. But that is not a safe refuge that is not the best refuge; a man is not delivered from all pains after having gone to that refuge.

Let us live happily, then, not hating those who hate us.

Let us live happily, then, though we call nothing our own.

Victory breeds hatred, for the conquered is unhappy. He who has given up both victory and defeat, he, the contented, is happy.

Health is the greatest of gifts; contentedness the best riches; trust is the best of relatives; perfect repose (Nirvána) the highest happiness.

He who possesses virtue and intelligence, who is just, speaks the truth, and does what is his own business, him the world will hold dear.

CCCCLXXII.

Unproductive Force.

Hindu.
Hitopadesa.
comp.

Of what use is wealth to him who neither gives nor enjoys it? What is strength to him who subdues not his own foes? What signifies a knowledge of the scripture to him who fails to practise virtue? What is the soul itself to him who cannot control himself?

CCCCLXXIII.

Frivolity.

Oppression maketh a wise man mad.
The heart of the wise is in the house of mourning;
But the heart of fools is in the house of joy.
Better is it to hear the rebuke of a wise man
Than to listen to the song of fools:
As the crackling of thorns under a pot,
Such is the laughter of fools.

<small>Heb. Ecclesiastes. comp.</small>

CCCCLXXIV.

Enjoyment.

I praised joy.
Lo! what I have seen to be good and beautiful;
That a man should eat and drink, and see the good of all his labour which he hath taken under the sun,
According to the days of life which God giveth him.
For God answereth man in the joy of his heart.
Say not, 'Why were the former days better than these?'
For thou dost not ask wisely concerning this.
To all the living there is hope.
Go eat thy bread with joy;
At all times let thy garments be white;
And in thy labour which thou endurest under the sun,
All that thy hand findeth to do, do with thy might.
Truly the light is sweet,
And to see the sun, pleasant to the eyes:
If a man live many years, in all of them let him rejoice.

<small>Heb. Ecclesiastes. comp.</small>

CCCCLXXV.
Accomplishments.

<small>Chinese. Tsze-Kung.</small>
Kih Tsze-Shing said, 'In a superior man it is only the substantial qualities which are wanted; why should we seek for ornamental accomplishments?'

<small>Analects.</small>
Tsze-Kung replied, 'Ornament is as substance; substance is as ornament. The hide of a leopard stripped of its hair is like the hide of a dog stripped of its hair.'

<small>Confucius. 'The Great Learning.'</small>
I have not seen any one who loves virtue as we love beauty.

Riches adorn a house, and virtue adorns the person.

The mind is expanded and the body acquires ease.

Therefore the accomplished man must have sincere thoughts.

The ode says, 'As we cut and then file, as we chisel and then polish, so has he cultivated himself.'

Let relaxation and enjoyment be found in the polite arts.

<small>'Doctrine of The Mean.'</small>
It is said in the Book of Poetry, 'Over her embroidered robe she puts a plain single garment,' intimating a dislike to the display of the elegance of the former. So is it the way of the superior man to prefer the concealment of his virtue, while it daily becomes more illustrious; and it is the way of the mean man to seek notoriety, while he daily goes more and more to ruin. It is the characteristic of the superior man, appearing insipid, yet never to produce satiety; while showing a simple negligence, yet to have his accomplishments recognised; while seemingly

plain, yet to be discriminating. He knows how what is distant lies in what is near; he knows how what is minute becomes manifest.

CCCCLXXVI.
Diligence.

The fault of others is easily perceived, but if a man look after the faults of others, and is always inclined to detract, his own weaknesses will grow. Burmese. Budh. Dhammapada. comp. (Müller.)

He who does not rise when it is time to rise, who, though young and strong, is full of sloth, whose will and thought are weak, that lazy and idle man will never find the way to knowledge.

Through zeal knowledge is gotten; through lack of zeal knowledge is lost.

If anything is to be done, let a man do it; let him attack it vigorously. A careless pilgrim only scatters the dust of his passions more widely.

CCCCLXXVII.
Good Things.

In aid of the proceedings that are among men, wisdom is good; in seeking renown, liberality is good; in the advancement of justice, devotedness is good; in the speaking of explanations, truth is good; in the progress of business, energy is good; in the attainment of benefit therefrom, thankfulness is good; in keeping one's self unblemished, the discreet speaking which is in truth is good; in keeping back misfortune, employment is good; before an assembly, eloquent discourse is good; for peace of mind, friendship is good; with an associate in one's own deeds, the giving of advantage is good; among the superior, mildness and humility are Parsí. Mainyo-i-Khard. 6th cent. Ab.

good; among the inferior, instruction and civility are good; in bodily health, moderate eating and keeping the body at work are good; among dependants and servants, good behaviour and dignity are good; for having little grief in one's self, contentment is good; for not coming to dishonour, knowledge of one's self is good; and in every place and time, to restrain one's self from evil, and to be diligent in the performance of good deeds are good. Occupation, and preserving pure language, are above everything.

CCCCLXXVIII.
Opportunity.

Persian.

A poor man watched a thousand years before the gate of Paradise. Then, while he snatched one little nap—it opened and shut.

CCCCLXXIX.
Truth.

Persian.

Seek truth from thought, not in mouldy books. Look in the sky to find the moon, not in the pool.

CCCCLXXX.
Limitation.

Persian.

Each is bounded by his nature, stand he in valley or on mountain. Scoop thou with hand, poor or rich, from ocean or fountain, thou canst but fill thy pitcher.

CCCCLXXXI.
Anger.

Hindu.

He who holds back rising anger like a rolling chariot, him I call a real driver; other people are but holding the reins.

Let a man overcome anger by love ; let him overcome evil by good ; let him overcome the greedy by liberality, the liar by truth. *Burmese. Budh. Dhammapada.*

CCCCLXXXII.
Blame.

This is an old saying, O Atula ! this is not only of to-day : ' They blame him who sits silent, they blame him who speaks much, they also blame him who says little ; there is no one on earth who is not blamed.' *Dhammapada.*

CCCCLXXXIII.
Proverbs.

On this coast ships have been wrecked ; why comest thou here with thy fragile skiff ? *Turkish. (Albitis.)*

One does not throw stones at a barren tree.

If we have not wealth let us have honour.

Before the carriage breaks many can show the right way.

The sluggard says, ' I want strength.'

The blow from a knife may be easily cured ; not so a blow from the tongue.

Death is a black camel that kneels down before every door.

CCCCLXXXIV.
Words.

Words are the key of the heart.

If conversation be not to the purpose, a single word is already too much. *Chinese. (Albitis.) comp.*

Raillery is the lightning of calumny.

When alone, think of your own faults ; when in company, forget those of others.

A little impatience causes great trouble.

When a word has once escaped, a chariot with four horses cannot overtake it. Learn then to watch over thy words.

CCCCLXXXV.

The Mean.

Life is affected by two evils—lust and anger. Restrain them within the proper mean. Till man can attain this self-control he cannot become a celestial.

<small>Persian.
Desâtír.
Sásán.</small>

CCCCLXXXVI.

The Body.

The populousness of my body is the solitude of my soul.

<small>Persian.
Mani.</small>

CCCCLXXXVII.

Fitness.

It is fit to perform no act tardily: if thou hurry it, it will itself become evil. If thou take and cast down a raw fruit, will it ripen?

If eaten out of due time, even food turns to poison.

A crocodile in the water can destroy an elephant; out of the stream it is discomfited even by a dog. Where he is not at home, the skilful is of no avail.

If a fool should find the philosopher's stone, it would melt in his hand like a hailstone.

<small>Hindu.
Yémaua.</small>

CCCCLXXXVIII.

Selfish Cares.

Why suffer anxiety, O my heart, for the belly? As to having a belly, the frog that lives in a rock is thy equal.

Could we perceive the future, surely this iron age would not proceed as it does.

<small>Vemana.</small>

Those who enjoy wealth, those who laud it, and those who long for it, look upon him as a superior who abstains from it.

CCCCLXXXIX.
Ignorance.

Empty are all quarters of the world to an empty mind. <small>Hindu. Hitopadesa.</small>

Many who read the scriptures are grossly ignorant; but he who acts well is a truly learned man.

CCCCXC.
Avarice.

A man of virtue may die, but he becomes not avaricious; as fire may be extinguished, but not cooled. <small>Hitopadesa.</small>

CCCCXCI.
Falsehood.

Silence for the remainder of life is better than speaking falsely. <small>Hitopadesa.</small>

CCCCXCII.
Servility.

It is better to abandon life than flatter the base. Impoverishment is better than luxury through another's wealth. Not to attend at the door of the wealthy, and not to use the voice of petition, these imply the best life of a man. <small>Hitopadesa.</small>

CCCCXCIII.
Contentment.

He who possesses a contented mind possesses all things, as the snake covered with his skin needs no slippers for his feet. <small>Hitopadesa.</small>

CCCCXCIV.
Wealth.

Hitopadesa.

What a rich man gives, and what he consumes, is his real wealth. Whose is the remainder which thou hoardest? Other covetous men will sport with that.

CCCCXCV.
Woman.

Hindu. Manu. comp.

That pain and care which a mother and father undergo in producing and rearing children cannot be compensated in a hundred years.

Even from poison may nectar be taken; even from a child, gentleness of speech; even from a foe, prudent conduct; and even from an impure substance, gold. From every quarter, therefore, must be selected knowledge, virtue, purity, gentle speech, liberal arts, and women bright as gems.

Where women are honoured, there the deities are pleased; but when they are dishonoured, there all religious acts become fruitless.

On whatever houses the women of a family, not being duly honoured, pronounce an imprecation, those houses, with all that belong to them, utterly perish. In whatever family the husband is contented with his wife, and the wife with her husband, in that house will fortune be assuredly permanent.

A wife being gaily adorned, her whole house is embellished; but if she be destitute of ornament, all will be deprived of decoration.

Families, enriched by knowledge, though possessing little temporal wealth, are numbered among the great, and acquire exalted fame.

CCCCXCVI.

Innocence.

As the butterfly alights on the flower,
And destroys not its form or its sweetness,   Chinese. Budh.
But taking a sip, forthwith departs,
So the lowly follower[1] of Buddha   [1] Lit. 'Mendicant.'
Takes not nor hurts another's possessions;
Observes not another man's actions or omissions;
Looks only to his own behaviour and conduct;
Takes care to observe if this is correct or not.

CCCCXCVII.

Purity.

Practising no evil way;
Advancing in the exercise of virtue;   Chinese. Budh. comp.
Purifying both mind and will:
The man who guards his mouth with virtuous motive,
And cleanses both his mind and will,
Permits his body to engage in nothing wrong;
This is the triple purification.
Scrupulously avoiding all wicked actions;
Reverently performing all virtuous ones;
Purifying this intention from all selfish ends:
This is the doctrine of all the enlightened.[1]   [1] Lit. 'Buddhas.'

CCCCXCVIII.

Purity.

By forgiveness of injuries the learned are purified;
by liberality, those who have neglected their duty; by   Hindu. Manu.
pious meditation, those who have secret faults.

Bodies are cleansed by water; the mind is purified by truth. The hand of an artist employed in his art is always pure.

CCCCXCIX.

Maxims.

Arabic.
(Albitis.)

You must not be ashamed to ask what you do not know.

A book is the best companion with which to spend your time.

He who asks from a friend more than he can do, deserves a refusal.

Temperance is a tree which has contentment for its root, and peace for its fruit.

How short would life be if hope did not prolong it!

Invariably speak the truth, even when you are aware of its being disagreeable.

He who learns sciences, and does not practise what they teach, resembles a man who digs, but does not sow.

We are slaves to a secret once it is published, instead of a secret being our slave as long as we keep it concealed.

Measure every one according to his measure.

Absolute solitude is madness.

A wise man's day is worth a fool's life.

D.

Pearls before Swine.

Hindu.
Hitopadesa.

A hundred good works are lost upon the wicked; a hundred wise words are lost upon fools; a hundred good precepts are lost upon the obstinate; a hundred sciences upon those who never reflect.

DI.
Reproof.

A serpent by drinking milk only increases his venom; thus a fool, being admonished, is provoked but not benefited. — Hindu. Hitopadesa.

DII.
Apprehension.

The destroyer of all successes is ill-timed apprehension of danger. — Hindu. Hitopadesa.

DIII.
Counsel.

Do nothing without advice; and when thou hast once done, repent not.

Be not confident (even) in a plain way.

In every good work trust thine own soul. — Heb. Ecclesiasticus. Apoc.

DIV.
Politeness.

Politeness is a mine destined to enrich not only those who receive, but those who dispense it. — Persian. (Albitis.)

DV.
Lying.

There are two things inseparable from lying,— many promises and many excuses. — Persian. (Albitis.)

DVI.
Courage.

Old age will give the coward no peace, though spears may spare him.

His destiny let no man know beforehand; his mind will be freest from care.

Cattle die, kindred die, we ourselves also die; but the fair fame never dies of him who has earned it.

Scand. Sæmund's Edda.

DVII.
Temperance.

Cattle know when to go home from grazing, but a foolish man never knows his stomach's measure.

Scand. Sæmund's Edda.

DVIII.
Experience.

At a hoary speaker laugh thou never: often is good that which the aged utter.

Scand. Sæmund's Edda.

DIX.
Silence.

A garrulous tongue, if not checked, sings often to its own harm.

Scand. Sæmund's Edda.

DX.
Patience.

Patience and resignation is the one road;
Buddha has declared no better path exists:
The disciple who is angry or impatient
Cannot really be called a saint.[1]
Destroy anger and there will be rest;
Destroy anger and there will be peace:
Anger is the poisonous root
Which overthrows the growth of virtue.
Without complaint, without envy;
Continuing in the practice of the precepts;
Knowing the way to moderate appetite;

Chinese. Budh. Catena. comp.

[1] Lit. 'Shaman.'

Ever joyous without any weight of care ;
Fixed and ever advancing in virtue :
This is the doctrine of the enlightened.[1]

[1] Lit. 'Buddhas.'

DXI.

Age.

The memorial of virtue is immortal. It weareth a crown, and ever triumpheth, striving for undefiled rewards. Honourable age is not that which standeth in length of years, nor that is measured by number of years ; but wisdom is the grey hair unto men, and an unspotted life is old age. Though the righteous be prevented with death, yet shall he be in rest. He being made perfect in a short time, fulfilled a long time. The righteous being dead shall condemn the unrighteous who are living ; and youth that is perfected shall condemn the old age of the unjust.

Heb. Wisdom of Solomon. Ab.

DXII.

Affection.

Abu Horiera used every day to visit Mustefa (Mohammed)—upon whom be the blessing and peace of God ! The Prophet said, 'O Abu Horiera ! come not every day, that so affection may increase.' They observed to a holy man, that, notwithstanding the benefits which we derive from the sun's bounteousness, we have not heard any one speaking of him with affection. He replied, 'That is because he can be seen every day, excepting in the winter, when, being veiled, he is beloved.'

There is no harm in visiting men, but let it not

Persian. Sádi. Gul.

be so often that they may say, 'It is enough.' If you correct yourself, you will not need reprehension from another.

DXIII.
Temperance.

<small>Sâdi.
Gul.</small> But for the cravings of the belly, not a bird would have fallen into the snare; nay, the fowler would not have spread his net. The belly is chains to the hands and fetters to the feet. He who is a slave to his belly seldom worships God.

DXIV.
Independence.

<small>Sâdi.
Gul.</small> Although a dress bestowed by a monarch is valuable, yet one's own coarse clothes are preferable; and although the great man's food is exquisite, still the scraps of one's own table are more delicious. Vinegar and potherbs, obtained by one's own labour, are preferable to bread and lamb received from the hand of the head man of the village.

DXV.
Contentment.

<small>Sâdi.
Gul.</small> An African mendicant at Aleppo, in the quarter occupied by the dealers in linen cloths, was saying, 'O wealthy sirs! if there had been justice amongst you, and we had possessed contentment, there would have been an end of beggary in this world.' O contentment! make me rich; for without thee there is no wealth. Lókman made choice of patience in retirement. Whosoever hath not patience, neither doth he possess philosophy.

DXVI.

Reproof.

He who listens not to advice, studies to hear reprehension. When advice gains not admission into the ear, if they reprehend you, be silent.

_{Sádi.}
_{Gul.}

DXVII.

Independence.

I heard of a Durwaish who was suffering great distress from poverty, and sewing patch upon patch, but who comforted himself with the following verse : 'I am contented with stale bread, and a coarse woollen frock, since it is better to bear the weight of one's own necessities than to suffer the load of obligation from mankind.' Somebody said to him, 'Why do you sit quiet, whilst such an one in this city has a liberal mind, and possesses universal benevolence, being ever willing to assist the pious, and always ready to comfort every heart ? If he were apprised of your condition, he would consider it an obligation to satisfy your wants.' He replied, 'Be silent; for it is better to die of want than to expose our necessities to any one ; for they have said that to sew patch upon patch and be patient is preferable to writing a petition to a great man for clothing.' Of a truth, it is equal to the torments of hell to enter into paradise by the help of one's neighbour.

_{Sádi.}
_{Gul.}

They asked Hátim Tái if he had ever seen or heard of any person in the world more noble-minded than himself. He replied, 'One day, after having sacrificed forty camels, I went along with an Arab chief to the skirt of a desert, where I saw a labourer who had made up a bundle of thorns, whom I asked why he did not go to the feast of Hátim Tái, to whose table people were repairing in crowds? he answered, 'Whosoever eateth bread from his own labour will not submit to be under obligation to Hátim Tái.' I considered this man as my superior in generosity and liberality.'

DXVIII.
Enterprise.

<small>Persian.
Háfiz.
(Emerson.)</small>

On prince or bride no diamond stone
Half so gracious ever shone,
As the light of enterprise
Beaming from a young man's eyes.

DXIX.
Superfluous Wealth.

<small>Sádi.
Gul.</small>

I saw an Arab sitting in a circle of jewellers of Básráh, and relating as follows: 'Once on a time, having missed my way in the desert, and having no provisions left, I gave myself up for lost: when I happened to find a bag full of pearls. I shall never forget the relish and delight that I felt on supposing it to be fried wheat; nor the bitterness and despair which I suffered on discovering that the bag contained pearls.'

DXX.
Contentment.

<small>Sádi.
Gul.</small>

I never complained of the vicissitudes of fortune, nor murmured at the ordinances of Heaven, excepting once, when my feet were bare, and I had not the means of procuring myself shoes. I entered the great mosque at Cufah with a heavy heart, when I beheld a man who had no feet. I offered up praise and thanksgiving to God for his bounty, and bore with patience the want of shoes.

DXXI.
Riches.

Riches are for the comfort of life, and not life for the accumulation of riches. I asked a holy wise man, <small>Sádi. Gul.</small> 'Who is fortunate and who is unfortunate?' He replied, he was fortunate who ate and sowed, and he was unfortunate who died without having enjoyed. Pray not over that worthless wretch who performed no act of piety; who spent his whole life in amassing money, without making any use of it.

DXXII.
Slow Growths.

I have heard that in the land of the East they are forty years in making a china cup: they make <small>Sádi. Gul.</small> a hundred in a day at Bagdad, and consequently you see the meanness of the price. A chicken, as soon as it comes out of the egg, seeks its food; but an infant hath not reason and discrimination. That which was something all at once, never arrives at much perfection; and the other by degrees surpasses all things in power and excellence. Glass is everywhere, and therefore of no value; the ruby is obtained with difficulty, and on that account is precious.

Affairs are accomplished through patience; and the hasty man faileth in his undertakings.

HUMILITY.

DXXIII.
Humility.

<small>Persian.
(Von
Hammer.)</small>
Whatever jewels thou wearest on thy brow, only humility can give them their lustre. To that talisman paradise opens its gate, and to it opens the heart of man. Dear to all hearts is he whom lowliness exalts; his bending is the graceful droop of the branch laden with fruit.

DXXIV.
Humility.

<small>Persian.
Sádi.
Gul.</small>
I saw bunches of fresh roses tied to a dome with some grass. I said, 'What is this worthless grass, that it should be in the company of roses?' The grass wept and said, 'Be silent; the benevolent forget not their associates; although I have neither beauty, nor colour, nor odour, still am I not the grass of God's garden? I am the servant of the munificent God, nourished from of old by his bounty.'

DXXV.
Humility.

<small>Hindu.
Vémana.</small>
If you say, 'I am humble,' this is no humility. In an unsuitable place let us never hold ourselves superior. To be low is no humiliation.

The light man will always talk big, but the excellent speaks coolly. Will gold ring like dull metal?

It is easy to talk, but hard to stay the mind; we may teach others, but cannot ourselves understand; it is easy to lay hold on the sword, but hard to become valiant.

He who says, 'I know nothing,' is shrewd; he who says, 'I am learned,' is a talker. He who holds his peace is the wisest and the best.

DXXVI.

Wisdom in Obscurity.

There was a little city, and the men in it were few; Heb.
Ecclesiastes.
And a great king came against it, and besieged it,
And he built up great towers against it.
And there was found in it a poor, wise man,
And he delivered the city by his wisdom;
Yet men remembered not that poor man.
Then I said, 'Wisdom is better than might;
Though the wisdom of the poor man is despised,
And his words are not heard.
The words of the wise in quietness are heard
More than the clamour of him who ruleth among fools.'

DXXVII.

Self-righteousness.

I remember that in my early youth I was overmuch religious and vigilant, and scrupulously pious Persian.
Sádi.
Gul. and abstinent. One night I sat up in attendance upon my father—on whom be God's mercy!—never closed my eyes during the whole night, and held the precious Koran open on my lap, while the company around us were fast asleep. I said to my father, 'Not an individual of these will raise his head that he may perform his genuflections or ritual of prayer ; but they are all so sound asleep that you might conclude they were dead.' He replied, 'O emanation of your father ! you also had better have slept, than that you should thus calumniate the failings of mankind.' The boaster sees nothing but himself, having a veil of conceit before his eyes. If he was endowed with an eye capable of discerning God, he would not discern any person weaker than himself.

DXXVIII.

Humility.

Persian.
Sádi.
Gul.
comp.

Make thyself dust to do anything well.

Obedience ensures greatness.

Near Casbin a man of the country of Parthia came forth to accost me mounted on a tiger. At this sight such fear seized me that I could not flee nor move. But he said, 'O Sádi ! be not surprised at what thou seest. Do thou only not withdraw thy neck from the yoke of God, and nothing shall be able to withdraw its neck from thy yoke.' Whosoever possesseth the qualities of righteousness placeth his head on the threshold of obedience.

DXXIX.

The Child and the Childlike.

Christian.
Matt.
Mark.
comp.

The disciples came to Jesus, saying, Who then is greatest in the kingdom of heaven ? And he called a child to him, and set him in the midst of them, and said, Truly do I say to you, unless ye are changed, and become as children, ye shall not even enter the kingdom of heaven. Whoever therefore shall have humility like this child, he is the greatest in the kingdom of heaven. If any one desire to be first, he will be last of all. And whoever receiveth one such child in my name, receiveth me. And whoever receiveth me, receiveth not me, but him that sent me. But whoever shall cause one of these believing little ones to fall away, it were better for him to have a great millstone hung round his neck, and be swallowed up in the depth of the sea.

And they brought children to him that he might touch them; and the disciples rebuked those that brought them. But Jesus seeing it, was much displeased, and said to them, Suffer the children to come to me: forbid them not; for to such belongeth the kingdom of heaven. Truly do I say to you, whoever shall not receive the kingdom of heaven as a child will not enter therein. And he took the children in his arms, and blessed them.

And when the chief priests heard the children in the temple crying Hosanna, they were much displeased, and said, Dost thou hear this? And Jesus answered, Have ye not read in the scripture, 'Out of the mouth of babes and sucklings thou hast prepared praise.'

Jesus rejoiced in spirit, and said, I thank thee, O Father, that though thou didst hide these things from the wise and discerning, thou didst reveal them to babes. Yea, Father, for so it seemed good in thy sight.

DXXX.
Childlikeness.

By undivided attention to the passion-nature and tenderness, it is possible to be a little child. By putting away impurity from the hidden eye of the heart, it is possible to be without spot. There is a purity and quietude by which one may rule the whole world. To keep tenderness, I pronounce strength.

    He who knows the masculine nature, and at the same time keeps the feminine, will be the whole world's channel, the centre of universal attraction. Being the whole world's channel, eternal virtue will not depart from him, and he will return again to the state of an infant. He who knows the light, and at the same time keeps the shade, will be the whole world's model. He who knows the glory, and at the same time keeps the shame, will be the whole world's valley. Being the whole world's valley, eternal virtue will fill him, and he will return home to simplicity. Of all the weak things in the world, nothing exceeds water; and yet of those which attack hard and strong things, I know not what is superior to it. Do not make light of this. The fact that the weak can conquer the strong, and the tender the hard, is known to all the world; yet none carry it out in practice. The reason of heaven does not strive, yet conquers well; does not call, yet things come of their own accord; is slack, yet plans well. The net of heaven is very wide in its meshes, yet misses nothing.

DXXXI.

Humility.

    Then came to him the mother of the sons of Zebedee with her sons, falling down before him, and asking a certain thing of him. And he said to her, What is thy wish? She saith to him, Grant that these my two sons may sit, one on thy right hand, and one on thy left, in thy kingdom.

And when the ten heard this, they were much displeased with the two brothers. But Jesus called them to him, and said, Ye know that the rulers of the nations lord it over them, and their great men exercise a strict authority over them. Not so shall it be among you; but whoever desireth to become great among you will be your minister, and whoever desireth to be first among you, will be your servant; even as the son of Man came not to be served, but to serve.

DXXXII.

Humility.

And he spoke a parable to those who were invited, when he observed how they chose out the highest places at the table, saying to them, When thou art invited by any one to a wedding, do not take the highest place, lest one more honourable than thou may have been invited by him, and he who invited thee and him come and say to thee, Give place to this man; and then thou wilt begin with shame to take the lowest place. But when thou art invited, go and recline in the lowest place, that when he who invited thee cometh, he may say to thee, Friend, go up higher. Then wilt thou have honour in the presence of all who are at table with thee. For every one that exalteth himself will be humbled; and he that humbleth himself will be exalted. *(Christian. Luke.)*

DXXXIII.

Humility.

And to some who trusted in themselves that they were righteous, and despised all others, he spoke this parable: Two men went up into the temple to pray; *(Christian. Luke.)*

the one a Pharisee, and the other a publican. The Pharisee stood and prayed by himself thus : O God, I thank thee that I am not as the rest of men, extortioners, unjust, adulterers, or even as this publican. I fast twice in the week; I give tithes of all that I gain. But the publican, standing afar off, would not even lift up his eyes to heaven, but smote his breast, saying, O God, be merciful to me a sinner! I tell you, this man went down to his house justified rather than the other; for every one that exalteth himself will be humbled, but he that humbleth himself will be exalted.

DXXXIV.

Rules for the Young.

Hear, attend, but speak little.

Sufi. (Palmer.)

Never answer a question not addressed to you; but, if asked, answer promptly and concisely, never feeling ashamed to say, 'I know not.'

Do not dispute for disputation's sake.

Never boast before your elders.

Never seek the highest place, nor even accept it if it be offered to you.

Do not be over-ceremonious, for this will compel your elders to act in the same manner towards you, and give them needless annoyance.

Observe in all cases the etiquette appropriate to the time, place, and persons present.

In indifferent matters, that is, matters involving no breach of duty by their omission or commission, conform to the practice and wishes of those with whom you are associating. Do not make a practice of anything which is not either a duty, or calculated to increase the comfort of your associates; otherwise it will become an idol to you; and it is incumbent on every one to break his idols and renounce his (bad) habits.

DXXXV.
Humility.

To attain God the heart must be lowly. Lowliness excites no man's envy. Trees are carried away by the flood, whilst rushes remain. Religious ceremonies and outward (ascetic) acts have no power to release from sin. Hindu.
Marátha.
Tukáráma.
(Mrs Manning.)

Sunití said, 'O son! be not uneasy at this slight, for none can take away what thou hast done, and none can supply what thou hast not done. An intelligent person remains contented with what (acknowledgment) proceeds from his degree of merit. If thou art aggrieved (by neglect), endeavour to accumulate religious merit. Be thou good-natured, reverential, friendly, devoted to the interest of all, and prosperity will hasten to its proper object, as water will fall to the low ground. Hindu.
Vishnu
Pur.
(Wilson MS.)
comp.

DXXXVI.
Humility.

There is nothing like keeping the inner man. The sage embraces unity, and so is a pattern for the world. Chinese.
Lao-Tsze.

He puts himself last, and yet is first; abandons himself, and yet is preserved. Is this not through his having no selfishness? Hereby he preserves self-interest intact. He is not self-displaying, and therefore he shines. He is not self-approving, and therefore he is distinguished. He is not self-praising, and therefore he has merit. He is not self-exalting, and therefore he stands high; and inasmuch as he does not strive, no one in all the world strives with him. That ancient saying, 'He that humbles himself shall be preserved entire,'—oh, it is no vain utterance!

DXXXVII.
Pride.

<small>Heb.
Prov.</small>

Be not wise in thine own eyes.
Pride goeth before destruction,
And a haughty spirit before a fall.
Better to be of a lowly spirit with the meek,
Than to share spoil with the proud.
Better is he who is slow to anger than a mighty man;
And greater he that ruleth his own spirit,
Than he who taketh a city.

DXXXVIII.
The Lowly Spirit.

<small>Heb.
Isa.</small>

Thus saith the high and lofty One
That inhabiteth eternity, whose name is Holy:
I inhabit the high and lofty place,
But dwell also with the contrite and lowly in spirit,
To revive the spirit of the humble,
And to revive the heart of the contrite,—
Lest the spirit should faint before me,
And the souls which I have made.

DXXXIX.
Haughtiness.

Now Korah was of the people of Moses: but he behaved haughtily toward them; for we had given him such treasure that its keys would have burdened a company of men of strength. When his people said to him, 'Exult not, for God loveth not those who exult; but seek, by means of what God hath given thee, to attain the future mansion; and neglect not thy part in this world, but be bounteous to others as God hath been bounteous to thee; and seek not to commit excesses on the earth, for God loveth not those who commit excesses,— Arabic.
Koran,
s. 28,
'The Story.'
comp.

He said, 'It hath been given me only on account of the knowledge that is in me.'

And Korah went forth to his people in his pomp. Those who were greedy for this present life said, 'Oh, that we had the like of that which hath been bestowed on Korah!'

But they to whom knowledge had been given said, 'The reward of God is better for him who believeth and worketh righteousness, and none shall win it but those who have patiently endured!'

And we clave the earth for Korah and his palace, and he was not among those who are succoured (by man).

There is no protector for the unjust!

DXL.

Modesty.

Of old we bestowed wisdom upon Lókman, who said, 'Be thankful to God; for whoever is thankful, is thankful to his own behoof; and if any shall be thankless, . . . God truly is self-sufficient. Koran,
s. 31,
'Lókman.'
comp.

And bear in mind when Lókman said to his son, 'O my son! join not other gods with God!

'Verily God will bring everything to light, though

it were but the weight of a mustard-seed, and hidden in a rock or in the heaven or in the earth; for God is subtile, informed of all.

'O my son! enjoin the right and forbid the wrong, and be patient under whatever shall betide thee;

'And distort not thy face at men, nor walk thou loftily upon the earth;

'But let thy pace be modest; and lower thy voice; for the least pleasing of voices is surely the voice of asses.'

DXLI.

Humility.

<small>Heb.
Ecclesiasticus.
Apoc.</small>

My son, go on with thy business in meekness; so shalt thou be beloved of him that is approved. The greater thou art, the more humble thyself. Many are in high place, and of renown; but mysteries are revealed unto the lowly. Seek not out the things that are too hard for thee, neither search the things that are above thy strength. But what is commanded thee, think thereupon with reverence: for it is not needful for thee to see with thine eyes the things that are in secret. Be not curious in unnecessary matters: more things are showed unto thee than men understand.

Many are deceived by their own vain opinion; and an evil suspicion hath overthrown their judgment. Without eyes thou canst not have light: profess not therefore the knowledge thou hast not.

DXLII.

Reverence.

Get thyself the love of the assembly, and bow thy head to a great man.

Let it not grieve thee to bow down thine ear to the poor, and give him a friendly answer with meekness. *Ecclesiasticus. Apoc. Ab.*

Wisdom exalteth her children.

Whoso giveth ear unto her shall judge nations.

Observe the opportunity, and beware of evil; and be not ashamed when it concerneth thy soul. For there is a shame that bringeth sin, and there is a shame which is glory and grace.

Accept no person against thy soul, and let not reverence for any man cause thee to fall.

And refrain not to speak when there is occasion to do good: hide not thy wisdom in her beauty. In nowise speak against the truth.

Be abashed (only) of the error of thine ignorance.

Be not ashamed to confess thy errors. Make not thyself an underling to a foolish man; neither accept the person of the mighty. Be not quick of tongue and slow of deed.

Strive for the truth unto death, and God shall strive for thee.

DXLIII.

Pride.

Why are dust and ashes proud?

He that is to-day a king, to-morrow shall die, and shall inherit creeping things. Pride is the beginning of sin. *Ecclesiasticus. Apoc. Ab.*

God hath cast down the thrones of proud princes, and set up the meek in their stead; he hath plucked up proud nations by the roots, and planted the lowly in their place. My son, glorify thy soul in humility, and give it honour according to the worthiness thereof.

Who will honour him that dishonoureth his own life?

Wisdom lifteth up the head of him that is of low degree, and maketh him to sit among great men. The bee is little, but its fruit is the chief of sweet things. Many kings have sat down upon the ground; and one not thought of hath worn the crown.

DXLIV.

Service.

<small>Persian.
Urfi.
10th cent.
comp.</small>

O thou who hast experienced happiness and trouble from good and bad events, and who art in consequence full of thanks, and sometimes of complaints!

Do not take high ground, that thy efforts be not vain; be rather like grass, that stands in the way of the wind, or like a bundle of grass, which others carry off on their shoulders.

DXLV.

Humility.

<small>Arabic.
(Tr. by Prof.
Carlyle, 1835.)</small>

Why should I blush that Fortune's frown
    Dooms me life's humble paths to tread,
To live unheeded and unknown,
    To sink forgotten to the dead?

'Tis not the good, the wise, the brave,
    That surest shine or highest rise;
The feather sports upon the wave,
    The pearl in ocean's cavern lies.

DXLVI.

Contentment.

A certain king, when arrived at the end of his days, having no heir, directed in his will that, in the morning after his death, the first person who entered the gate of the city, they should place on his head the crown of royalty, and commit to his charge the government of the kingdom. It happened that the first person who entered the city gate was a beggar, who all his life had collected scraps of victuals, and sewed patch upon patch. The ministers of state and the nobles of the court carried into execution the king's will, bestowing on him the kingdom and the treasure. For some time the Durwaish governed the kingdom, until part of the nobility swerved their necks from his obedience, and all the surrounding monarchs, engaging in hostile confederacies, attacked him with their armies. In short, the troops and peasantry were thrown into confusion, and he lost the possession of some territories. The Durwaish was distressed at these events, when an old friend, who had been his companion in the days of poverty, returned from a journey, and finding him in such an exalted state, said, 'Praised be the God of excellence and glory, that your high fortune has aided you, and prosperity been your guide, so that a rose has issued from the brier, and the thorn has been extracted from your foot, and you have arrived at this dignity ! Of a truth, joy succeeds sorrow ; the bud sometimes blossoms and sometimes withers; the tree is sometimes naked and sometimes clothed.' He replied, 'O brother ! condole with me, for this is not a time for congratulation. When you saw me last, I was only anxious how to obtain bread ; but now I have all the cares of the world to encounter. If the times are adverse, I am in pain; and if they are prosperous, I am captivated with worldly enjoyments. There is no calamity greater than worldly affairs, because they distress the heart in

Persian. Sádi. Gul.

prosperity as well as in adversity. If you want riches, seek only for contentment, which is inestimable wealth. If the rich man should throw money into your lap, consider not yourself obliged to him; for I have often heard it said by pious men that the patience of the poor is preferable to the liberality of the rich. If Bahram should roast an onager to be distributed amongst the people, it would not be equal to the leg of a locust to an ant.'

DXLVII.
Patience.

Sádi.
Gul.

A great river is not made turbid by a stone; the religious man who is hurt at injuries is as yet but shallow water. If any misfortune befalleth you, bear with it, that, by forgiving others, you may yourself obtain pardon. O my brother! seeing that we are at last to return to earth, let us humble ourselves in ashes before we are changed into dust.

DXLVIII.
Ambition.

Sádi.
Gul.

Attend to the following story :—In the city of Bagdad there happened a contention between the flag and the curtain. The flag, disgusted with the dust of the road and the fatigue of marching, said to the curtain in displeasure, 'You and myself are schoolfellows, both servants of the Sultan's court. I never enjoy a moment's relaxation from business, being obliged to travel at all seasons; you have not experienced the fatigue of marching, the danger of storming the fortress, the perils of the desert, nor the inconveniences of whirlwinds and dust: my foot is more forward in enterprise,—why, then, is thy dignity greater than mine? You pass your time amongst youths beautiful as the moon, and with virgins odoriferous as jasmine. I am carried in the hands of menial servants, and travel with my feet in bands, and my head agitated by the wind.' The curtain replied, 'My head is placed on the threshold, and not, like yours, raised up to the sky. Whosoever through folly exalts his neck, precipitates himself into distress.'

DXLIX.
Humility.

A raindrop fell into the sea. 'I am lost!' it cried; 'what am I in such a sea?' Into the shell of a gaping oyster it fell, and there was formed into the orient pearl which now shines fairest in Britain's diadem. Humility creates the worth it underrates. Persian. (after Sir W. Jones.)

DL.
Ornament of the Lowly.

In the last day men shall wear
On their heads the dust,
As ensign and as ornament
Of their lowly trust. Persian. Háfiz. (Emerson.)

DLI.
Strength.

A holy man saw a wrestler distracted and foaming at the mouth with rage: he inquired the cause, and was told some one had given him abuse. He said, 'This paltry fellow, who can lift a stone of a thousand pounds weight, is not able to bear a single word! Show your power by engaging others to speak kindly to Sádi. Gul.

you : it is not courage to drive your fist against another man's mouth if you are able to tear the front of an elephant ; he is no man who hath not humanity. The sons of Adam are formed of humble earth ; if you possess not humility, neither are you a man.'

GREATNESS.

DLII.
Our Fathers.

Let us now praise famous men, and our fathers that begat us. _{Heb. Ecclesiasticus. Apoc. Ab.}

God hath wrought great glory by them through his great power from the beginning :

Such as did bear rule in their kingdoms, men renowned for their power, giving counsel by their understanding, and declaring prophecies :

Leaders of the people by their counsels, and by their knowledge of learning meet for the people, wise and eloquent in their instructions :

Such as found out musical tunes, and recited verses in writing :

Rich men, furnished with ability, living peaceably in their habitations :

All these were honoured in their generations, and were the glory of their times.

There be of them that have left a name behind them, that their praises might be reported. And some there be which have no memorial; but these were merciful men, whose righteousness hath not been forgotten : with their seed shall remain a good inheritance, and their glory shall not be blotted out.

Their bodies are buried in peace, but their name liveth for evermore.

The people will tell of their wisdom, and the congregation will show forth their praise.

DLIII.

Greatness.

Ecclesiasticus.
Apoc.
Ab.

He that giveth his mind to the law of the Most High, and is occupied in the meditation thereof, will seek out the wisdom of all the ancients, and study prophecies.

He will keep the sayings of the renowned men; and where subtile fables are, he will be there also. He will seek out the secrets of grave sentences, and be conversant in dark parables.

He shall serve among great men, and appear before princes: he will travel through strange countries; for he hath tried the good and the evil among men.

When the great God will, he shall be filled with the spirit of understanding; he shall pour out wise sentences.

The Most High shall direct his counsel and knowledge, and in his secrets shall he meditate. He shall show forth that which he hath learned, and shall glory in the law of God.

Many shall commend his understanding; and so long as the world endureth it shall not be blotted out: his memorial shall not depart away, and his name shall live from generation to generation.

Nations shall show forth his wisdom, and the assembly shall declare his praise.

DLIV.

Nobility.

I have heard these words, 'Living in solitude to master their aims, practising rectitude to carry out their principles;' but I have not seen such men. Chinese. Confucius. Analects.

To sit in silence and recall past ideas, to study and feel no anxiety, to instruct men without weariness,— have I this ability in me?

The man of character does not go out of his place; he is modest in speech, but exceeds in action.

He will hold rectitude essential, bringing it forth in humility, performing it with prudence, completing it with sincerity. What he seeks is in himself.

There is a divine nobility and a human nobility.

Benevolence, justice, fidelity, and truth, and to delight in virtue without weariness, constitute divine nobility. To be a prince, a prime minister, or a great officer, constitutes human nobility. The ancients adorned divine nobility, and human nobility followed it. Mencius, &c. 'Four Books.'

It has never been the case that he who possessed genuine virtue could not influence others, nor that he who was not sincere could influence others.

The principles of great men illuminate the universe.

DLV.

Greatness in Adversity.

When the year becomes cold, we shall note that the pine and the cypress are the last to lose their leaves. Confucius. Analects.

The Duke-king of Ts'e had a thousand teams; but on the day of his death the people did not praise him for a single virtue. Pᵉih-e and Shuh-ts'e died of hunger at the foot of the Show-Yang mountain, and the people, down to the present time, praise them.

Chee-Kung said, 'Were they discontented?' The sage replies, 'They sought and obtained complete virtue; how then could they be discontented?'

Coarse rice for food, water to drink, and the bended arm for a pillow,—happiness may be enjoyed even in these. Without virtue, riches and honour seem to me like a passing cloud.

A wise and good man was Hooi. A piece of bamboo was his dish, a cocoa-nut his cup, his dwelling a miserable shed. Men could not sustain the sight of his wretchedness. But Hooi did not change the serenity of his mind.

DLVI.

Virtue.

Hindu.
Rámáyana.
'The Iliad of the East.'
(Richardson.)

'Even so, —, my soul shall triumph.' Thus spake Rama.

'I was wrong,' he said, and dashed a spray of softened tears from his eyes. 'Virtue is a service man owes himself; and though there were no heaven, nor any God to rule the world, it were not less the binding law of life. It is man's privilege to know the right and follow it. Betray and prosecute me, brother men! Pour out your rage on me, O malignant devils! Smile, or watch my agony with cold disdain, ye blissful gods! Earth, hell, heaven, combine your might to crush me,—I will still hold fast by this inheritance! My strength is nothing—time can shake and cripple it; my youth is transient—already grief has withered up my days; my heart—alas! it seems well nigh broken now! Anguish may crush it utterly, and life may fail; but even so my soul, that has not tripped, shall triumph, and dying, give the lie to soulless Destiny, that dares to boast itself man's master.'

DLVII.
Lowliness and Grandeur.

The Grand Being, having left the palace, sat all day by the riverside, in a spot perfumed with the fragrant flowers of the forest trees. Then royally he marched, till he came to a great Bo-tree, perfect in the beauty of its trunk and branches, and brilliant dark-green foliage. And he met a certain Brahman, named Sotiya, and from him accepted eight handfuls of long grass. The Master then spread the grass on the ground to the east of the Bo-tree, and the grass became a jewelled throne. The Lord seated thereon, with upright figure and well-steadied mind, turned his whole thought to attain through purity and charity the exaltation of knowledge. And around him gathered the angels of many worlds with fragrant offerings, and the strains of their heavenly concert resounded in the most distant universe.

<small>Siamese. Life of Buddha. comp.</small>

DLVIII.
Resting.

The poem says, 'The twittering yellow-bird rests on a corner of the mound.' When it rests, it knows where to rest. Shall a man not be equal to this bird? Profound was King Wan. With how bright and unceasing a feeling of reverence did he regard his resting-places! As a sovereign, he rested in benevolence. As a minister, he rested in reverence. As

<small>Confucius. 'The Great Learning.'</small>

a son, he rested in filial piety. As a father, he rested in kindness. In communication with his subjects, he rested in good faith. The point where to rest being known, the aim is determined. By that determination calmness is attained. In calmness may be found the deliberation by which is reached the desired end.

DLIX.

Woman.

Ye heavens! let your sweetest benedictions descend on Solima. May her name blossom in the songs her bounty hath called to our hearts! She bade her bower arise, entwined with lily and rose, not in pride, not for her repose, but that the wayfarer might find rest, and the lost find shelter. Her grove is the couch of the aged, the home of the widow; and the orphan regains both parents in her tender eyes. No sorrow hath oppressed, no pain hath wasted, but the heart of Solima hath listened to it with tears which soft-eyed angels wear for pearls. The stranger and the pilgrim well know, when the sky is dark and the north wind rages, when the clouds give no rain, when the babe is without sustenance from its mother, that thou, O Solima, art bountiful to them as the spring, that thou art their harvest, that thou art a sun to them by day, and a moon in the cloudy night!

[Arabic. (Par. after Sir W. Jones.)]

DLX.

Honour.

In the reign of Noshirvan, a person sold a piece of ground to another, who in ploughing it discovered a buried treasure, which he instantly carried to the seller of the field; but he would not receive it, and

[Persian. Zofet al Muj-jaliso.]

said, 'I disposed of my land to thee with all its advantages, therefore whatever it may contain is thine.' The purchaser contended, saying, 'I only bought the soil, therefore whatever is under it must be thine.'

The Emperor, to whom the dispute was submitted, decided that a marriage should take place between the son and daughter of such virtuous men, and the treasure be theirs.

It is further related that the purchased field that year produced ears of corn so large and full, that they are still preserved in the cabinets of the rich.

DLXI.
Eminence.

The wise, virtuous, prudent, intelligent, teachable man will become eminent. Singálo Wada. Buddha. Gogerly.

The persevering, diligent man, unshaken in adversity, and of inflexible determination, will become eminent.

The well-informed, friendly-disposed, prudent-speaking, generous-minded, self-controlled man, calm and self-possessed, will become eminent.

In this world, generosity, mildness of speech, public spirit, and courteous behaviour, are worthy of respect under all circumstances, and will be valuable in all places.

The wise man who carefully cultivates these will obtain both prosperity and honour.

DLXII.
Fame.

The spider holds the veil in the palace of Cæsar; the owl stands sentinel on the watchtower of Afrasial. Persian. Sádi. (Sir W. Jones.

DLXIII.

Leaders.

<small>Christian.
Ep. to Heb.
comp.</small>
Remember your leaders, who spoke to you the word of God; and considering well the aim of their life, imitate their faithfulness.

We have an altar of which they cannot eat who serve the tabernacle.

Jesus suffered without the gate: let us go forth to him without the camp, bearing his reproach.

Obey your leaders, and submit yourselves to them; for they keep watch in behalf of your souls, as those who must give an account; that they may do this with joy, and not with grief.

DLXIV.

Continuity.

<small>Christian.
1 Cor.
comp.</small>
For I would not have you ignorant, brethren, that all our fathers were under the cloud, and all passed through the sea, and were all baptized to Moses in the cloud and in the sea, and all ate the same spiritual food, and all drank the same spiritual drink.

These things were recorded for our admonition, to whom the ends of the ages have come. Wherefore let him that thinketh he standeth take heed lest he fall. No temptation hath come upon you but such as is common to man; but God is faithful, who will not suffer you to be tempted beyond what ye are able to endure, but will with the temptation furnish also the way to escape, that ye may be able to endure it.

DLXV.

Faithfulness.

Now faith is assurance of things hoped for, a conviction of things not seen. For by it the elders obtained a good report. <small>Christian. Ep. to Heb. comp.</small>

By faith Abraham, when called, obeyed to go forth to a place which he was afterward to receive for an inheritance, and went forth, not knowing whither he was going. By faith he sojourned in the land of the promise, as in a foreign country, dwelling in tents with Isaac and Jacob, the heirs with him of the same promise; for he was looking for the city which hath foundations, whose maker and builder is God.

These died in faith, not having received the promised blessings, but having seen them from afar, and greeted them, and having professed that they were strangers and sojourners on the earth. For they who say such things show plainly that they are seeking a country. And if indeed they had been mindful of that from which they came out, they would have had opportunity to return; but now they desire a better country, that is, a heavenly.

By faith Moses, when he was come to years, refused to be called the son of Pharaoh's daughter, choosing rather to suffer affliction with the people of God than to enjoy the pleasures of sin for a season; esteeming the reproach of a deliverer greater riches than the treasures of Egypt; for he looked to the recompense of reward. By faith he forsook Egypt, not fearing the wrath of the king; for he endured, as seeing him who is invisible.

And what shall I say more? For the time would

fail me to tell of Gideon, of Barak, and Samson, and Jephthah, of David and Samuel, and the prophets; who through faith subdued kingdoms, wrought righteousness, obtained promised blessings, stopped the mouths of lions, quenched the power of fire, escaped the edge of the sword, out of weakness were made strong, became mighty in war, put to flight the armies of the aliens. Women received back their dead as by a resurrection; but others were tortured, not accepting deliverance, that they might obtain a better resurrection; and others had trial of mockings and scourgings, and also of bonds and imprisonment; they were stoned, they were sawn asunder, were tempted, were slain with the sword; they went about in sheep-skins and goat-skins, being destitute, afflicted, tormented; they wandered in deserts and mountains, and caves and the clefts of the earth,—they, of whom the world was not worthy.

And these all, having obtained a good report through faith, received not the promised blessing, God having provided for us some better thing, that they might not be made perfect without us.

Therefore let us also, being surrounded by so great a cloud of witnesses, lay aside every weight, and the sin which doth easily beset us, and let us run with perseverance the race that is set before us.

DLXVI.
Royal Virtues.

[Buddhist. Játakas. (R. C. Childers.) 6th cent. B.C.]

There was once a king of Benares named Brahmadatta, whose righteous administration of justice put an end to litigation in his kingdom, and left him time to turn his attention to his own faults, with a view to their correction. He accordingly questioned first his own retinue, then the public officials, then the citizens of Benares, then the suburban inhabitants, and lastly, mounting his chariot, he drove through the length and breadth of the land, begging all whom he met to tell him his faults. But all with one accord told him only of his virtues, and he was returning baffled from his expedition, when in a narrow defile his chariot met that of Mallika, King of Kosala, who was bound on a precisely similar mission. It at once became evident that one of the chariots must make way for the other, and the charioteers of the rival monarchs commenced a dispute for the precedence, which seemed hopeless when it was ascertained that neither could claim any advantage over the other in age, wealth, fame, or military power. At length, however, it was decided that the more virtuous should have the precedence; and the charioteer of King Mallika, challenged to describe the virtues of his royal master, replies as follows, 'King Mallika overthrows the strong by strength, the mild by mildness, good he overcomes with good, and evil with evil.' The other charioteer said, 'If these are his virtues, what are his faults?' Then he said of his own master, 'With meekness he conquers anger, he overcomes evil with good, he disarms avarice with liberality, and the liar with truth.' Hearing this, Mallika and his charioteer alight, and their chariot is drawn aside.

DLXVII.

Magnanimity.

And it came to pass, when Saul had returned from following the Philistines, that it was told him, saying,

Heb.
1 Sam.
Ab.

Behold, David is in the wilderness of En-gedi. Then Saul took three thousand chosen men out of all Israel, and went to seek David and his men upon the rocks of the wild goats. And he came to the sheep-cotes by the way, where was a cave ; and Saul went in to cover his feet: and David and his men were remaining in the inner part of the cave. And the men of David said unto him, Behold, I will deliver thine enemy into thy hand, that thou mayest do to him as it shall seem good unto thee. Then David arose and cut off the skirt of Saul's robe privily.

David stayed his men, and suffered them not to rise against Saul ; but Saul rose up out of the cave, and went on his way.

Then David arose afterward, and went out of the cave, and cried after Saul, saying, My lord the king ! And when Saul looked behind him, David stooped with his face to the ground and bowed himself. And David said to Saul, Wherefore hearest thou men's words, saying, 'Behold, David seeketh thy hurt ?' Behold, this day thine eyes have seen how that Jehovah had delivered thee to-day into my hand in the cave ; and some bade me kill thee, but mine eye spared thee. Behold, my father, the skirt of thy robe in my hand ; for in that I cut off the skirt of thy robe, and killed thee not, know thou and see that there is neither evil nor transgression in my hand, and I have not sinned against thee ; yet thou huntest my life, to take it.

Then Saul said, Is this thy voice, my son David ? And Saul lifted up his voice and wept. And he said to David, Thou art more righteous than I ; for thou hast requited me good, whereas I have requited thee evil. For if a man find his enemy, will he let him go well away? And now, behold, I know that thou shalt surely be king.

DLXVIII.
Bountiful Natures.

Large rivers, great trees, wholesome plants, and wealthy persons, are not born for themselves, but to be of service to others. _{Hindu. (Albitis.)}

DLXIX.
Advice to a Son.

Seek science, and learn real greatness, that thou mayest daily improve. Thy noble ancestry ranks but second to thine own merits. Birth and high pedigree are idle and vain, and avail thee nothing in yonder spheres, where true greatness alone is rewarded. _{Persian. Nizámi.}

DLXX.
Three Jewels.

The gem of the sky is the sun; the gem of the home is the child: in the assembly shines the brow of the wise man. _{Singhalese. Buddhist.}

DLXXI.
Fame.

A stately pleasure-house built Mahmoud in the gardens of Ghusni, and there prepared a banquet for his father. But when he looked for admiration in the father's eye, he saw only sadness. 'My son,' said the king, 'any of my wealthy subjects could have built this bauble with gold; 'twere nobler work to erect the more durable structure of good fame, which shall stand for ever, to be imitated, but never to be equalled!' _{Persian. Nizámi.}

Mahmoud lived and died. Of all the gorgeous palaces he built, not one stone is now left upon another, but the edifice of his fame triumphs over time.

DLXXII.

Destiny.

<small>Persian.
Nizámi.</small>

More kingdoms wait thy diadem than are known to thee by name. Thee may sovereign Destiny lead to victory day by day!

DLXXIII.

Good-will.

<small>Páli.
Buddha.
Khuddaka
Pátha.
comp.</small>

This is what should be done by him who is wise in seeking his own good, and gaining a knowledge of the tranquil lot of Nirvána:—

Let him be diligent, upright, and conscientious; not vain-glorious, but gentle and lowly;

Contented and cheerful; not oppressed with cares; not burdened with riches; tranquil, prudent, free from arrogance and avarice.

Let him not do any mean action, nor incur the reproval of wise men.

Let all creatures be prosperous and happy, let them be of joyful mind; all beings that have life, be they feeble or strong, be they minute or vast:

Seen or unseen, near or afar, born or seeking birth, let all beings be joyful.

Let no man deceive another; let none be harsh to any; let none wish ill to his neighbour.

Let the love that fills the mother's heart as she watches over an only child, even such love, animate all.

Let the good-will that is boundless, immeasurable,

impartial, unmixed with enmity, prevail throughout the world—above, below, around.

If a man be of this mind, wherever he moves, and in every moment, the saying is come to pass, 'This place is the abode of holiness.'

JUSTICE AND GOVERNMENT.

DLXXIV.
Government.

Chinese.
Confucius.
'Doctrine of the Mean.'
6th cent. B.C.

The poem says, 'That is the right imperial domain where the people have repose.'

Make happy those who are near, and those who are far will come.

The great man will cultivate himself with reverential carefulness, that he may give rest to all the people.

Where rulers love justice, the people respond readily with service.

The path is not far from men. The ode says, 'As we cut axe-handles, we grasp one handle to hew another.' So the wise governor uses what is in man to reform men.

The acts of a wise ruler are for ages a law to the empire; his words are for ages a lesson to the empire.

Chung-Ne handed down the doctrines of the sages as if they were his ancestors. He harmonised with heaven above, and beneath with sea and land. In alternating progress he was as the four seasons.

What needs no display is virtue.

The wise man does not use rewards, and the people are stimulated to virtue; he does not show anger, and the people are awed more than by battle-axes.

Heaven and earth are without doubleness.

The superior man being sincere and reverential, the whole world is conducted to a state of happy tranquillity.
Great energies are traced in great transformations.

DLXXV.

Justice.

The Arabs say, 'There is no better ruler than judgment, no safer guardian than justice, no stronger sword than right, no ally surer than truth.' (Arabic. (D'Herb.))

Justice is an unassailable fortress, built on the brow of a mountain which cannot be overthrown by the violence of torrents, nor demolished by the force of armies.

'Do you desire,' said Abdallah, 'to bring the praise of mankind upon your action? Then desire not unjustly, or even by your right, to grasp that which belongs to another.'

Tamerlane said, 'If you would preserve the state in repose, let the sword of justice repose not.'

DLXXVI.

Equity.

To every period its men; and the rise of every one is according to his creed, and his watching for opportunity. (Arabic. 16th cent. (Jo R.A.S.) comp.

The chief quality of leadership is the jewel of equity, by which is justified the obedience of every man to his leader.

The exercise of equity for one day is equal to sixty years spent in prayer.

It is said, 'Man after his existence is but a subject of conversation.' Be thou a good subject for those who shall mention thee.

DLXXVII.

Equality.

<small>Persian. Khèyam. 11th cent.</small>

Justice is the soul of the universe. The universe is a body ; the senses are its angels ; the heavens, the elements, and all beings, its limbs : behold the eternal unity—the rest is only illusion.

Why should a man who possesses a bit of bread securing life for two days, and who has a cup of fresh water—why should such a man be commanded by another who is not his superior, and why should he serve one who is only his equal ?

In this world he who possesses a morsel of bread, and some nest in which to shelter himself, who is master or slave of no man, tell that man to live content ; he possesses a very sweet existence.

DLXXVIII.

Humanity.

<small>Chinese. Confucius.</small>

A soldier of the kingdom of Ci lost his buckler, and having sought it in vain, consoled himself by saying, 'A soldier has lost his buckler, but a soldier of our camp will find and use it.' It had been better had he said, 'A man has lost his buckler, but a man will find it.' The abject man sows that himself or his friends may reap: the love of the perfect man is universal.

DLXXIX.
Brotherhood.
>Have we not one father?
>Why do we act treacherously
>Every one towards his neighbour,
>By profaning the covenant of our fathers?

<small>Heb. Mal. comp.</small>

DLXXX.
Equality.

Mandhata said to Narada, 'I see persons of every colour in all orders, and we are all subject to love, anger, fear, thought, grief, hunger, and labour. Where then is the difference of castes?'

<small>Hindu. Padma Pur. Swarga Khanda. (Wilson MS.) comp.</small>

Narada replied, 'There is no difference of castes: all the universe is pervaded by the Supreme Being. The creatures of God have passed into classes by their actions.'

Learning should be rescued from every consideration of high rank or low, a consideration that cannot for a moment be compatible with instruction; and the heart should be kept free from all (such) infatuation.

He is a devotee and a wise man all of whose engagements are pursued through every obstruction he may meet with; who is devoted, ignorant of cruelty, and lives as a friend of all creatures; who, uninfluenced by favour, is directed only by infallible reason; and who is master of his senses.

Truth is God himself, and it is divine meditation; by it the world is caused, governed, and preserved. Falsehood is darkness. Those two are the stations of heaven and hell.

There is no virtue in the world greater than that of doing good to others.
Without virtue everything would cease to be.

DLXXXI.
Age and Youth.

Persian.
(Albitis.)

Woe to the nation where the young have already the vices of old age, and where the aged retain the follies of youth!

DLXXXII.
Graduated Duties.

Hindu.
Hitopadesa.
c. 500 B.C.

Let a man desert a single person for the sake of his tribe, his tribe for the sake of his native city, his native city for the sake of his country, and the whole world for the sake of his own soul.

DLXXXIII.
Judgment.

Singhalese.
Kusa Játakya.
6th cent. B.C.
(Steele.)

A poor woman went to a tank to bathe her child. Having bathed and dressed it, she set it on the bank to play while she herself bathed. An evil-minded woman approached, saying, 'May I take care of your babe for a little?' The mother consented. The evil woman then ran off with the child, the mother pursuing with lamentations. Having overtaken her, the evil woman claimed the child, and the two came to the hall of Buddha, who walked the earth as a great judge. Having heard what each woman had to say, the judge drew a line on the floor, and laid the child upon it. Then said he to one, 'Lay hold of the child's arms,' to the other, 'Lay hold of the child's legs; then let each pull, and she that draws this child over the line shall be adjudged its mother.' But as the two struggled the babe cried, and the mother said, 'No; let her have it,' and stood aside weeping. But the judge said, 'Let her who hath compassion take the child.' And to the evil woman he said, 'Go, but amend thy ways, lest a heavy after-fortune await thee.'

DLXXXIV.

Judgment.

There came unto Solomon two women, and they stood before him. And the first woman said, O my lord! I and this woman dwell in one house; and I brought forth a child in the house. And it came to pass that on the third day afterwards this woman also was delivered of a child. And it came to pass that this woman's child died in the night; and she arose in the middle of the night, when thy handmaid was asleep, and took my child from beside me, and she laid her own dead child in my bosom. And I arose in the morning and examined the child, and behold it was not that which I had brought forth. And the other woman said, Nay; but the living child is mine, and the dead child is thine. And the king said, The one saith, 'This living child is mine;' and the other saith, 'Nay; but it is mine.' Then he said, Bring me a sword. And they brought a sword unto the king. And the king said, Cut the living child in two, and give half to the one, and half to the other. And the woman whose the living child was spake to the king, for her heart yearned for her child—O my lord! give unto her the living child, and by no means put it to death. But the other said, Let it be neither

Heb.
1 Kings.
Ab.

thine nor mine, but divide it. And the king answered, Give unto that one the living child; she is its mother.

DLXXXV.

The Peaceful.

<small>Singhalese. Buddhist.</small> Three cubs the lioness brings forth, five the tigress, but one the cow; yet many are the meek cattle, few the beasts of prey. The fierce and grasping soon decay; the universe preserves to the peaceful the heritage of the earth.

DLXXXVI.

Mercy and Forbearance.

<small>Singhalese. Buddhist.</small> With mercy and forbearance shalt thou disarm every foe. For want of fuel the fire expires: mercy and forbearance bring violence to nought.

DLXXXVII.

Capital Punishment.

<small>Confucius. Analects.</small> Ke K'ang, distressed about the number of thieves in his kingdom, inquired of Confucius how he might do away with them. The sage said, 'If you, sir, were not covetous, the people would not steal, though you should pay them for it.'

Ke K'ang asked, 'What do you say about killing the unprincipled for the good of the principled?' Confucius said, 'In carrying on your government why use killing at all? Let the rulers desire what is good, and the people will be good. The grass must bend when the wind blows across it.'

How can men who cannot rectify themselves, rectify others?

DLXXXVIII.

Office.

Lew Hea Hooi did not refuse an inferior office. Although he lost his place, he grumbled not. In poverty he repined not. He lived in harmony with men of little worth, and could not bear to abandon them. He said, ' You are you, and I am I ; although you sit by my side with your body, how can you defile me ?' Hence, when the fame of Lew Hea Hooi is heard of, the mean man becomes liberal, and the miserly becomes generous. Confucius. Analects.

DLXXXIX.

Clemency and Justice.

When the enemy has failed in all other artifices, he will propose friendship, that under its appearance he may effect what he could not compass as an open adversary. Persian. Sádi.

Forgiveness is commendable, but apply not ointment to the wounds of an oppressor. Knoweth he not that whosoever spareth the life of a serpent committeth injury towards the sons of Adam? Be not so severe as to cause disgust, nor so lenient as to encourage audacity. Severity and leniency should be tempered together ; like the surgeon, who, when he uses the lancet, applies also a plaster.

DXC.

A Happy State.

    That our sons may be like plants,
        Growing up in their youth;
    Our daughters like corner-pillars, Heb. Ps.

Hewn for the structure of a palace ;
Our granaries filled,
Sending forth store after store ;
Our flocks bringing forth thousands,
Ten thousands in our fields ;
Our oxen bearing loads ;
No breaking in, no going out ;
Nor any clamour in our streets.
Happy the people that is in such a state !

DXCI.

Captivity.

By the rivers of Babylon there we sat down,
And wept when we remembered Zion.
We hanged our harps upon the willows,
For they who had carried us away captives
 required of us a song.
How can we sing a song of the Lord
In a strange land ?
May they who sowed in tears
Reap in joy !
May he who went out weeping,
Bearing a cast of seed,
Come again with rejoicing,
Bringing his sheaves with him !

Heb.
Ps.
comp.

DXCII.

Peace.

The superior man in his home makes the left hand —the weak side—the place of honour; but he who goes forth to use weapons of war honours the right— the strong hand. Weapons are instruments of evil

Chinese.
Lao-Tsze.
B.C. 604.

omen. They are not the tools of the superior man. He uses them only when he cannot help it.

He is brave in need, but never overbearing. His actions are such as he would have rendered to himself again.

Peace is his highest aim. When he conquers, he is not elated. To be elated is to rejoice in the destruction of human life; and he who rejoices at the destruction of human life is not fit to be entrusted with power in the world. He who has been instrumental in killing many people should move on over them with bitter tears. Those who have been victorious in battle are disposed after the order of a funeral. Begin to regulate before disorder comes. Where legions are quartered, briers and thorns grow. In the track of great armies must follow bad years.

DXCIII.
Peace.

Peace, peace, to far and to near!
Saith the Lord.
But the wicked are like the troubled sea,
That cannot rest:
Its waters send up mire and dirt.
There is no peace, saith my God, to the wicked.

Heb.
Isa.

DXCIV.
The Agitator.

For Zion's sake will I not hold my peace,
And for Jerusalem's sake will I not rest,
Until the righteousness thereof go forth as brightness,
And the salvation thereof as a lamp that burneth.

Heb.
Isa.

Upon thy walls, O Jerusalem, have I set watchmen,
Who shall never hold their peace, day and night.
Go through, go through the gates;
Prepare ye the way of the people!
Lift up a standard to the peoples!

DXCV.
Peace.

<small>Heb.
Isa.
comp.</small>

It shall come to pass in the latter days that the house of God shall be established above every height, and all nations shall flow unto it. And many peoples shall say—
Let us go up to the mountain of God,
And he will teach us his ways,
And we will walk in his paths:
And he shall judge among the nations,
And decide for many peoples.
And they shall beat their swords into ploughshares,
And their spears into pruning-hooks;
Nation shall not lift up sword against nation,
Neither shall they learn war any more.

DXCVI.
Peacefulness.

<small>Christian.
James.
comp.</small>

The tongue is a little member, and boasteth great things. Behold how great a forest a little fire kindleth! And the tongue is a fire. Every kind of beasts and of birds, of creeping things and things in the sea, is tamed and hath been tamed by mankind; but the tongue can no man tame. Therewith bless we God, and therewith curse we men, made after the likeness of God. Out of the same mouth proceedeth blessing and cursing. My brethren, these things ought not so to be. Doth a fountain from the same opening send forth sweet water and bitter? Who is wise and endued with knowledge among you? let him show out of a good course of conduct his works in meekness of wisdom. But if ye have bitter rivalry and strife in your hearts, do not glory and lie against the truth. This wisdom is not that which descendeth from above, but earthly, sensual, diabolical. For where there is rivalry and strife there is confusion, and every evil work. But the wisdom from above is first pure, then peaceable; gentle, easy to be entreated, full of mercy and good fruits; without partiality, without hypocrisy. And the fruit of righteousness is sown in peace by those who make peace.

Whence are wars and whence are fightings among you? Are they not hence, from your lusts that war in your members? Ye lust, and have not; ye kill, and earnestly covet, and cannot obtain; ye fight and war. The husbandman waiteth for the precious fruit of the earth, and is patient about it until it hath received the early and latter rain. Be ye also patient.

DXCVII.

War against War.

Come see the works of God,
What desolations he hath made in the land,— Heb.
Ps.
Causing wars to cease to the ends of the land:
The bow he hath broken, and he hath cut in two
    the spear:
The chariots he hath burned with fire.
' Be ye still, and know that I am God.'

DXCVIII.

The King.

<small>Hindu. Cural. comp.</small>

Never to fail in fearlessness, liberality, wisdom, and energy, this is the kingly character.

The whole world will exalt the country of a king who is easy of access, and whose words are gentle.

The world will praise and submit itself to the mind of the king who is able to give with affability, and to protect all who come to him.

The whole world will dwell under the shade of the king who can bear words that embitter the ear.

He is the light of kings who has beneficence, benevolence, rectitude, and care for his people.

That king will be esteemed a god among men who performs his own duties and protects mankind.

Let a king daily examine the conduct of his servants; if they do not act crookedly, the world will not act crookedly.

To cherish great men, and make them his own, is the most difficult of all things.

The king who is without the guard of men who can rebuke him will perish, though there be no one to destroy him.

It is tenfold more injurious to lose the friendship of the good than to incur the hatred of the many.

There will be nothing left for enemies to do against him who has the power of acting so as to secure the fellowship of worthy men.

The falling tears of a people will wear away the support of any throne.

DXCIX.

Sympathy.

The sage is ever the good saviour of men; he rejects none. He is ever the good saviour of things; he rejects nothing.

<small>Chinese. Lao-Tsze. B.C. 604.</small>

He who knows eternity is magnanimous. Being magnanimous, he is catholic. Being catholic, he is a king. Being a king, he is heaven.

Being heaven, he is reason.

Being reason, he is enduring.

The spirit, like the perennial spring of the valley, never dies.

His I call the comprehensive intelligence. For the good men are the instructors of other good men; and the bad men are the material for the good men to work upon.

The sage, when he wishes to be above the people so as to rule them, must keep below them. When he wishes to be before the people, he must in person keep behind them. In this way, while in position over the people, they do not feel his weight. Therefore the world delights to exalt him, and no one is offended.

He makes the mind of the people his mind.

The good I would meet with goodness. The not good I would meet with goodness also. The faithful I would meet with faith. The not faithful I would meet with faith also. Virtue is faithful. Recompense injury with kindness.

The sage lives in the world with a timid reserve, but his mind blends in sympathy with all. The people all turn their eyes and ears up to him; and he regards them all as his children.

He who bears the calamities of his country shall be called the king of the world.

DC.
The Righteous Ruler.

<small>Heb.
Isa.
comp.</small>
The spirit of God shall rest upon him,
The spirit of wisdom and understanding,
The spirit of counsel and might.
With righteousness shall he judge the poor,
And decide with equity for the afflicted of the earth.
With the breath of his lips he shall slay the wicked.
Justice and faithfulness shall be the girdle of his loins.
Then the wolf shall dwell with the lamb,
And the leopard shall lie down with the kid,
And the calf and the young lion and the fatling together,
And a little child shall lead them.
They shall not hurt nor destroy in all my holy mountain;
For the earth shall be full of the knowledge of God,
As the waters cover the sea.

DCI.
A Nation's Hope.

<small>Heb.
Isa.
comp.</small>
Behold, a king shall reign in righteousness,
And princes shall rule with justice;
And they shall be as a hiding-place from the wind,
And a covert from the tempest;
As springs of water in a dry place,

As the shadow of a great rock in a weary land.
The eyes of them that see shall not be dim,
And the ears of them that hear shall attend.
The heart even of the rash shall gain knowledge,
And the tongue of stammerers hasten to speak plainly.
No more shall the fool be called noble,
Nor the fraudulent be said to be generous;
For the fool speaketh foolishness
To make empty the soul of the hungry.
The fraudulent deviseth craftily
To destroy the poor with lying words,
Even when the needy pleadeth a just cause.
But the noble deviseth noble things,
And by noble things shall he stand.
The work of righteousness shall be peace,
And the effect of justice quietness and trust for ever.

DCII.
Bad Ministers.

I have heard a tale, that in the farthest limits of Marv there was a prince, a youth vigorous as the cypress. The old ministers reproved his inexperience, and through them the needy land was in peril of disturbance. In the anxious sleep of the young prince a sage came to him, and said, 'O new moon! be not imprisoned in the old zodiac. The new bough cannot raise its head from the grove unless it pierce through the dead stem.' When the prince raised his head from heavy sleep, he removed the obstructive ministers. He erased the old and raised the new; and the realm became fresh for the young prince. No task is well performed by a reluctant hand.

Persian.
Nizámi.
A.C. 1157.
Ab.

DCIII.

Helpfulness.

<small>Hindu.
Hitopadesa.</small>

He is the excellent man from whose presence none who seek aid or protection depart hopeless.

DCIV.

Union.

<small>Hindu.
Hitopadesa.</small>

The union of the small and weak performs great works. By blades of grass twisted together the elephant is tied fast. The birds caught in the fowler's net plied their wings in concert, and bore away the net through the air.

DCV.

Majorities.

<small>Confucius.
Analects.</small>

Tsăng the philosopher said, 'What ten eyes behold what ten hands point to, is to be regarded with reverence.'

Tsze-Kung asked, saying, 'What do you say of a man who is loved by all the people in his village?' Confucius answered, 'We may not for that accord our approval of him.' 'And what do you say of him who is hated by all the people in his village?' The Master said, 'We may not for that conclude that he is bad. It is better than either of these cases that the good in the village love him and the bad hate him.'

The Duke of Gae asked, 'What should be done to secure the submission of the people?' The sage said, 'Advance the upright and set aside the crooked, then the people will submit. Advance the crooked and set aside the upright, and the people will not submit.'

DCVI.

Wrongs.

The wise exhibit, as clearly as if it were displayed before our eyes, the doctrine belonging to the science of ethics, that danger arises from pointing out evil, and success from pointing out a remedy.

<small>Hindu. Hitopade</small>

DCVII.

In the Night.

One calleth to me out of Seir,
'Watchman, what of the night?
Watchman, what of the night?'
The watchman said, 'The morning cometh,
And also the night.
If ye will inquire, inquire ye : come to me again.'
O God, thou art my God !
Thy counsels of old are faithfulness and truth.
Thou hast been a stronghold to the poor,
A refuge from the storm, a shadow from the heat.
Open ye the gates,
That the righteous nation may enter in
Which keepeth the truth.
A steadfast mind thou wilt keep in perfect peace.
The way of the just is straight :
Thou, the most upright, makest his path plain.
We have waited for thee ;
My soul hath desired thee in the night ;
My spirit within me shall seek thee early.
Awake and sing, ye that dwell in the dust ;
For thy dew is a life-giving dew,
And the earth shall bring forth the dead.

<small>Heb. Isa. comp.</small>

DCVIII.

The Reformer.

<small>Heb.
Isa.
comp.</small>

The Lord hath given me the tongue of the instructed,
That I may know how to assist the weary with my word.
He wakeneth, morning by morning,
He wakeneth mine ear to hear as the instructed.
And I was not rebellious, neither turned away backward.
I gave my back to the smiters,
And my cheek to them that plucked off the hair.
I made my face like a flint;
And I know that I shall not be put to shame.
He that justifieth me is near.
Who is mine adversary? let us stand up together.
Lo! they shall all wax old as a garment:
The moth shall consume them.

DCIX.

Radicalism.

<small>Chinese.
Confucius.
'The Great
Learning.'
comp.</small>

Things have their root and their completion. It cannot be that when the root is neglected, what springs from it will be well ordered.

The ancients, who wished to illustrate illustrious virtue throughout the empire, began, said Confucius, with investigation. Things being investigated, knowledge became complete. Knowledge being complete, their thoughts were sincere. Their thoughts being sincere, their hearts were then rectified. Their hearts being rectified, their persons were cultivated. Their persons being cultivated, their families were regulated. Their families being regulated, their states were rightly governed. Their states being rightly governed, the whole empire was made tranquil and happy.

DCX.

The Tyrant's Fall.

Upon the bare mountain lift ye up a banner! Heb.
Isa.
comp.
Exalt the voice unto them, wave the hand,
That they may enter into the gates of the tyrants.
I have given charge to my appointed ones,
And will lay low the haughtiness of the terrible.
I will make a man more precious than fine gold,
Even a man than the gold of Ophir.
The whole earth is at rest and is quiet;
They break forth into singing :
How art thou fallen from heaven,
O bright shining son of the morning !
Is this the man that made the earth to tremble,
That did shake kingdoms,
Which made the world as a wilderness ?
This is the purpose that is purposed upon all the earth,
And this the hand that is stretched out upon all nations :
The poorest shall feed,
And the needy lie down in safety.
Thy throne shall be established in mercy.

DCXI.

Brotherhood.

Thus saith God :—
Observe ye justice, and do righteousness ; Heb.
Isa.
comp.
For my salvation is near to come :
Blessed is the man that doeth this,

That keepeth his hand from doing any evil.
Neither let the stranger say,
'God hath utterly separated me from his people;'
The stranger will I bring to my holy mountain.
Cast up, cast up, prepare the way;
Take the stumbling-block from the way of my people!
Arise, shine; for thy light is come,
And the glory of the Lord is arisen upon thee!
For behold darkness covereth the earth,
And gross darkness the peoples.
The nations shall come to thy light,
And kings to the brightness of thy rising;
Therefore thy gates shall be open continually,
They shall not be shut day nor night.
Violence shall be no more heard in thy land.
The little one shall become a thousand,
And the small one a strong nation.
Behold, I create a new heaven and a new earth,
And the former shall not be remembered;
But be ye glad and exult for ever in that which I create.
For behold, I make the city an exaltation,
And her people a joy.

DCXII.

Mercy misplaced.

<small>Persian. Sádi. Gul.</small>
The rain, in whose nature there is no partiality, produces tulips in the garden, but only weeds in a barren soil. A sterile soil will not yield spikenard; waste not then seed upon it. To show favour to the wicked is in fact doing injury to the good.

Showing mercy to the wicked is doing injury to the good, and pardoning oppressors is injuring the oppressed. When you connect yourself with base men, and show them favour, they commit crimes with your power, whereby you participate in their guilt.

DCXIII.

Justice.

In a certain year I was sitting retired in the great mosque at Damascus, at the head of the tomb of Yáhiyá the prophet (on whom be peace!) One of the kings of Arabia, who was notorious for his injustice, happened to come on a pilgrimage, and having performed his devotions, he uttered the following words : ' The poor and the rich are servants of this earth, and those who are richest have the greatest wants.' He then looked towards me, and said, ' Because Durwaishes are strenuous and sincere in their commerce with heaven, unite your prayers with mine, for I am in dread of a powerful enemy.'

Sádi. Gul.

I replied, ' Show mercy to the weak peasant, that you may not experience difficulty from a strong enemy. It is criminal to crush the poor and defenceless subjects with the arm of power. He liveth in dread who befriendeth not the poor; for should his foot slip, no one layeth hold of his hand. Whosoever soweth bad seed, and looketh for good fruit, tortureth his imagination in vain, making a false judgment of things. Take the cotton out of thine ear, and distribute justice to mankind; for if thou refusest justice, there will be a day of retribution.

' The children of Adam are limbs of one another, and are all produced from the same substance ; when the world gives pain to one member, the others also suffer uneasiness. Thou who art indifferent to the sufferings of others deservest not to be called a man.'

DCXIV.
Beginnings.

<small>Sádi.
Gul.</small>

Karoon, who had forty chambers full of treasure, was destroyed; but Nowshirvan died not, having left an immortal name.

They have related that Nowshirvan, being at a hunting-seat, was about to have some game dressed, and as there was not any salt, a servant was sent to fetch some from a village, when the monarch ordered him to pay the price of the salt, that the exaction might not become a custom, and the village be desolated. They say to him, 'From this trifle what injury can ensue?' He replied, 'Oppression was brought into the world from small beginnings, which every newcomer has increased, until it has reached the present degree of enormity. If the monarch were to eat a single apple from the garden of a peasant, the servants would pull up the tree by the roots; and if the Sultan orders five eggs to be taken by force, his soldiers will spit a thousand fowls. The iniquitous tyrant remaineth not, but the curses of mankind rest on him for ever.'

DCXV.
The Orphan.

<small>Sádi.
Bust.</small>

If the orphan come to cry, who will soothe him? if he be pettish, who will put up with his ill-humours? Take heed that he weep not; for the throne of the Almighty is shaken to and fro when the orphan sets a-crying. Beware of the groans of the wounded souls,

since the inward sore will at length break out;
oppress not to the utmost a single heart, for a single
sigh has power to overset a whole world. On the
crown of Káikusrou was the following inscription:
'For how many years, during what space of time,
shall men pass over my grave? As the kingdom came
to me by succession, in like manner shall it pass to
the hands of others.'

DCXVI.
Power.

A solitary Durwaish had taken up his abode in a
corner of a desert. The king passed him, and the ^{Sádi.}_{Gul.}
Durwaish, because retirement is the kingdom of contentment, did not lift up his head, nor show any signs
of politeness. The monarch, conscious of his superior
dignity, was chagrined, and said, 'This tribe of ragged
mendicants resemble the brute beasts.' His vizier
said to the Durwaish, 'When the monarch of the
terrestrial globe passed by you, why did not you do
him homage, nor behave even with common good
manners?' He replied, 'Tell the monarch of the
earth to expect service from him who hopes to receive
benefits; and let him know also that the monarch is
for the protection of his subjects, and not the subjects
for the service of the king. The king is the sentinel
of the poor, although affluence, pomp, and power are
his portion. The sheep are not for the shepherd, but
the shepherd is for their service.'

DCXVII.
Independence.

There were two brothers, one of whom was in the
service of the king, and the other ate the bread of his

own industry. Once the rich man said to his poor brother, 'Why do you not enter into the service of the king, to relieve yourself from the affliction of labour?' He asked, 'And why do you not work, that you may be relieved from the baseness of servitude? for the sages have said that to eat one's bread, and to sit down at ease, is preferable to wearing a golden girdle, and standing up in service; to use your hands in making mortar of quicklime is preferable to placing them on your breast in attendance on the Umeer.' Precious life has been spent in these cares, 'What shall I eat in the summer, and with what shall I be clothed in the winter?' O ignoble belly! satisfy yourself with a loaf of bread, that you may not bend your back in servitude.

Sádi. Gul.

DCXVIII.
Vanity.

A certain king said to a religious man, 'Do you ever think of me?' He answered, 'Yes, whenever I forget God.'

Sádi. Gul.

DCXIX.
Mercy.

Whosoever hath his adversary in his power, and doth not destroy him, is an enemy to himself. When there is a stone in the hand, and the head of a snake under the stone, the prudent man delayeth not execution. To show mercy to the sharp-teethed tiger would be doing injury to the sheep. But others have advanced the contrary, and said that in the execution of a prisoner delay is best, because you retain the power of killing or of releasing; but should he be put

Sádi. Gul.

to death without deliberation, good counsel may perchance be lost, since reparation is impossible. It is easy to take away life, but impossible to restore it. It is a rule of reason that the archer should have patience; for when the arrow has left the bow, it will not return.

DCXX.
Power.

A purpose without power is fraud and deceit, and power without design is ignorance and madness. The first requisites are judgment, prudence, and wisdom, and then a kingdom; because putting power and wealth into the hand of the ignorant is furnishing weapons against themselves.

Sádi. Gul.

DCXXI.
Experience.

Know you not that you will see your feet in fetters when you listen not to the admonition of mankind.

Sádi. Gul.

DCXXII.
Implora pace.

>Peace be within thy walls!
>Prosperity within thy palaces!
>For my brethren and companions' sake
>I will now say, Peace be within thee!

Sádi. Gul.

ACTION.

DCXXIII.

Assent and Action.

<small>Chinese.
Confucius.
Analects.</small>

Can men refuse to assent to the words of strict admonition? But it is reforming the conduct because of them which is valuable. Can men refuse to be pleased with words of gentle advice? But it is unfolding their aim which is valuable.

There are cases in which the blade springs, but the plant does not go on to flower. There are cases when it flowers, but no fruit is produced.

They who know the truth are not equal to those who love it, and they who love it are not equal to those who find delight in it.

DCXXIV.

The Heaven of Actions.

<small>Hindu.
Vishnu
Puràna.
(Wilson MS.)
comp.</small>

Blessed above all heavenly abodes is Bháráta Vársha, for it is the seat of actions, while others are those of enjoyment. There it is difficult to be born. The Devatás sing, 'Glorified are they that are born there, for they will obtain final emancipation. They are above the gods themselves who perform good actions and resign their rewards.

'Their minds are purified, and at last they are

liberated in the deity. We know not where we shall be born after the fruits of the actions which have gained this heaven; but happy are they who, possessing their senses perfect, are born in the Bháráta Vársha (heaven of good actions).'

DCXXV.
Radicalism.

The superior man bends his attention to what is radical. Chinese. Analects.

The root being established, all right practical courses naturally grow up.

When agreements are made according to what is right, what is spoken can be made good.

Confucius said, 'Yew could with half a word settle litigations.'

Yew never slept over a promise.

When he (Yew) heard anything which he had not yet carried into practice, he was afraid of hearing anything else.

Confucius said, 'Dressed himself in a tattered robe quilted with hemp, yet standing up by the side of men dressed in ermine, and not ashamed;—ah! it is Yew who is equal to this.'

DCXXVI.
Words and Actions.

Confucius said, 'Fine words and an insinuating appearance are seldom associated with virtue. Confucius. Analects.

'I hate the manner in which purple takes away the lustre of vermilion. I hate the way in which the (licentious) songs of Ch'ing confound the music of the Ya (Odes.)'

The Master said, 'I would prefer not speaking.' Tsze-Kung said, 'If you, Master, do not speak, what shall we, your disciples, have to record?'

Confucius said, 'Does heaven speak? The four seasons pursue their courses, and all things are being continually produced, but does heaven say anything?'

DCXXVII.
Industry.

<small>Heb.
Prov.</small>

Go to the ant, thou sluggard ;
Consider her ways, and be wise,
Which, having no leader,
No inspector, or ruler,
Provideth her food in the summer,
Collecteth her meat in the harvest.
How long, O sluggard, wilt thou lie ?
When wilt thou arise from thy sleep ?
A little sleep, a little slumber,
A little folding of the hands to rest ;
So shall thy poverty come like one who travelleth,
And thy want like an armed man.

DCXXVIII.
Labour.

<small>Chinese.
(Albitis.)</small> To enjoy the pleasures of wealth, you ought first to partake the bitterness of labour.

Every grain of rice you eat has been watered by the sweat of the labourer.

DCXXIX.
Skill.

<small>Chinese.
(Albitis.)</small> A hammer can make a needle out of a beam.

DCXXX.
Labour.

It is labour which makes known the true worth of a man, as fire makes the perfume of the incense evaporate. Hindu. (Albitis.)

DCXXXI.
Work.

A sower of seeds is as great in the eyes of Ormuzd as if he had given existence to a thousand creatures. Persian. (Albitis.)

DCXXXII.
Agriculture.

There was once a giantess who had a daughter, and the child saw a husbandman ploughing in the field. Then she ran and picked him up with her finger and thumb, and put him and his plough and his oxen into her apron, and carried them to her mother and said, 'Mother, what sort of beetle is this I found wriggling in the sand?' But the mother, said, 'Child, go put it in the place where thou hast found it. We must begone out of this land, for these little people will dwell in it.' Scandinavian Fable.

DCXXXIII.
Taciturnity.

When the rosebush blossomed in the bower, a nightingale said to the falcon, 'How is it that thou, being silent, bearest the prize from all birds? Thou hast not spoken a pleasing word to any one; yet thy abode is the wrist of the king, and thy food the deli- Persian. Nizámi. A.C. 1157.

cate partridge. I who produce a hundred musical gems in a moment have the worm for my food and the thorn for my mansion.' The falcon replied, ' For once be all ear. I who perform a hundred acts repeat not one. Thou who performest not one deed, displayest a thousand. Since I am all intelligence in the hunt, the king gives me dainty food and his wrist. Since thou art one entire motion of a tongue, eat worms and sit on thorns; and so peace be with you!'

DCXXXIV.
Deeds.

Parsí Catechism. (Quoted by W. J. Potter. Free Rel. Assoc., America. 1870.)

Your saviour is your deeds, and God himself.

To do virtuous deeds, to give in charity, to be kind, to be humble, to speak sweet words, to wish good to others, to have a clean heart, to acquire learning, to speak the truth, to suppress anger, to be patient and contented, to be friendly, to feel shame, to pay due respect to the old and young, to be pious, to respect our parents and teachers,—all these are the friends of the good men, and the enemies of the bad men.

To tell untruths, to steal, to gamble, to look with wicked eye upon a woman, to commit treachery, to abuse, to be angry, to wish ill to another, to be proud, to be idle, to slander, to be avaricious, to be disrespectful, to be shameless, to be hot-tempered, to take what is another's property, to be revengeful, unclean, obstinate, envious, to do harm to any man, to be superstitious, and to do any other wicked and iniquitous action,—these are all the friends of the wicked and the enemies of the virtuous.

DCXXXV.

Action Determinative.

No act of virtue should be delayed which could be performed to-day; for death does not consider whether the man he approaches has done his duty or not. Death knows not regard nor antipathy; it owns neither friend nor foe. The life of man is the cause of action; and action passes into the destiny, good or evil, that is the principle upon which we exist, and on it depends the task each must perform.

_{Hindu.
Agni
Purána
comp.}

DCXXXVI.

Thought, Word, Deed.

They say that once upon a time the pious Zoroaster made the religion which he had received current in the world; and till the completion of three hundred years the religion was in purity, and men were without doubts. This religion, namely all the Avesta and Zend, written upon prepared cowskins, and with gold ink, were deposited in the archives of Stákhar Pápakán. But Alexander the Great, who was dwelling in Egypt, burnt them up, and after that there was confusion and contention among the people of the country of Iran. They were doubtful in regard to God, and religions of many kinds and various codes of law were promulgated.

_{Ardá-Víráf.
Pahlavi MS.,
about A.C.
1321, after
much older
tradition.
Ab.}

And it is related that the wise men and teachers of religion assembled, and agreed that they would give to some one among them a sacred narcotic, that he might pass into the invisible world and bring them intelligence. The lot for this task fell on Ardá-Víráf. Then those teachers of religion filled three golden cups with wine and the narcotic of Vishtasp : and they gave one cup over to Víráf with the word 'Well thought,' and the second cup with the word 'Well said,' and the third cup with the word ' Well done.'

While Víráf slept, the teachers and the seven sisters kept the ever-burning fire, and chanted the Avesta. On the seventh day the soul of Víráf returned, and he rose up as from a pleasant sleep, inspired with good thoughts, and full of joy. An accomplished writer sat before him, and whatsoever Víráf said he wrote down clearly and correctly, as followeth :—

'Taking the first footstep with the good thought, the second with the good word, and the third with good deed, I entered paradise.

' I put forth the first footstep to the star-track, on Húmat, where good thoughts are received with hospitality. And I saw those souls of the pious whose radiance, which ever increased, was glittering as the stars.

'And I asked Ataro the angel, " Which place is this ? and which people are these ? "

' And he answered, " This place is the star-track, and these are they who in the world offered no prayers and chanted no liturgies ; they also exercised no sovereignty. Through other good works have they attained felicity."

' I came to a place and saw the souls of the liberal, adorned above all other souls in splendour. And it seemed to me sublime.

' I saw the souls of the great and truthful speakers, who walked in lofty splendour. And it seemed to me sublime.

'I saw the souls of agriculturists in a splendid place, as they stood and offered praise before the spirits of water and earth, trees and cattle. Their throne also is great. And it seemed to me sublime.

'I saw also the souls of artisans seated on embellished thrones. And it seemed to me sublime.

'I saw the souls of the faithful, the teachers and inquirers, in the greatest gladness on a splendid throne. And it seemed to me sublime.

'I also saw the friendly souls of interceders and peace-seekers, who ever increased thereby their brilliance, and they ever walked happily in the light of the atmosphere.

'I also saw the pre-eminent world of the religious, which is the light, full of glory and every joy, with which no one is satiated.'

DCXXXVII.

The Beauty of Actions.

In paradise I beheld one departed from earth, over whom a spirit sang, 'Well is he by whom that which is his benefit becomes the benefit of another.' Ardâ-Vîrâf.

Then in the dawn the soul of that departed one passed amid pleasant trees, whose fragrance was wafted from God.

And there met him a beautiful maiden, whose form and face were charming to heart and soul. To her he said, 'Who art thou, than whom none so fair was ever seen by me in the land of the living.'

The maiden replied, 'O youth, I am thy actions.'

DCXXXVIII.

Character.

On the bathing-tub of K'ang the following words were engraved :—'If you can, renovate yourself each day.'

Chinese. Mencius. 'The Four Books.'

All things are contained complete in ourselves. There is no greater joy than to turn round on ourselves and become perfect.

The human figure and colour possess a divine nature, but it is only the sage who can fulfil what his nature promises.

The superior man's nature consists in this, that benevolence, justice, propriety, and wisdom, have their root in his heart, and are exhibited in his countenance. They shine forth in his face and go through to his back. They are manifested in his four members.

His errors are like the eclipses of the sun and moon. His errors all men see, and his reformation all men look for.

Wherever the superior man passes, renovation takes place. The divine spirit which he cherishes above and below, flows on with influence in heaven and earth.

DCXXXIX.

Circumstance.

Heb. Ecclesiastes. comp.

I saw under the sun
That the race is not to the swift,
Nor the battle to the mighty;
Nor yet riches to men of understanding,
Nor yet favour to men of skill:
For time and chance happeneth to them all.
He who observeth the wind will not sow,
And he who regardeth the clouds will not reap.
In the morning sow thou thy seed,
And in the evening withhold not thy hand:
Thou knowest not which will prosper, this or that,
Or whether both will be alike good.

SORROW AND DEATH.

DCXL.

Shadows.

Vines hold not their clusters all the year; now are they fruitful, and now they shed their leaves like tears. _{Persian. Sádi.} Like the sun, the pure are clouded. On them the _{Bóstán. Ab.} envious crowd may hurl its hate; but it is as sparks falling on the clear stream—the sparks perish, the water goes shining on. Fear not the dark, friend; perchance the Water of Life may be found in the dark abyss of sorrow. Let not thy gloom end in despair; for night is pregnant with the day.

In Suna my child's life passed away. How can I tell the sadness of that hour! It is not strange the rose should spring up from the earth where so many roselike forms sleep. In my agony I longed to behold once more my buried child, and tore the heavy stone from above its form. Then fear seized upon me, and a little voice came from beneath the shroud, 'Dost thou feel terror amid this darkness? Let then thy life brighten it. If thou wouldst have thy grave as light as day, let the lamp of life fed by virtue descend with thee to illumine it!'

DCXLI.
Sorrow.

> He who has seen no evil and sorrow
> May not become king on the plain of gladness.
> He whose soul is not pierced with a diamond
> Is still unworthy a royal crown.

<small>Amir Khusrau, court poet and librarian to Julal-ud-din. Vihilgy. A.C. 1288.</small>

DCXLII.
Sorrow.

Destiny will not be altered by our uttering a thousand lamentations and sighs, nor by our praises.

O brother who art in distress! be not disheartened; for God hath many hidden mercies. Repine not at the versatility of fortune; for patience is bitter, but the fruit is sweet.

<small>Persian. Sádi. Gul. comp.</small>

DCXLIII.
Dejection.

> As the hart panteth after water-brooks,
> So panteth my soul after thee, O God.
> My soul thirsteth for God, for the living God:
> When shall I go and behold the face of God?
> My tears are my food day and night,
> While daily it is said to me, 'Where is thy God?'
> These things I remember, and pour out my soul within me.
> Deep calleth to deep at the sound of thy water-spouts:
> All thy waves and thy billows pass over me.
> Why art thou bowed down, O my soul?
> And why art thou disquieted within me?
> Hope thou in God, that I shall yet praise him,
> The health of my countenance and my God.

<small>Heb. Ps.</small>

DCXLIV.
The Teaching of Pain.

The reed bewailed departed bliss and present woe: 'Torn untimely from my native banks, my heart is torn, that through me may sound the notes that charm the grave and gay. Who that hears my strains knows the secret of my bleeding heart.' Not fruitless was the pain of the reed which made it melodious. And thou, brave heart, arise; be free of every chain, though blazing with gold; be nobly bold; follow the true bride of thy life, though her name be Sorrow. Let the shell perish that the pearl may appear. Men may not know the secret of thy sad life, but through a pierced heart must be breathed the strain of love and hope which shall enrapture human souls.

<small>Sufi.
Maulavi.
comp.
and par.</small>

DCXLV.
Sorrow.

Grief, not mirth, is my ware. Why dost thou wish to know its price? I know that thou wilt not buy it, and that I shall not sell it.

<small>Persian.
Shikebí.
10th cent.</small>

DCXLVI.
Instability.

That opinion is contemptible which considers those things to be enduring which are not enduring.

<small>Hindu.
Cural II.</small>

The acquisition of wealth is like the gathering of an assembly for dancing; its expenditure is like the breaking up of that assembly.

Wealth is perishable: let those who obtain it immediately practise those virtues which are imperishable.

The day which shines as if real, the wise see it as a saw cutting down life.

Let virtuous deeds be done quickly, before the cough comes, making the tongue silent.

The world possesses the greatness of one who yesterday was and to-day is not.

Multitudinous thoughts occupy unwise minds, not knowing that they shall live another moment.

It seems as if the soul had taken shelter in a body, but not attained a home.

DCXLVII.
Renunciation.

<small>Hindu.
Cural II.</small>

Whatever thing a man has renounced, by that thing he cannot suffer pain.

He who destroys the pride which says 'I,' 'mine,' passes into a world which is above the gods.

When desire ceases, instability disappears.

DCXLVIII.
Sorrow and Death.

<small>Burmese.
Buddhagosha's
Parables.
Ab.</small>

A Hindu girl named Kiságotamí gave birth to a son. When the boy was able to walk by himself, he died. The young girl carried the dead child clasped to her bosom, and went from house to house, asking if any one would give her medicine for it. Some regarded her as mad; but a wise man said, 'My good girl, I cannot cure your son, but I know of a doctor who can attend to it. You must go to Pará Taken; he can give medicine.' Kiságotamí went to him, and said, 'Lord and Master, do you know any medicine that will be good for my boy?' Pára Taken said, 'I know of some.' She asked, 'What medicine do you require?' The sage replied, 'I require a handful of mustard-seed taken from a house where no son, husband, parent, or servant has died.' The girl said, 'Very good,' and went about with her dead child, asking for the mustard-seed. The people said, 'Here is some mustard-seed, take it.' Then the girl asked, 'In my friend's house has there died a son, a husband, a parent, or a servant?' They replied, 'Lady, what is this you say? The living are few, but the dead are many.' Then she went to other houses; but one said, 'I have lost my son,' another, 'I have lost my parent,' until at last she said, 'This is a heavy task I have undertaken. I am not the only one whose son is dead. In the whole Sávatthi country children are dying, parents are dying.' The girl went and laid her child down in a forest, then came to Pará Taken. He said to her, 'Have you received the handful of mustard-seed?' She answered, 'I have not. The people of the village told me the living are few, but the dead are many.' Pará Taken said to her, 'You thought that you alone had lost a son; the law of death rules all, there is no permanence.' Then Kiságotamí became a votary. Once when she was engaged in her devotions, she observed the lights in a house now shining now extinguished, and reflected, 'My state is like those lamps.' Then in a vision the lord appeared to her, and said, 'All living beings resemble the flame of those lamps, one moment lighted, the next extinguished; they only who have arrived at Nirvána are at rest.' Kiságotamí, on hearing this, became possessed of intuitive knowledge.

DCXLIX.
Dust to Dust.

I swear by the Declining Day,

Koran,
s. 103,
'The Afternoon.'
comp.
S. 18.

Verily, man's lot is cast amid destruction,
Save those who believe and do the things which be right, and enjoin truth, and enjoin steadfastness on each other.

Verily, we have made all that is on earth as its adornment, that we might make trial who among mankind would excel in works.

But we will surely reduce all that is thereon to dust.

S. 16.

All that is with you passeth away, but that which is with God abideth.

S. 30.

First and last is the affair with God.

DCL.
Earth-Song.

The Earth laughs with all her colours of autumn at the credulity of those mortal kings who do not curb their passions, but are absorbed in the care of worldly affairs. There is an old song of the Earth, ' Why are human kings, though wise and learned, affected by the love of transient objects ? why are they so credulous when they are themselves as transient as the foam ?

Hindu.
Vishnu
Purána.
comp.

' No mortal can obtain victory over anything, unless he be the master of himself. No mortal king can make others obedient, until he has learned rightly to conduct himself.

' Kings would bring the terraqueous world under subjection to them. They see not that Death hovers near.

For a moment's possession of me—the Earth—in

what deadly conflicts do they engage with one another!

'Many kings in turn have said, 'The world is mine: I am lord of it.' Such have passed away. But their sons are here, having inherited their passion, each demanding the earth as his right.

Beholding this, I cannot refrain from laughter, nor yet from compassion of these stupid and absurd men.'

These are the verses sung by the Earth, O Maitreya, and, hearing them, lust for the transient world dissolves like ice beside the fire.

DCLI..

Problems of Life.

There was in the land of Uz a man whose name was Job; and this man was perfect and upright, and one who feared God, and turned aside from evil. [Heb. or Persian. Ab.] And there were born to him seven sons and three daughters. And his possessions were seven thousand sheep, and three thousand camels, and five hundred yoke of oxen, and five hundred she-asses, and a very numerous household;. so that this man was greater than all the sons of the East.

Now on a certain day his sons and his daughters were eating and drinking wine in the house of their eldest brother. And a messenger came to Job, and said, ' The oxen were ploughing, and the she-asses were feeding near them; and the Sabæans rushed upon them, and carried them away, and smote the young men with the edge of the sword; and I only am escaped alone to tell thee.'

He was yet speaking when another came, and said, 'The fire of God hath fallen from the heavens and burned the sheep and the young men, and consumed them ; and I only am escaped alone to tell thee.'

He was yet speaking when another came, and said, 'The Chaldæans formed themselves in three troops, and rushed upon the camels, and carried them away, and smote the young men with the edge of the sword ; and I only am escaped alone to tell thee.'

He was yet speaking when another came, and said, 'Thy sons and thy daughters were eating and drinking in the house of their eldest brother, when, lo ! a great wind came from the desert and struck the four corners of the house, and it fell upon the youths, so that they are dead ; and I only am escaped alone to tell thee.'

Then Job arose, and rent his mantle, and shaved his head, and fell upon the ground, and bowed his head, and said :

'Naked came I forth from my mother's womb,
And naked shall I return thither.
Jehovah gave, and Jehovah hath taken away ;
Blessed be the name of Jehovah !'

In all this Job sinned not, and spake not foolishly against God.

His wife said to him, 'Dost thou still hold fast thine integrity ? Renounce God, and die.' But he said to her, 'Thou speakest as one of the foolish women speaketh. Shall we indeed receive good from God, and shall we not receive evil ?' In all this Job sinned not with his lips.

And three friends of Job heard of all this evil which had befallen him, and they came each from his place ; Eliphaz the Temanite, and Bildad the Shuhite, and Zophar the Naamathite ; for they had agreed together to come to mourn with him, and to comfort him. And they lifted up their eyes from afar, and knew him not; and they raised their voices and wept; and they rent each his mantle, and they threw dust over their heads towards the heavens. And they sat down with him on the ground seven days and seven nights; and no one spake to him a word, for they saw that his grief was exceedingly great.

At length Job opened his mouth, and cursed the day of his birth; and Job exclaimed and said:
'Perish the day in which I was born !
Why died I not at my birth?
For now I should have been lying down, and I should
    be quiet;
There the wicked cease from troubling,
And there the wearied are at rest:
The prisoners are at ease together;
They hear not the voice of the taskmaster:
Small and great are there,
And the servant set free from his master.
Why giveth He light to the miserable,
And life to the bitter in soul,
Who long for death, but it cometh not,
And would dig for it more than for hidden treasures;
Who would rejoice to exultation,
Who would leap for joy, could they find a grave;
To the man whose path is hidden,
And whom God hath fenced around?'
Then Eliphaz the Temanite answered and said:
'If one attempt to speak to thee, wilt thou be weary?
Yet who can refrain from speaking?
Lo! thou hast instructed many,
And the weak hands thou hast strengthened.

Him who was stumbling thy words have upholden,
And the feeble knees thou hast made firm.
But now it is come upon thee, and thou art wearied;
It hath reached thee, and thou art troubled.
Is not thy piety thy confidence,
Thy hope also the uprightness of thy ways?
Recollect, I pray thee; who is the innocent man that hath perished,
And where have the righteous been cut off?
Now, a word was secretly conveyed to me,
And mine ear received the whisper thereof,
Amidst troubled thoughts from the visions of the night,
When deep sleep had fallen upon men.
Fear came upon me and trembling,
And made all my bones to shake.
Then a spirit passed before my face;
The hair of my flesh rose on end.
There stood—but I could not discern its form—
An image before mine eyes.
There was stillness; then I heard a voice,—
" Shall mortal man be deemed just by God?
Shall a man be pure before his Maker?
Lo! in his servants he putteth no trust,
And to his angels he imputeth frailty;
How much more to those who dwell in houses of clay,
Whose foundation is in the dust,
Who are crushed like the moth!
From morning till evening they are beaten down;
While no one regards it, they perish for ever.
Is not the excellency that was in them taken away?
They die, and without wisdom."

  Surely sorrow cometh not forth from the dust,

Nor from the ground doth trouble spring up.
Surely man is born to trouble,
As birds of prey soar aloft in flight.
Truly I would betake myself unto God,
And to God I would commit my cause ;
Who doeth great and unsearchable things—
He frustrateth the designs of the crafty,
So that their hands cannot accomplish their design ;
Taking the wise in their own craftiness,
So that the counsel of the subtle cometh hastily to an
    end :
In the daytime they encounter darkness,
And in the noonday they grope as in the night.
But he saveth the desolate from their mouth,
And the oppressed from the hand of the strong ;
That the poor man may have hope,
And iniquity may stop her mouth.
Lo ! happy is the man whom God correcteth !
The chastening of the Almighty therefore despise not ;
For he woundeth, and he bindeth up ;
He smiteth, and his hands make whole.
From the scourge of the tongue thou shalt be hidden,
And thou shalt not be afraid of destruction when it
    cometh.
At devastation and at famine thou shalt laugh,
And of the beasts of the earth thou shalt not be afraid.
For with the stones of the field shall be thy covenant,
And the beasts of the field shall be at peace with thee.
Thou shalt go in full age to the grave,
As a sheaf of corn gathered in its season.'

   Then Job answered and said :
' Oh ! that my impatience were carefully weighed,
And my calamity laid with it in the balance !

For now would it be found heavier than the sand of
    the sea :
Therefore are my words vehement.
    Instruct me, and I will be silent ;
And cause me to understand how I have erred.
How forcible are right words !
But what do your reproaches prove ?
Is there iniquity in my tongue ?
Cannot my palate discern calamity ?
Is there not a service appointed for man upon earth,
And are not his days as the days of a hireling ?
As a servant panteth for the shade,
And as a hireling earnestly desireth his wages,
So I am made to inherit months of affliction,
And wearisome nights are numbered out to me.
When I lie down, I say,
" When shall I arise ? " but the darkness is prolonged,
And I am full of restlessness until the dawn.
If I have sinned, what have I done to thee,
O thou observer of man ?
Why hast thou set me up as thy mark,
So that I am a burden to myself ?
And why dost thou not take away my transgression,
And cause mine iniquity to pass away ?
For soon shall I lie down in the dust ;
Even shouldst thou seek me earnestly, I shall not
    be.'
    Then answered Bildad the Shuhite, and said :
' How long wilt thou utter these things,
And the words of thy mouth be a vehement wind ?
Shall God pervert judgment ?
Or shall the Almighty pervert justice ?
As thy children have sinned against him,

He hath sent them away in the power of their transgressions;
But if thou wouldst earnestly seek to God,
And to the Almighty make supplication,
If thou thyself be pure and upright,
Surely now he will rise up for thee,
And prosper thy righteous habitation;
So that thy former state should be small,
And thy latter state become exceedingly great.
Lo! God will not reject a perfect man,
Nor will he strengthen the hands of those who do evil.
He will yet fill thy mouth with laughter,
And thy lips with the shout of joy;
They who hate thee shall be clothed with shame;
And the tent of the wicked shall not be.'
    Then Job answered and said:
'Truly I know that it is so;
For how can a man be justified with God?
If he desireth to contend with him,
He cannot answer him as to one charge in a thousand.
Shall I contemn my own life?
It is all one—therefore I said,
The perfect and the wicked he destroyeth.
If the scourge slay the simple,
The dissolution of the innocent he also mocketh.
A land is given into the hand of the wicked,
The face of its judges he covereth.
If now it be not he, who is it?
For he is not a man like myself, that I should answer him,
That we should enter together on a trial.
There is not between us an umpire,
Who might put his hand upon us both.

Let him remove from off me his rod,
And let not the fear of him terrify me ;
Then will I speak and not be afraid of him,
For I am not so at heart.
My soul is weary of my life :
I will give free course to my complaint ;
I will speak in the bitterness of my soul.
I will say to God, " Condemn me not :
Show me wherefore thou contendest with me.
Is it good for thee to oppress,
To despise the labour of thy hands,
And to shine upon the counsels of the wicked?
Have thy hands fashioned me, and made me
Completely in every part, that thou mightest destroy me ?
Remember, I pray thee, that thou hast made me as clay,
And to the dust wilt thou bring me again ?
Are not my days few ? Cease, then,
And leave me, that I may be joyful for a little while,
Before I go away, not to return,
To a land of darkness and the shadow of death."'

    Then Zophar the Naamathite answered, and said :
' Shall not one of many words be answered ?
Or shall a man full of talk be justified ?
Shall thy vain boasts put men to silence ?
And shalt thou mock, and no one make thee ashamed ?
Now thou hast said, " My doctrine is pure,
And I am clean in thine eyes."
But oh that God would speak,
And open his lips with thee !
And that he would show thee the secrets of wisdom,

For they are doubly sufficient for instruction :
Then wouldst thou know that God remitteth to thee
    of thine iniquity.
The deep things of God canst thou find out ?
Canst thou find out the Almighty to perfection?
'Tis high as heaven—what canst thou do?
Deeper than the grave—what canst thou know ?
If thou wilt prepare thy heart,
And spread out to him thy hands ;
If thou put away the iniquity in thy hand,
And suffer not wickedness to dwell in thy tents,
Surely thou shalt then lift up thy face without spot;
And thou shalt be steadfast, and shalt not fear :
Surely thou shalt forget trouble ;
As waters that have passed away thou shalt remem-
    ber it,
And brighter than noon shall be thine age.'
    Then Job answered and said :
' Truly ye are the people,
And wisdom will die with you !
Yet I have understanding like you ;
I fall not below you ;
And who knoweth not such things as these ?
One derided by his friend am I ;
Calamity is despised ; prosperity is at ease ;
They who are slipping with their feet are smitten.
But ask now the beasts, and they will teach thee ;
And the fowls of the heavens, and they will tell thee.
With him is wisdom and might ;
He hath counsel and understanding.
Lo, he overthroweth, and it shall not be rebuilt ;
He bindeth a man, and he shall not be set free.
The misled and the misleader are his.

He leadeth away counsellors spoiled,
And judges he maketh foolish.
He dissolveth the authority of kings,
And bindeth a belt about their loins.
He leadeth priests away spoiled,
And overthroweth the powerful.
He sealeth the lips of the eloquent,
And the discernment of elders he taketh away.
He poureth contempt upon princes,
And the girdle of the powerful he looseneth.
He revealeth deep things out of darkness,
And bringeth forth to light the shadow of death.
He maketh nations to increase, and he destroyeth them :
He enlargeth nations, and he leadeth them away captive.
He taketh away understanding from the chiefs of a land,.
And causeth them to wander in a pathless waste :
They grope in darkness without light,
And he causeth them to reel like a drunken man.
Lo, all this mine eye hath seen,
Mine ear hath heard and understood it.
As ye know, I also know ;
I fall not below you.
Truly I would plead with the Almighty,
And to contend with God I earnestly desire :
Since truly ye are forgers of lies ;
Physicians of no value are ye all.
Oh that ye would be altogether silent !
For that would be your wisdom.
    Hear now my defence,
And attend to the pleadings of my lips.

Let not Thy terrors make me afraid,
Then call upon me, and I will answer!
Why hidest thou thy face,
And accountest me an enemy to thee?
The driven leaf wouldst thou crush?
The parched stubble wouldst thou pursue?
 Man, that is born of woman,
Is of few days and full of trouble.
As a flower he springeth up and withereth;
Yea, he fleeth away as a shadow, and continueth not.
Upon such a one wilt thou open thine eyes?
And wilt thou bring me into trial with thyself?
For there is hope of a tree, if cut down,
That it will sprout again,
And that its tender branches will not cease;
Though its root grow old in the earth,
And its stock die in the ground,
At the scent of water it will bud,
And send forth branches as a young plant.
But man dieth, and he is gone for ever!
Yea, man expireth, and where is he?
 If a man die, will he live again?
All the days of my appointed service I will wait,
Till my relief shall come.
Thou wilt call, and I shall answer thee.'
 Then Eliphaz the Temanite answered and said:
'Should a wise man answer with empty knowledge,
And fill his breast with the east wind?
Reasoning with speech that profiteth not,
And with sayings by which he can do no good?
Surely thou makest the fear of God void,
And discouragest prayer before him.
Truly thine own mouth discovereth thine iniquity,

Though thou choosest the tongue of the crafty.
Thine own mouth condemneth thee, and not I ;
And thine own lips bear witness against thee.
 I will show thee, hear me ;
And that which I have seen I will relate ;
What wise men have declared,
And have not concealed, having received it from their fathers ;
To whom alone the land was given,
And a stranger wandered not among them.
During all the days of a wicked man he is in pangs,
And the number of his years is hidden from the oppressor.
A sound of terrors is in his ears ;
In the midst of prosperity the destroyer cometh upon him.
He hath no confidence that he shall escape from darkness,
But he is set apart for the sword.
He wandereth about seeking bread ;
He knoweth that a day of darkness is close at hand.
Distress terrifieth him,
And anxiety presseth upon him,
As a king ready for an onset ;
Because he had stretched forth his hand against God,
And against the Almighty he had put forth his strength.'
 Then Job answered and said :
' I have heard such things as these in abundance :
Miserable comforters are ye all !
Shall there be an end to words of wind ?
Or what inciteth thee that thou shouldst answer ?

I also, like you, could speak,
If ye were in my place :
I could heap together old sayings against you,
And against you shake my head.
 O earth ! hide no blood shed by me,
And let there be no limit to its cry against me !
Even now, lo, my witness is in the heavens,
And mine eye-witness is on high !
My friends are they who scorn me ;
Therefore to God mine eye poureth forth tears.
Oh that a man might plead with God,
As a son of man pleadeth with his neighbour !
For when a few years have passed,
I must go the way by which I cannot return.
My breath is oppressed, my days are extinct,
The grave is ready for me.
Have pity on me, have pity on me, O my friends,
For the hand of God hath touched me !
 Oh that now my words were written !
Oh that they were inscribed in a book !
That with an iron pen, and with lead,
They were engraven for ever on a rock !
For I know that my Vindicator liveth,
And that at length he will rise up on the earth.
And after my skin hath been thus wasted,
And without my flesh, I shall see God ;
Whom I shall behold on my side,
And mine eyes shall see, but not as an adversary.'

 Then answered Zophar the Naamathite, and said :
'Knowest thou this ? From of old,
From the time when man was placed on the earth,
The triumphing of the wicked is short,
And the joy of the profane but for a moment.'

And Job answered and said :
'Listen attentively to my speech,
And after I have spoken do thou mock.
Why do the wicked live,
Grow old, and become mighty in power ?
Their seed is established in their presence with themselves,
And their offspring before their eyes.
Their houses are safe from fear,
And the rod of God is not upon them.
Their bull gendereth, and faileth not ;
Their cow bringeth forth, and casteth not.
They send forth their little ones like a flock,
And their children dance.
Can any one teach God knowledge ?
Since he ruleth those on high.
One man dieth in his full strength,
Wholly at ease and quiet ;
His sides are filled with fat,
And his bones are moist with marrow :
Another man dieth in the bitterness of his soul,
And tasteth not good.
Together they lie down in the dust,
And the worm covereth them.'
Then Eliphaz the Temanite answered and said :
'Can a man be profitable to God,
Because a wise man may be profitable to himself ?
Can it be any pleasure to the Almighty that thou justifiest thyself,
Or any gain that thou provest thy way upright ?
Through fear of thee will he plead with thee ?
Will he come with thee into judgment ?
Is not thy wickedness great,

And thine iniquities without end?
Surely thou hast taken a pledge from thy brother
    without cause,
And the raiment of the naked thou hast stripped off.
Thou hast not given water to the weary to drink,
And from the hungry thou hast withholden bread.
But as for the powerful man, the land was his,
And the man whose person was accepted dwelt in it.
Widows thou didst send away empty,
And the arms of orphans thou didst break.
Therefore snares are all around thee,
And sudden fear troubleth thee;
Or darkness in which thou canst not see,
And a flood of waters covereth thee.'
    Then Job answered and said:
'Even yet is my complaint rebellion?
My wound is heavier than my sighing.
Oh that I knew where I might find him!
I would go even to his judgment-seat.
I would order my cause before him,
And fill my mouth with arguments.
I should know with what words he would answer me,
And I should understand what he would say to me.
With his great power, would he contend with me?
No; surely he would give heed to me.
There the upright might plead with him;
And I should be acquitted once for all by my judge.
Lo, I go forward, but he is not there;
And backward, but I cannot perceive him;
To the left, where he worketh, but I cannot behold
    him;
He hideth himself on the right hand, so that I cannot
    see him.

But he knoweth the way which is in my heart.
He proveth me ; as gold shall I come forth ;
In his paths my foot hath firmly kept ;
His way I have observed, and have not turned aside ;
The orders of his lips I have not removed from me ;
In my bosom I have laid up the words of his mouth.
But he is in one mind, and who can turn him ?
And what he desireth he doeth.
Surely he will perfect what is decreed for me.'
  Then answered Bildad the Shuhite, and said :
' Dominion and terror are with him ;
He maketh retribution in his high places.
Is there any number to his troops ?
And on whom riseth not his light ?
How then can man be justified with God ?
Or how can he be pure who is born of woman ?
Lo, even the moon, it shineth not,
And the stars are not pure, in his sight.
How much less man, a worm !
And the son of man, a reptile !'
  Then Job answered and said :
' The Grave is naked before Him,
And there is no covering to Destruction.
He hath described a circle on the surface of the waters,
To the boundary of light and darkness.
By his spirit he hath adorned the heavens ;
His hand hath formed the winding serpent.
Lo, these are the outlines of his way.
How faint the whisper we have heard of him !
But the thunder of his power who can understand ?
As God liveth, who hath rejected my cause ;
Even the Almighty, who hath embittered my soul ;
So long as my breath is in me,

And the spirit of God is in my nostrils,
My lips shall not speak wickedness,
Nor my tongue utter falsehood.
Far be it from me to justify you :
Till I expire I will not renounce my integrity.
My righteousness I will hold fast, and will not let it go.
My heart shall not reproach me during my life.
   Truly there is a vein for silver,
And a place for gold, which men refine.
Iron is taken out of the earth,
And the stone is smelted into brass.
Man putteth an end to darkness,
And to the lowest depths he searcheth
For the stone of darkness and of the shadow of death.
He openeth a shaft out of the mountain ;
Unsupported by the feet,
They are suspended, they swing away from men.
The earth, out of which cometh food,
In its lowermost parts is turned up as by fire.
Its stones are the place of the sapphire,
And she has grains of gold for man.
This path the bird of prey knoweth not,
The eye of the vulture hath not glanced upon it ;
Wild beasts have not trodden it,
The lion hath not passed over it.
On the flinty rock man putteth forth his hand,
He turneth up mountains from the roots.
He cutteth out channels in the rocks :
Thus his eye seeth every precious thing.
He restraineth the streams from oozing,
And that which was hidden he bringeth to light.
   But wisdom, where shall that be found ?
And where is the place of understanding ?

Man knoweth not its price,
Nor can it be found in the land of the living.
The deep saith, "It is not in me;"
And the sea saith, "It is not with me."
Gold shall not be given for it,
Nor shall silver be weighed as its worth.
It cannot be purchased with the gold of Ophir,
With the precious onyx or the sapphire.
Gold or crystal cannot be its price;
Nor its barter jewels of fine gold.
Coral or the beryl shall not be mentioned,
And wisdom is more precious than pearls.
The topaz of Cush shall not be its price;
With purest gold it shall not be purchased.
  Wisdom, whence then shall it come?
And where is the place of understanding?
Since it is hidden from the eyes of every living thing,
And concealed from the birds of the heavens.
Destruction and Death say:
"With our ears we have heard the report of it."
God understandeth the way of it,
And he knoweth its place.
For he looketh to the ends of the earth;
What is under the whole heavens he seeth.
When he appointed the weight of the wind,
And disposed the seas by measure;
When he gave laws to the rain,
And a path for the glittering thunderbolt;
Then he saw it and declared it;
He prepared it, and also searched it out.
But to man he said—
"Lo, the fear of the Lord, that is wisdom,
And to depart from evil is understanding."'

And Job renewed his discourse, and said :
'Oh that I were as in months past,
As in the days when God preserved me.
When his lamp shone above my head,
When by its light I walked through darkness.
As I was in the days of my prosperity,
When the counsel of God was over my tent.
When the Almighty was yet with me,
When my children were around me.
When the ear heard me, it blessed me ;
When the eye saw me, it bore witness to me ;
For I delivered the poor man who cried,
And the fatherless, and him who had no helper.
The blessing of him that was ready to perish came
    upon me,
And I caused the widow's heart to sing for joy.
I put on equity, and it clothed me as a robe,
And justice was my robe and diadem.
Eyes was I to the blind,
And feet was I to the lame.
A father was I to the needy ;
And the cause which I knew not I searched out.
And I brake the tusks of the unjust man,
And from his teeth I snatched the prey.
And I said, " In my nest I shall expire,
And like the sand I shall multiply my days.
My root will lie open to the waters,
And the dew will lodge all night upon my branches.
My glory will be ever fresh with me,
And my bow will be renewed in my hand."
They heard me and waited,
And were silent for my counsel.
After I had spoken, they spake not again ;

And my speech dropped upon them ;
And they waited for me as for the rain,
And they opened their mouth, as for the latter rain.
But now I am become like dust and ashes.
I cry to thee, but thou answerest me not :
I persevere, but thou lookest calmly upon me.
Thou art turned to be cruel to me ;
Did I not weep for the miserable ?
Was not my soul grieved for the needy ?
Yet when I expected good, then came evil ;
And I looked for light, but darkness came.
My harp is also turned to mourning,
And my pipes to the voice of weepers.
If I have walked with falsehood,
And my foot hath hastened to deceit,
Let him weigh me in a just balance,
And let God know my integrity.
If my step hath turned from the right way,
And my heart hath gone after mine eyes,
And a stain hath cleaved to my hands,
May I sow, and another eat,
And may my produce be rooted up.
If I have despised the cause of my man-servant or my maid-servant
When they would contend with me,
Then what should I do should God rise up,
And should he make inquisition, what should I answer him ?
If I have seen one perishing for want of clothing,
And a poor man who had no covering ;
If I have made gold my hope,
Or to fine gold have said, "My confidence ! "
If I have rejoiced at the calamity of him who hated me,

And triumphed when evil had befallen him ;
Behold my signature ;—let the Almighty answer me,
And let my adversary write a bill of accusation!
If my land crieth out against me,
And its furrows also weep ;
If I have eaten its produce without pay,
And caused the spirit of the hirelings to fail ;
Instead of wheat, let the bramble grow,
And instead of barley, the aconite !'

The words of Job are ended.

Then God spake unto Job out of the whirlwind, and said :
' Who is this that darkeneth counsel
By words without knowledge ?
Gird up now thy loins like a mighty man ;
I will question thee, and do thou inform me.
Where wast thou when I founded the earth ?
Declare, since thou hast understanding.
Who appointed its measure ? since thou knowest ;
Or who stretched over it the line ?
On what are its foundations sunk ;
Or who laid its corner-stone,
When the morning stars sang together,
And all the sons of God shouted for joy ?
And who shut up the sea with doors,
When it brake forth issuing from the womb ?
When I made a cloud its vesture,
And thick darkness its swathing-band ;
When I brake up for it my decreed place,
And placed a bar and gates,
And said, " Hitherto shalt thou come, but no further,

And here shall thy proud waves be stayed?"
Since thy days began, hast thou given charge to the
   morning?
Hast thou caused the dawn to know its place,
That it might take hold of the ends of the earth,
That the wicked might be driven out of it?
It is changed as clay by the seal,
And all things stand forth as in rich apparel;
Then their light is withholden from the wicked,
And the high-raised arm is broken.
Which is the way to the place where light dwelleth?
And darkness, where is its abode?
That thou shouldst lead each to its boundary,
And shouldst discern the paths to its mansion.
Hast thou gone to the treasuries of the snow?
And the treasuries of hail hast thou seen?
Where is the way by which lightning is portioned out;
By which the east wind is diffused over the earth?
Who hath opened a channel for the overflowing waters;
And a way for the bolt of the thunder;
To give rain upon a land where no one is,
The desert, in which there is no man;
To water abundantly the barren and desolate place,
And to cause the bud of the herbage to spring forth?
Canst thou bind the sweet influences of the Pleiades,
Or loosen the bands of Orion?
Canst thou bring forth the Signs in their season?
Or canst thou lead the Bear and his sons?
Who prepareth for the raven his food,
When his young cry to God,
When they wander for want of meat?
Hast thou given to the horse strength?
Hast thou clothed his neck with thunder?

And from afar he smelleth the battle,
The thunder of the chieftains, and the shouting.
By thy understanding doth the hawk fly,
Spreading his wings towards the south?
At thy bidding doth the eagle soar aloft,
Building his nest on high?
On a rock he lodgeth and abideth,
On a craggy rock and a cliff.
Thence he exploreth his food,
From afar his eyes behold it.'

And God spake again to Job, and said:
'Will he who blameth contend with the Almighty?
Let him who reproveth God, answer.'

Then Job answered Jehovah, and said:
'Lo, I am of no account, what shall I reply to thee?
I put my hand upon my mouth.
Once have I spoken, but I will not answer;
And twice; but I will say no more.'

Now when God had spoken these words to Job, he said to Eliphaz the Temanite, 'My wrath is kindled against thee, and against thy two friends; for ye have not spoken concerning me that which is right, like my servant Job.'

DCLII.

Time.

Time is the root of all beings, born and unborn; of pleasure and pain. In Time hath existence birth, and in it all passeth away. Watching while others sleep, Time for ever destroys, for ever renews. Unvanquished Time!

Hindu.
Máharbáráta.
Adiparva.

DCLIII.
Death.

<small>Sádi. Gul. comp.</small>

'Alas !' I said, 'how grateful didst thou prove to my heart so long as the verdure of thy existence flourished in the garden!' 'Have patience,' he replied, 'O my friend, till the return of the spring, and thou mayest again see verdure and flowers shooting from my bosom.'

In every moment of thy life a breath is expended, so that what remaineth is but of small account. Alas ! thou hast spent fifty years in sleep, excepting these five days that thou hast been awakened to reflection. Shame on that man who departed without finishing his work ; who, when the drum was beaten for marching, had not made up his burden ! Sweet sleep on the day of marching withholds the traveller from his way. Every one who came erected a new fabric ; he departed and evacuated the tenement for another to enter. And this, in like manner, formed new schemes ; but no one ever finished the building.

DCLIV.
The World.

<small>Sádi. Gul.</small>

On the portico of the hall of Fèredoun was written, 'The world, O my brother, continueth not to any one ; place your affections on the Creator of the universe, and that will suffice. Make no reliance, neither rest upon the kingdom of this world ; seeing how many like yourself it hath nourished and killed.' When the pure soul is about to depart, what is the difference between expiring on a throne or on the bare ground ?

DCLV.

Death.

Each spot where tulips prank their state
Has drunk the life-blood of the great;
The violets yon field which stain
Are moles of beauties Time hath slain.

Persian.
Omar
Khèyam.
(Emerson.)

DCLVI.

Charity.

We saw him in the garden, the pleasant garden,
With his companions and his children, the children he loved.
His children and his servants blessed him.
His home was the shelter of happiness.
    Peace be upon him!
We saw him giving food to the hungry,
And clothing to the naked.
We saw him give help and succour to the aged,
And good counsel to the young.
He suffered not the stranger to sleep in the streets:
He opened his door to the wayfarer.
    Peace be upon him!

Syrian.
Dirge.
(Miss Rogers.)
comp.

DCLVII.

Opportunity.

Happy is the man whose conscience hath not condemned him! He that gathereth by defrauding his own soul, gathereth for others that shall spend his goods riotously. He that is evil to himself, to whom will he be good?

According to thy ability do good to thyself. Death will not be long in coming, and the covenant

Ecclesiasticus.
Apoc.
Ab.

of the grave is not showed unto thee. Do good unto thy friend before thou die. Defraud not thyself of the good day, and let not the part of a good desire overpass thee.

Shalt thou leave thy travails to another, and thy tasks to be divided by lot ? Give and take, and sanctify thy soul. All flesh waxeth old as a garment.

DCLVIII.

Life short, Art long.

Lord, thou hast been our refuge
<small>Heb. Ps.</small> In all generations.
Thou turnest man to dust,
And sayest, 'Return, ye sons of man.'
For a thousand years in thy sight
Are as yesterday when it is past,
And as a watch in the night.
Thou carriest them away with a flood ; they are asleep.
As grass which groweth in the morning ;
In the morning it flowereth and groweth,
In the evening it is cut down and withereth.
The days of our years are threescore years and ten ;
And if by strength they be fourscore years,
Yet is their pride trouble and sorrow ;
For it is soon cut off, and we fly away.
So teach us to number our days
That we may apply our hearts to wisdom.
Let thy work appear to thy servants,
And thy majesty to their children.
And let the beauty of God be upon us,
And the work of our hands establish thou for us ;
Yea, the work of our hands establish thou it.

DCLIX.

The Inevitable.

A father went daily to weep at the tomb of his son. The son from his abode of happiness looked with pity on his father, and at length, taking on human form again, descended on earth, and throwing himself down near the tomb where his father was, began to weep with violence. The father approaching, said, 'Young man, why are you weeping?' 'I am weeping,' he replied, 'because I want the sun and the moon to make a pair of wheels for my cart.' 'Young man,' said the father, 'you must be mad; who can make cart-wheels out of the sun and moon?' The youth replied, 'You are weeping for a mortal whose transient life has passed away, but I weep for the sun and moon which I continually have before me.'

Buddhagosha's Parables. comp.

DCLX.

Life and Death.

I entered the workshop of a potter, and watched him at his mill fashioning the necks and handles of pitchers. Those were made of the heads of kings, these of the feet of beggars.

In this palace, which rivalled the heavens in splendour when king succeeded king in emulation, I saw the turtle sitting, and heard it crying, 'Where? where?'

They who are endowed with knowledge and virtue, who by their wisdom have become the torch of their disciples, even they have not taken a step beyond this profound night of mystery; they have only

Persian. Khèyam. 11th cent.

bequeathed us a few fables ere returning to the slumber of death.

This wheel of the heavens will revolve after thy death and mine, friend; it conspires against thy life and mine. Come, sit thee on the grass, for but little time remains to us before other grass shall spring from thy dust and mine. When thou and I have passed away, they will place a pair of bricks over us. Then the brickmaker will fashion for other tombs other bricks made of thy dust and mine.

Think not that I fear the world, nor my departure from it. Death being a fact, I have no fear of it. That which I alone fear is not having lived well enough. What does it matter whether we live in the world a hundred years, or but one day? Let us take care that the bowl of our form hold the heart's good wine before we become mere clay again for the potter to mould into other shapes. To buy this wine, sell thy Koran!

DCLXI.

Dust to Dust.

<small>A Brahman Burial-Service, comp.</small>

O Earth! to thee we commend our brother. Of thee he was formed, by thee he was sustained, and unto thee he now returns.

O Fire! thou hadst a claim in our brother during life. He subsisted by thy influence in nature; to thee we commit his body, thou emblem of purity; may his spirit be purified on entering a new state of existence!

O Air! while the breath of life continued, our brother respired by thee; his last breath is now departed, to thee we yield him!

O Water! thou didst contribute to the life of our

brother; thou wert one of his sustaining elements. His remains are now dispersed, receive thy share of him who has now taken an everlasting flight!

DCLXII.
Death.

O Death! how bitter is the thought of thee to a man that liveth at rest in his possessions, unto the man that hath nothing to vex him, and hath prosperity in all things; yea, unto him that is yet able to enjoy his food. Ecclesiasticus. Apoc. Ab.

O Death! acceptable is thy sentence unto the needy, and unto him whose strength faileth, that is now in the last age, and troubled in all things; to him that despaireth, and hath lost patience.

Fear not the sentence of death: remember them that have been before thee and that shall come after thee; for this is the law of God over all flesh.

There is no inquisition in the grave.

Have regard to thy name; for that shall remain with thee beyond a thousand treasures of gold.

A good life hath but few days; but a good name endureth for ever.

DCLXIII.
Death.

An Indian prince, Tisso, one day riding in the forest, saw a herd of elk sporting. 'See how happy,' he said, 'these browsing elk are! Why should not priests, lodged and fed comfortably in the temples, also amuse themselves?' Returning home, he imparted this reflection to the king. The king on the next day conferred the sovereignty on him, saying, 'Prince, admin- Hindu Story.

ister this empire for seven days; at the termination of that period I shall put thee to death.' At the end of the seventh day the king inquired, 'From what cause hast thou become so emaciated?' He answered, 'From the horror of death.' The monarch rejoined, 'Live, my child, and be wise. Thou hast ceased to take recreation, saying to thyself, In seven days I shall be put to death. These priests in the temple incessantly meditate on death; how can they enter into healthful diversions?'

DCLXIV.
Virtues Immortal.

Burmese. Buddha.

The brilliant chariots of kings are destroyed; the body also approaches destruction; but the virtues of good people never approach destruction. Thus do the good say to the good.

DCLXV.
Permanence.

Persian. Anik of Buchara.

With victorious skill and irresistible arrow I vanquished the world. Strongholds fell where I raised my hand; where I moved, the lines of battle gave way. All this availed little. Swift death came, saying, 'Permanence and power belong alone to God.'

DCLXVI.
The Unknown Future.

Hindu. Bhágavat. Gita. comp.

Death is certain to all things which are subject to birth, and regeneration to all things which are mortal. Wherefore it doth not behove thee to grieve about that which is inevitable. The former state of beings is unknown, the middle state is evident, and their future state is not to be discovered. Why then shouldst thou trouble thyself about such things as these ? Some regard the soul as a wonder, while some speak, and others hear of it with astonishment; but no one knoweth it, although he may have heard it described.

Just to thy wish the door of heaven is found open before thee. Be free from duplicity, and stand firm in the path of truth ; be free from care and trouble, and turn thy mind to things which are spiritual. Let the motive be in the deed, and not in the event. Be not one whose motive for action is the hope of reward. Let not thy life be spent in inaction. Depend upon application, perform thy duty, abandon all thought of the consequence, and make the event equal, whether it terminate in good or evil. Seek an asylum then in wisdom alone ; for the miserable and unhappy are so on account of the event of things.

DCLXVII.

Progress.

It needs not that I swear by the sunset redness,
And by the night and its gatherings,
And by the moon when at her full,
That from state to state shall ye be surely carried
    onward !

<small>Koran, s. 84, 'The Splitting Asunder.'</small>

DCLXVIII.

Life and Death.

On parent knees a naked, new-born child
Weeping thou sat'st, while all around thee smiled :
So live that, sinking in thy long last sleep,
Thou then mayest smile, while all around thee weep.

<small>Arabian. Ali Ben Ahmed. (Sir W. Jones.)</small>

SANCTIONS.

DCLXIX.
Thorns.

<small>Persian.
Anwarí.
(Cowell and Palmer.)
comp.</small>

The dragon-toothed thorn in the garden
A sting like a scorpion's shows;
He hath posted it there as a warden
To watch o'er the delicate rose.
The honey, delicious in flavour,
He teacheth the bee to secrete,
And joineth with infinite favour
The sting and the sweet.

DCLXX.
Heaven and Hell.

<small>Persian.
Omar Khèyam.
11th cent.
comp.</small>

In mosque and school, in church and synagogue, they have a horror of hell, and a seeking of paradise; but the seed of this anxiety has never germinated in the heart that has penetrated the secret of the Most High.

If the revolutions of the universe have brought thee no joy, why count whether there be seven heavens or eight?

Each heart that God hath illumined with the light of affection—be it found in mosque or in synagogue—if its name be written in the Book of Love, is set free from anxieties about hell, and from longings for paradise.

Hell is but a spark of the useless troubles which we have given ourselves; paradise only an instant of the repose which we have sometimes enjoyed on earth.

DCLXXI.
Cause and Effect.

As surely as the pebble cast heavenward abides not there, but returns to the earth; so, proportionate to thy deed, good or ill, will the desire of thy heart be meted out to thee in whatever form or world thou shalt enter. <small>Singhalese. Buddha.</small>

DCLXXII.
Self-judgment.

Take care that your final account shall be settled before death. Undergo here your indictment and your trial; pass on yourself just sentence and punishment; then will you pass into the future without further trial, chastisement, or fear. <small>Turkish. Lamai. (D'Herb.)</small>

DCLXXIII.
A Bad Conscience.

Between two physicians, in consequence of their living together, a few words of altercation took place. It is not right for two to be spoken of as one; both cannot reap the same crop. Who ever saw a place for two swords in one sheath? The desire came to those two sages that one of the two should have the house to himself. When anger caught the waist of revenge, it set about devising a plan to settle the matter. They would drink two draughts of their own making, so as <small>Persian. Nizámi. (MS.) Ab.</small>

to see who was the strongest of heart, and whose poison was the most deadly.

The first rival made a little poison, which with its putrescence would melt a black stone. The other took a draught of it, and as it reminded him of sugar, drank it easily. Then he made a decoction of herbs, and stopped the course of the poison with an antidote. He burnt like the moth, but found his wings again; he appeared again in the assembly. He brought a flower from the garden, recited a charm over it, and breathed upon it; then gave to his enemy this flower more effectual than his own poison. His enemy, receiving that flower, was overwhelmed with fear, became senseless, and expired. One with a remedy drove the poison out of his body; the other died through imagination of a single flower.

Such among the many-coloured flowers which are in the garden of the earth is a drop of blood from the heart of a man.

DCLXXIV.

The Voice of Blood.

Heb.
Gen.

And Cain said to Abel his brother, 'Let us go into the field.' And when they were in the field, Cain rose up against Abel his brother, and slew him. And Jehovah said to Cain, 'Where is Abel thy brother?' And he said, 'I know not. Am I my brother's keeper?' And Jehovah said, 'What hast thou done? the voice of thy brother's blood crieth to me from the ground. And now art thou cursed from the earth which hath opened its mouth to receive thy brother's blood from thy hand. If thou tillest the ground, it will no more yield to thee its strength: a fugitive and a wanderer shalt thou be in the earth.' And Cain said to Jehovah, 'My punishment is greater than I can bear. Lo! thou drivest me out this day from the face of this land, and from thy presence I shall be hidden ; and I shall be a fugitive and a wanderer in the earth ; and it shall come to pass that whosoever findeth me will slay me.' God set a mark upon Cain, that no one should slay him.

DCLXXV.

Recoil.

Whoso casteth a stone on high casteth it on his own head ; and a deceitful stroke maketh (two) wounds. Heb.
Ecclesiasticus.
Apoc.
comp.

Whoso diggeth a pit shall fall therein ; and he that setteth a trap shall be taken therein.

He that worketh mischief, it shall fall upon him, and he shall not know whence it cometh.

Malice and wrath, even these are abominations ; and the sinful man shall have them both.

When the evil man curseth Satan, he curseth his own soul.

DCLXXVI.

The Right Fear.

The excellent will fear to do wrong.

Because evil produces evil, therefore should it be feared more than fire. Hindu.
Cural.

To do no evil even to enemies will be called the chief of virtues.

Justice will meditate the ruin of him who meditates the ruin of another.

Commit not wrong, saying, 'I am poor ;' if you do, you will become poorer still.

Let not him do evil to others who desires not that sorrows should pursue himself.

Men may live amid many enmities, but will not escape the enmity and pursuit of their own sin. This shadow at their heels will not leave them, which means destruction.

If a man love himself, let him commit no wrong, however small.

DCLXXVII.
Reality.

<small>Sufi.
Abdal Khalek.
(D'Herb.)</small>

Tremble in the presence of an earnest believer: he possesses the art of physiognomy in perfection, and has a discernment of his own which pierces to that which is most secret in the heart of men.

DCLXXVIII.
Patience.

<small>Persian.
(D'Herb)</small>

Have patience, and thou shalt see reduced to dust those who have trampled others in the dust.

Have patience, and thou shalt see those whom the world hated as thorns blooming as roses.

DCLXXIX.
Two Serpents.

<small>Oriental Fables.</small>

The learned Saib, who was entrusted with the education of the son of the Sultan Carizama, related to him each day a story. One day he told him this from the annals of Persia:—' A magician presented himself before King Zohak, and breathing on his breast, caused two serpents to come forth from the region of the king's heart. The king in wrath was about to slay him, but the magician said, "These two serpents are tokens of the glory of your reign. They must be fed, and with human blood. This you may obtain by sacrificing to them the lowest of your people; but they will bring you happiness, and whatever pleases you is just." Zohak was at first shocked; but gradually he accustomed himself to the counsel, and his subjects were sacrificed to the serpents. But the people only saw in Zohak a monster bent on their destruction. They revolted, and shut him up in a cavern of the mountain Damavend, where he became a prey to the two serpents whose voracity he could no longer appease.'

'What a horrible history!' exclaimed the young prince, when his preceptor had ended it. 'Pray tell me another that I can hear without shuddering.' 'Willingly, my lord,' replied Saib. 'Here is a very simple one:—A young sultan placed his confidence in an artful courtier, who filled his mind with false ideas of glory and happiness, and introduced into his heart pride and voluptuousness. Absorbed by these two passions, the young monarch sacrificed his people to them, insomuch that in their wretchedness they tore him from the throne. He lost his crown and his treasures, but his pride and voluptuousness remained, and being now unable to satisfy them, he died of rage and despair.'

The young prince of Carizama said, 'I like this story better than the other.' 'Alas, prince!' replied his preceptor, 'it is nevertheless the same.'

DCLXXX.
Consuming Fire.

Love is the hell-spark that burneth up the mountain of iniquity. Mahomet. (Tradition.)

DCLXXXI.

Pleasure: Transient and Permanent.

Heb.
Wisdom of
Solomon.
Ab.

Some have said, reasoning with themselves, but not aright :—Our life is short and tedious, and in the death of a man there is no remedy, neither was there any man known to have returned from the grave. We are born at all adventure, and we shall be hereafter as though we had never been, for the breath in our nostrils is as smoke, and a little spark in the moving of our heart, which being extinguished, our body shall be turned into ashes, and our spirit shall vanish as the soft air. Our name shall be forgotten in time, and no man shall have our works in remembrance, and our life shall pass away as the trace of a cloud. Our time is a very shadow that passeth away. Come on, therefore, let us enjoy the good things that are present. Let us fill ourselves with costly wine and ointments. Let no flower of the spring pass by us. Let us crown ourselves with roses before they be withered. Let none of us go without his part of voluptuousness : let us leave tokens of our joyfulness in every place ; for this is our portion, and our lot is this. Let our strength be the law of justice ; for that which is feeble is found to be nothing worth. Let us lie in wait for the righteous. He abstaineth from our ways as filthiness, saying,—' He pronounceth the end of the just to be blessed, and maketh his boast that God is his father. Let us see if his words be true ; for if the just man be the son of God, he will help him.'

Such things they did imagine, and were deceived ; for their own wickedness hath blinded them. They hoped not for the wages of justice, nor discerned a reward for blameless souls. For God made man to be the image of his own eternity. They that put their trust in him shall understand the truth; and such as be faithful in love shall abide with him.

Whoso despiseth wisdom and nurture, he is miserable; his hope is vain, his labours unfruitful. Glorious is the fruit of good labours, and the root of wisdom shall never fall away.

DCLXXXII.
Poverty and Wealth.

Poverty which is through honesty is better than wealth which is from the treasure of others, since it is said, 'Even he who is the poorest and most helpless one, if he always keep his thoughts and actions just, obtains a share of every good work done in the world.' <small>Parsí. Mainyo-i-Khard. 6th cent. Ab.</small>

These men are to be considered rich :—he who is perfect in wisdom; he who has health; he that is fearless; he who is contented; he who through honesty has made fate his friend. And these are poor :—he with whom wisdom is not; he who is unhealthy; he who lives in fear and falsehood; he who is not master of himself.

The sage asked, 'In the creation of God is there anything on which Ahriman cannot bring misfortune?' The Spirit of Wisdom replied, 'On a wise and contented man it is impossible to bring misfortune.'

DCLXXXIII.
Self-control.

Self-control will place a man among the gods; the want of it will drive him into the dark abyss. <small>Hindu. Cural.</small>

Let it be guarded as a treasure; there is no greater

source of good for man than that, though he guard nothing else, he guard his tongue. The wound burnt in by fire may heal; but a wound burnt in by the tongue will never heal.

One word of evil intent will change good into evil.

He who, like a tortoise, can draw in his five senses, will obtain happiness.

Virtue seeking for an opportunity will come into the path of the man who guards against anger and has learned restraint.

Humility is good in all, but especially in the rich; it is the excellence of a higher riches.

More lofty than a mountain will be the greatness of that man who without swerving from his proper state controls himself.

All other creatures will worship him who has attained the control of his own soul.

DCLXXXIV.

Envy.

Hindu. Cural.
Among all those who stand on the outside of virtue, there are no greater fools than those who stand outside their neighbour's door.

To those who cherish envy, that is enough. Though other enemies fail, that will bring destruction.

The wealth of the envious man, and the poverty of the upright, these exist not.

Do you ask, What is the indestructibility of wealth? It is to be free from coveting the possessions of others.

It is magnanimity that will give victory.

DCLXXXV.

The Earth.

The earth is the Lord's, and the fulness thereof ; _{Heb.}
The world, and all who dwell therein. _{Ps.}
Who shall ascend into the hill of the Lord ?
And who shall stand in his holy place ?
The clean of hands, and the pure of heart ;
He who hath not lifted up his soul to vanity,
Nor sworn deceitfully ;
He shall receive a blessing from the Lord,
And righteousness from the God of his salvation.

DCLXXXVI.

Songs in the Night.

From the heavens thou didst cause thy sentence
    to be heard ; _{Heb. Ps. comp.}
The earth was afraid, and was still,
When God rose up to give sentence,
To save all the oppressed of the land.
I remember my song in the night ;
Thy way was in the sea,
And thy paths in the great waters,
And thy footsteps were not known.
I will hear what God shall speak :
Mercy and truth will meet together ;
Righteousness and peace will kiss each other ;
Truth will spring forth from the earth,
And justice will look down from the heavens.
The Lord will surely give what is good,
And our land will yield its increase.
Righteousness will go before him,
And tread firmly on the way.

2 E

DCLXXXVII.
Requital.

Heb.
Ps.

God hath requited me according to my righteousness,
According to the cleanness of my hands in his sight.
With the merciful thou wilt show thyself merciful;
With the upright thou wilt show thyself upright;
With the pure thou wilt show thyself pure;
And with the perverse thou wilt show thyself perverse.
Surely an afflicted people thou wilt save,
But lofty looks thou wilt bring down.

DCLXXXVIII.
Trust.

Heb.
Ps.

Trust in the Lord, and do good;
Delight thyself, also, in the Lord,
And he will give to thee the desires of thy heart.
Trust in him, and he will accomplish;
He will bring forth thy righteousness as the light,
And thy judgment as the noonday.
Wait silently for God, and place thy hope in him.
Fret not thyself because of him that prospereth in his way,
Because of the man who accomplisheth his evil devices.
Cease from anger, and forsake wrath;
Fret not thyself so as in any wise to do evil.
Yet a little while, and the wicked man shall not be:
Thou shalt search for his place, but it shall not be:
But the lowly shall inherit the land,
And shall delight themselves in abundant prosperity.
Better is a little that a righteous man hath,
Than the abundant riches of the wicked.
The mouth of the righteous man uttereth wisdom,

And his tongue speaketh justice :
The law of his God is in his heart ;
His steps shall not slip.
I have seen the wicked man terrible,
And spreading himself like a green native tree :
Yet he passed away, and lo ! he was not ;
And I sought him, but he was not to be found.
Mark the perfect man, and behold the upright ;
For the end of that man is peace.

DCLXXXIX.

Exaltation of Evil Men.

Save me, O God, for the godly man faileth,
For the faithful cease from among the sons of men.   Heb. Ps.
They speak falsehood every one to his neighbour :
With flattering lips, but with a double heart they
    speak.
May God cut off all flattering lips,
The tongue that speaketh boastful things !
Of those who say, ' By our tongue we shall prevail.
Our lips are our own ; who is lord over us ? '
' On account of the desolation of the poor,
On account of the moaning of the needy,
I will now arise,' saith the Lord ;
' I will place in safety him who is scorned.'
The words of the Lord are pure words—
Silver tried in a crucible,
Purified from earth seven times.
Thou, O God, wilt keep them,
Thou wilt preserve them from this generation for ever.
The wicked walk on every side
When the vilest men are exalted.

DCXC.

Retribution.

<small>Heb.
Prov.
comp.</small>

My son, if base men entice thee,
Consent thou not.
Walk not in the way with them :
Keep back thy foot from their paths ;
For their feet run to evil.
Surely in vain the net is spread
In the sight of any bird ;
But these lay snares for their own lives.
Such are the ways of every one greedy of gain ;
The life of those addicted to it, it taketh away.
Because they hated knowledge,
Therefore they shall eat of the fruit of their own way,
And from their own counsel they shall be filled.
For the turning away of the simple shall slay them,
And the carelessness of fools shall destroy them.

DCXCI.

Rebuke of the Just.

<small>Heb.
Ps.</small>

Let not my heart incline to an evil thing,
To do evil deeds wickedly with men who work iniquity ;
Nor let me eat of their dainties !
Let a righteous man smite me, it will be kindness ;
And let him reprove me, it will be oil for the head.

DCXCII.

Guilelessness.

<small>Heb.
Ps.</small>

Guard thy tongue from evil,
And thy lips from speaking deceit.
Depart from evil, and do good ;

Seek peace, and pursue it.
The face of God is against those who do evil,
To cut off the remembrance of them from the land.
He is near to the contrite of heart,
And the lowly of spirit he saveth.

DCXCIII.
The Reward.
I said, 'I have laboured vainly,
I have spent my strength for naught; Heb. Isa. comp.
Yet surely my work is with God.'
Then said God,
'Is it a slight thing that thou shouldst be my servant?'

DCXCIV.
Self-Delusion.
Now go, write it before them upon a tablet,
And inscribe it in a book; Heb. Isa.
That it may be for a future day, for a testimony for ever:
For a rebellious people is this, lying children,
Children that will not hear the law of God;
Who say to the seers, 'See not,'
And to the prophets, 'Prophesy not to us right things;
Speak unto us smooth things, prophesy deceits,
Depart from the way, turn aside from the path,
Cause the Holy One to cease from before us.'
Wherefore, thus saith the Holy One,
'Because ye have refused this word,
And trust in oppression and perverseness,
This iniquity shall be to you
As a breach in a lofty wall,
Whose breaking cometh suddenly, in a moment.'

DCXCV.

False Peace.

<small>Heb.
Jer.</small> From the least even unto the greatest of them
Every one is greedy of gain;
From the prophet even unto the priest,
Every one dealeth falsely.
They have healed the wounds of my people slightly,
Saying, ' Peace, peace !' when there is no peace.
Are they ashamed that they have done what is base?
Nay, they are not at all ashamed,
Neither know they how to blush.
Behold, I will bring evil upon this people,
Even the fruit of their own thoughts.

DCXCVI.

Conscience.

<small>Wisdom of
Solomon.
Apoc.
Ab.</small> When unrighteous men thought to oppress the holy nation, they lay in their own houses prisoners of darkness, fettered with the bonds of a long night, exiled from the eternal providence. No power of the fire might give them light, neither could the bright beams of the stars lighten that horrible night.

For wickedness, condemned by her own witness, is very timorous, and being pressed with conscience, always forecasteth grievous things. For fear is nothing else but a betraying of the succours which reason offereth. They sleeping the same sleep that night—which was indeed intolerable, coming upon them from the bottom of inevitable hell—were partly troubled with monstrous apparitions, and partly fainted, their heart failing them; for a sudden fear, and not looked for, came upon them. Whoever then fell down was fast shut in a prison that had no iron bars. They were all bound with one chain of darkness. Whether it were a whistling wind, or melodies of birds among the spreading branches, or a pleasing sound of falling water, or a terrible sound of stones cast down, or of leaping invisible beasts, or roaring of wild beasts, or a rebounding echo from the hollow mountains : these things made them swoon for fear. The whole world shined with clear light, and none were hindered in their labour: over them only was spread a heavy night. Yet were they unto themselves more grievous than the darkness.

DCXCVII.

Radicalism.

In those days came John the Baptist preaching in the wilderness of Judea, saying, Repent, for the kingdom of heaven is at hand. For this is he that was spoken of through Isaiah the prophet, saying, 'The voice of one crying in the wilderness, Prepare the way of the Lord, make straight his paths!' And John himself had his raiment of camel's hair, and a leathern girdle about his loins; and his food was locusts and wild honey.

Christian.
Matt.

Then went out to him Jerusalem, and all Judea, and all the country about the Jordan, and were baptized by him in the river Jordan, confessing their sins. But seeing many of the Pharisees and Sadducees coming to be baptized, he said to them, Brood of vipers! who warned you to flee from the coming wrath? Bring forth therefore fruit worthy of repentance, and think not to say within yourselves, We have Abraham for our father; for I say to you that God is able out of these stones to raise up children to Abraham. And already is the axe lying at the root of the trees; every tree therefore that beareth not good fruit is to be cut down, and cast into the fire. I indeed baptize you in water, for repentance; but he that cometh after me is mightier than I, whose sandals I am not worthy to bear; he will baptize you in the sacred spirit and in fire. His winnowing-shovel is in his hand, and he will thoroughly cleanse his threshing-floor, and gather his wheat into the garner; but the chaff he will burn up with unquenchable fire.

DCXCVIII.
Power of Leasts.

Christian.
Matt.
comp.

Another parable he put forth to them, saying, The kingdom of heaven is like a grain of mustard, which a man took and sowed in his field. Which is the least indeed of all seeds; but when it is grown, it is greater than the herbs, and becometh a tree, so that the birds of the air come and lodge in its branches.

Another parable he spoke to them: The kingdom of heaven is like leaven, which a woman took and hid in three measures of meal, till the whole was leavened.

Again, it is like a merchant seeking goodly pearls. Having found one pearl of great price, he went and sold all that he had, and bought it.

DCXCIX.
Covetousness.

Christian.
Luke.

And he said to them, Take heed, and beware of all covetousness; for even when one hath great abundance, his life doth not depend upon his possessions.

And he spoke a parable to them, saying, The ground of a certain rich man brought forth plentifully. And he thought within himself, saying, What shall I do? for I have not where to store my crops. And he said, This will I do; I will pull down my barns, and build greater; and there will I store all my crops and my goods; and I will say to my soul, Soul, thou hast many goods laid up for many years; take thine ease, eat, drink, be merry. But God said to him, Fool! this night will thy soul be required of thee; and whose will those things be which thou hast laid up? So is he that layeth up treasure for himself, and is not rich towards God.

DCC.

Opportunity.

Then the kingdom of heaven will be like ten virgins, who took their lamps, and went out to meet the bridegroom. And five of them were foolish, and five wise. For the foolish took their lamps, and took no oil with them. But the wise took oil in their vessels with their lamps. And as the bridegroom tarried, they all slumbered and slept. But at midnight there was a cry, Lo! the bridegroom! go out to meet him. Then all those virgins arose, and trimmed their lamps. And the foolish said to the wise, Give us of your oil, for our lamps are going out. But the wise answered, saying, Perhaps there will not be enough for us and you; go rather to those who sell, and buy for yourselves. And while they went to buy, the bridegroom came; and they who were ready went in with him to the wedding; and the door was shut.

_{Christian.
Matt.}

DCCI.

Culture.

Christian.
Matt.

For it will be as when a man going abroad called his own servants, and entrusted to them his property; and to one he gave five talents, to another two, and to another one, to each according to his ability, and went abroad. He that had received the five talents went immediately and traded with the same, and gained five talents more. In like manner, he that had received the two gained two more. But he that had received the one went and dug in the earth, and hid his lord's money. And after a long time the lord of those servants cometh, and reckoneth with them. And he that had received the five talents came and brought five talents more, saying, Lord, thou entrustedst to me five talents; see, I have gained five talents more. His lord said to him, Well done, good and faithful servant! thou hast been faithful over a little, I will place thee in charge of much; enter into the joy of thy lord. He also that had received the two talents came and said, Lord, thou entrustedst to me two talents; see, I have gained two talents more. His lord said to him, Well done, good and faithful servant! thou hast been faithful over a little, I will place thee in charge of much; enter into the joy of thy lord. Then he also that had received the one talent came and said, Lord, I knew thee to be a hard man, reaping where thou didst not sow, and gathering where thou didst not scatter seed; and I was afraid, and went and hid thy talent in the earth. See! thou hast thine own. But his lord answered and said to him, Wicked and slothful servant! didst thou know that I reap where I sowed not, and gather where I did not scatter seed? Thou oughtest then to have put my money with the money-dealers, and on my coming I should have received mine own with interest. Take therefore the talent from him.

DCCII.
Light Unrecognised.

There was a man sent from God whose name was John. He came as a witness, to bear witness of the light, that through him all might believe. The true light, which enlighteneth every man, was coming into the world. In him was life, and the life was the light of men; the light shone in the darkness, and the darkness comprehended it not. He was in the world, and the world knew him not. He came to his own, and his own received him not. Christian.
John.
comp.

This is the condemnation, that the light hath come into the world and men loved darkness rather than light; for their deeds were evil. Every one that doeth evil hateth the light, lest his deeds should be reproved. But he that doeth the truth cometh to the light, that his deeds may be made manifest that they are wrought in God.

DCCIII.
Rejected Truth.

And he began to speak to the people this parable :— A man planted a vineyard, and let it out to husbandmen, and went abroad for a long time. And at the season he sent a servant to the husbandmen, that they should give him of the fruit of the vineyard; but the husbandmen beat him, and sent him away empty-handed. And he sent still another servant; and they beat him also, and treated him shamefully, and sent Christian.
Luke.
comp.

him away empty-handed. And he went on to send a third ; and they wounded him also, and cast him out. And the lord of the vineyard said, What shall I do ? I will send my beloved son ; perhaps they will respect him. But when the husbandmen saw him, they reasoned among themselves, saying, This is the heir ; let us kill him, that the inheritance may become ours. So they cast him out of the vineyard, and killed him. What then will the lord of the vineyard do to them ? He will come and destroy these husbandmen, and will give the vineyard to others. And when they heard this, they said, God forbid ! But he, looking upon them, said, What then is this which is written, 'The stone which the builders rejected, the same hath become the corner-stone ?' Every one who falleth upon that stone will be broken ; but on whomsoever it falleth, it will grind him to powder.

And when he came near, as he beheld the city, he wept over it, saying, If thou hadst known, even thou, and that in this thy day, the things that concern thy peace ! but now they are hidden from thine eyes. For the days will come upon thee when thine enemies will cast up a mound about thee, and compass thee round, and shut thee in on every side, and will level thee with the ground, and thy children within thee ; and they will not leave in thee one stone upon another ; because thou knewest not the time of thy visitation.

And he was teaching daily in the temple ; but the chief priests, and the scribes, and the leading men of the people sought to destroy him. And they could not find an opportunity of doing anything, for all the people hung upon him listening.

DCCIV.

Sowing and Reaping.

The fruit of the Spirit is love, joy, peace, longsuffering, kindness, goodness, faithfulness, humility, temperance. <small>Christian. Gal. comp.</small>

Let us not become vainglorious, provoking or envying one another.

If a man be detected in a fault, do ye who are spiritual restore such a one in the spirit of meekness; considering thyself, lest thou also be tempted. Bear ye one another's burdens, and thus fulfil the law of Christ. For if a man thinketh himself to be something when he is nothing, he deceiveth himself. But let each one prove his own work, and then will he have his ground for boasting in himself alone, and not in comparison with another; for every one must bear his own load.

Let him that is taught in the word share with the teacher in all good things. Be not deceived, God is not mocked; for whatever a man soweth, that shall he also reap. For he that soweth to his flesh, shall of the flesh reap corruption; but he that soweth to the spirit, shall of the spirit reap life everlasting. And let us not be faint-hearted in well-doing; for in due season we shall reap if we faint not.

DCCV.

Woes.

My people are destroyed through lack of knowledge. Woe unto them that draw down punishment with cords of sin! Woe unto them that call evil good, and good evil,—bitter for sweet, and sweet for bitter,— <small>Heb. Isa. comp.</small>

darkness for light, and light for darkness! Woe unto them that are wise in their own eyes, and prudent in their own sight! Woe unto them that are mighty to mingle strong drink! Woe to them who absolve the guilty for reward, and take away the righteousness of the righteous from him! As a tongue of fire devoureth stubble, their root shall be rottenness, and their blossom shall be ashes.

> Woe unto them that make unrighteous decrees,
> And that write, causing misery by what they have written!
> To turn aside the needy from judgment,
> And to take away the right of the poor;
> That widows may be their prey,
> And that they may rob the fatherless!

DCCVI.
Danger.

Persian.

Deem it not safe to pass through the thicket of Lust: there crouches the tiger Pain.

DCCVII.
Happiness and Misery.

Koran, s. 92, 'The Night.' comp.

> By the night when she spreads her veil;
> By the day when it brightly shineth;
> By him who made male and female;
> At different ends truly do ye aim!
> As to him who giveth, and feareth God
> (Who giveth of his substance that he may become pure,
> Who offereth not favours to any one for a recompense),
> And yieldeth assent to the Good,

To him will we make easy the path to happiness.
But as to him who is covetous and bent on riches,
And calleth the Good a lie,
To him will we make easy the path to misery.

DCCVIII.
Recoil.

Lo! the wicked is in labour with iniquity;   Heb.
He hath conceived mischief,   Ps.
And he is bringing forth falsehood.
He hath dug a pit, and made it deep;
But he shall fall into the pit which he hath made.
His mischief shall return upon his own head,
And upon the crown of his head his violence shall descend.

DCCIX.
Evil.

Even an evil-doer sees happiness as long as his evil deed has not ripened; but when his evil deed has ripened, then does the evil-doer see evil.   Burmese. Dhammapada. comp. (Müller.)

Let no man think lightly of evil, saying in his heart, 'It will not come near unto me.' Even by the falling of water-drops a water-pot is filled; the fool becomes full of evil, even if he gathers it little by little.

He who has no wound on his hand may touch poison with his hand; nor is there evil for one who does not commit evil.

If a man offend a harmless, pure, and innocent person, the evil falls back upon that fool like light dust thrown up against the wind.

Not in the sky, not in the midst of the sea, not if

we enter into the clefts of the mountains, is there known a spot in the whole world where a man might be freed from an evil deed.

DCCX.

Justice.

Hindu. Manu.
Iniquity, committed in this world, produces not fruit immediately, but, like the earth, in due season, and advancing by little and little, it eradicates the man who committed it.

He grows rich for a while through unrighteousness; then he beholds good things; then it is that he vanquished his foes; but he perishes at length from his whole root upwards.

Justice, being destroyed, will destroy; being preserved, will preserve; it must never therefore be violated. Beware, O judge! lest justice, being overturned, overturn both us and thyself.

The only firm friend who follows men, even after death, is justice; all others are extinct with the body.

DCCXI.

Slavery.

Scand. Sæmund's Edda. (Paraphrased from Gratta-Savngr.)
Far in the morning-time of the world was Frothi's peace. Then did none harm another, and the gem lay untouched by any thief on Jalaugursheath. There was found in Danmaurk the mighty Quern called Grotti, which to the grinder's will ever produceth.

Then King Frothi called his slaves renowned for strength, Fenia and Menia, and bade them grind him gold. The maidens ground through many years, they ground endless treasures; but at last they grew weary. Then Frothi said, 'Grind on! Rest ye not, sleep ye not, longer than the cuckoo is silent, or a verse can be sung!' The weary slaves ground on, till lo ! from the mighty Quern is poured forth an army of men. Now lieth Frothi slain amid his gold. Now is Frothi's peace for ever ended.

DCCXII.

Necessity.

When the gods in the Norse fable were unable to bind the Fenris Wolf with steel, or with weight of mountains—the one he snapped, the other he spurned with his heel—they put round his foot a limp band softer than silk or cobweb, and this held him—the more he spurned, the stiffer it drew. So soft and so stanch is fate. Scandinavian Fable.

DCCXIII.

The Unchanging.

Verily God holdeth fast the heavens and the earth that they pass not away.

Their haughtiness on earth and their plotting of evil! But the plotting of evil shall only enmesh those who make use of it. Look they then for aught but God's way with the peoples of old ? Thou shalt not find any change in the way of God ; yea, thou shalt not find any variableness in the way of God ! Arabic. Koran, s. 35, 'The Creator, or the Angels.'

DCCXIV.

Fate.

What is stronger than fate ? If we think to avert it, it is with us before the thought. Hindu. Cural.

They who gather millions enjoy only as is determined. Whatever is not conferred by fate cannot be

2 F

preserved, though guarded with painful care : what fate has given cannot be lost, though thrown away.

Fate has ordained two properties—wealth and knowledge—sought by different men. In the acquisition of that not appointed to either, everything favourable becomes unfavourable ; in accordance with fate everything unfavourable becomes favourable.

Although a man may study the most polished treatises, the knowledge which fate has decreed to him will still prevail.

Adverse fate is no disgrace to any one ; to be without exertion, and not to know what should be known, this is disgrace. Although, through destiny, the end cannot be obtained, the earnest endeavour will yield its reward.

DCCXV.

Restoration.

Arabian.
(Von Hammer.)

In the last day, when all things save paradise shall have passed away, God will look upon hell, and at that instant its flames shall be extinguished for ever.

DCCXVI.

Judgment and Charity.

Christian.
John.
(Text of Tregilles.)

And they went each to his house ; but Jesus went to the Mount of Olives. And early in the morning he came again to the temple, and all the people were coming to him. And he sat down and taught them. And the scribes and the Pharisees bring to him a woman taken in adultery ; and having set her in the midst, they say to him, Teacher, this woman was taken in adultery, in the very act. Now in the Law Moses commanded us to stone such persons ; what then dost thou say? But this they said to try him, that they might be able to accuse him. But Jesus stooped down, and with his finger wrote on the ground. But when they continued asking him, he lifted himself up, and said to them, Let him that is without sin among you first cast a stone at her. And again he stooped down, and wrote on the ground. And when they heard this, they went out one by one, beginning with the oldest; and Jesus was left alone, and the woman who was in the midst. And Jesus lifted himself up and said to her, Woman, where are they? Did no one condemn thee? And she said, No one, Lord. And Jesus said, Neither do I condemn thee; go, and sin no more.

DCCXVII.

Truth.

He who knows truth, knows the Divinity, and this will enable him to slay all evil lusts. Will he who has swallowed a delicious plantain swallow bitter venom? *Hindu. Vémana.*

If thy word be truth, this is a hundred additional years of life.

DCCXVIII.

Sowing and Reaping.

I was sitting in a boat, in company with some persons of distinction, when a vessel near us sunk, and two brothers fell into a whirlpool. One of the company promised a mariner a hundred dinars if he would save both the brothers. The mariner came and saved one, and the other perished. I said, 'Of a truth, the other had no longer to live, and therefore he was taken out of the water the last.' The mariner, *Persian. Sádi. Gul.*

laughing, replied, 'What you say is true; but I had also another motive for saving this in preference to the other; because once, when I was tired in the desert, he mounted me on a camel; and from the hand of the other I received a whipping in my childhood.' I replied, 'Truly the great God is just, so that whosoever doeth good shall himself experience good, and he who committeth evil shall suffer evil.' As far as you can avoid it, distress not the mind of any one, for in the path of life there are many thorns. Assist the exigencies of others, since you also stand in need of many things.

DCCXIX.
Opportunity.

Koran,
s. 32,
'Adoration.

When the guilty shall droop their heads and cry, 'O our Lord! we have seen and heard: return us then; we will do that which is right'—*it shall be said*, 'Taste the recompense of your having forgotten the meeting with your day.'

DCCXX.
Responsibility.

Persian.
Urfí.
10th cent.

O 'Urfí! live with good and evil men in such a manner that Muslims may bathe thee after death in holy water, and Hindus burn thee.

If thou wishest to see thy faults clearly, lie for a moment in ambush for thyself, as if thou didst not know thee.

'Urfí has done well to stand quietly before a closed door, which no one would open. He did not knock at another door.

To pine for the arrival of young spring shows

narrowness of mind: hundreds of beauties are on the heap of rubbish in the backyard which are not met with in a rose-garden.

On the day when all shall give an account of their deeds, and when the virtues of both Sheik and Brahman shall be scrutinised, not a grain shall be taken of that which thou hast reaped, but a harvest shall be demanded of that thou hast not sown.

Alas! thou leavest behind and losest that which once belonged to thee. Thou oughtest to have taken it with thee; but hast thou taken it with thee?

DCCXXI.

Seeming and Being.

A certain pious man saw in a dream a king in paradise and a holy man in hell. He asked what could be the meaning of the exaltation of one, and the degradation of the other, as the contrary is generally considered to be the case? They replied, 'The king has obtained paradise in return for his love of holy men; and the religious man, by associating with kings, has got into hell.' Of what use are the coarse frock, the beads, and patched garments? Abstain from evil deeds, and there is no need of a cap of leaves; possess the virtues of a Durwaish, and wear a Tartarian crown. Sádi. Gul.

DCCXXII.

Reproof.

There was a king who oppressed his subjects. An informer came to him, and said, 'A certain old man has in private called thee a tyrant, a disturber, and bloodthirsty.' The king, enraged, said, 'Even now Persian. Nizámi. Ab.

I put him to death.' While the king made preparations for the execution, a youth ran to the old man, and said, 'The king is ill-disposed to thee; hasten to assuage his wrath.' The sage performed his ablution, took his shroud, and went to the king. The tyrant, seeing him, clapped his hands together, and with eye hungry for revenge, cried, 'I hear that thou hast given loose to thy speech; thou hast called me revengeful, an oppressive demon.' The sage replied, 'I have said worse of thee than what thou repeatest. Old and young are in peril from thy action; town and village are injured by thy ministry. Apply thy understanding, and see if it be true; if it be not, slay me on a gibbet. I am holding a mirror before thee; when it shows thy blemishes truly, it is a folly to break the mirror: break thyself.'

The king saw the rectitude of the sage, and his own crookedness. He said, ' Remove his burial-spices and his shroud; bring to him sweet perfumes, and the robe of honour.' He became a just prince, cherishing his subjects. Bring forward thy rough truth : truth from thee is victory from God; it shall shine as a pearl.

DCCXXIII.

Seeming and Being.

Sâdi.
Gul.

Be thou good, although mankind speak evil of you, which is better than being bad, whilst they think you good.

I lamented to a venerable Sheik that some one had accused me falsely of lasciviousness. He replied, ' Put him to shame by your virtue. Let your conduct be virtuous, when it will not be in the power of the detractor to convict you of evil. When the harp is in tune, how can it suffer correction from the hand of the musician?'

DCCXXIV.
The World.

Come, look at this glittering world, like unto a royal chariot; the foolish are immersed in it, but the wise do not cling to it. _{Burmese. Budh. Dhammapada. comp. (Müller.)}

He whose evil deeds are covered by good deeds brightens up this world, like the moon when freed from clouds.

Better than sovereignty over the earth, better than going to heaven, better than lordship over all worlds, is the reward of the first step in holiness.

DCCXXV.
Time.

Time is a portion of the revolution of the great heaven, and the relation of one transient thing with another; the events of the world move with the movement of the spheres. _{Persian. Desâtír Sâsán.}

DCCXXVI.
Temperance.

A certain man having made many vows which he broke, a venerable personage said to him, 'I know that you make it a practice to eat a great deal, and that your inclination to restrain your appetite is weaker than a hair, whilst your appetite, in the manner you indulge it, would break a chain; but a day may come when this intemperance may destroy you. Somebody nourished a wolf's whelp, which when full grown tore its master to pieces.' _{Sádi. Gul.}

DCCXXVII.
Retribution.

Hindu.
Manu.

As the seasons of the year attain respectively their distinctive marks in due time and of their own accord, even so the actions of every being attend it naturally.

The scorned may sleep sweetly; with pleasure he may awake, and with pleasure pass through life; but the scorner perishes.

He who shall each day honour all beings will go to the highest regions in a straight path, with an irradiated form.

Let not a man be querulous, even though in pain; let him not injure another in deed or in thought; let him not utter even a word by which his fellow-creature may suffer uneasiness, since that will obstruct his own progress to beatitude.

DCCXXVIII.
The Shadow.

Persian.
Ardâ
Vîrâf.

In a region of bleak cold wandered a soul which had departed from the earth; and there stood before him a hideous woman, profligate and deformed. 'Who art thou?' he cried—'who art thou, than whom no demon could be more foul or horrible?' To him she answered, 'I am thy own actions!'

DCCXXIX.
Retribution.

Sâdi.
Gul.

He who, when he hath the power, doeth not good, when he loses the means, will suffer distress. There is not a more unfortunate wretch than the oppressor; for in the day of adversity nobody is his friend.

DCCXXX.
Good Imperishable.
I saw in hell one whose body a noxious creature gnawed, but his right foot was not gnawed. The angel said to me, 'This is the soul of a lazy man, who when living never did any good work; but with that right foot which suffers not a bundle of grass was cast before a ploughing ox.'
Ardá Víráf.

DCCXXXI.
Envy.
Wish not ill to the envious man, for the unfortunate wretch is a calamity to himself. Where is the need of your showing enmity towards him who has such an adversary at his heels?
Sádi. Gul.

DCCLXXXII.
Responsibility.
I saw the souls of a man and woman dragged, the man to heaven, the woman to hell. The woman said, 'How is it that though we shared every benefit when living, they are now bearing thee to heaven, me to hell?' The man said, 'Because I practised good thoughts, words, and deeds; but thou didst worship idols.' The woman said, 'Among the living thou wast completely lord and sovereign over me—my body, life, and soul were thine; then why hast not thou taught me the reason of thy excellence, whereby thou mightest have caused excellence in me?'
Ardá Víráf.

The woman sat in darkness, but without other affliction; the man sat in light, but covered with shame.

DCCXXXIII.

Action.

Koran
s. 99,
'The Earth-
quake.'
comp.

When the earth with her quaking shall quake,
And the earth shall cast forth her burdens,
And men shall say, 'What aileth her?'
On that day shall she tell out her tidings,
Because thy Lord shall have inspired her.
On that day shall men come forward in throngs to behold their works;
And whosoever shall have wrought an atom's weight of good shall behold it,
And whosoever shall have wrought an atom's weight of evil shall behold it.

DCCXXXIV.

Reward of Virtue.

Sâdi.
Gul.

A Durwaish, in his prayer, said, 'O God! show pity towards the wicked, for on the good thou hast already bestowed mercy by having created them virtuous.'

DCCXXXV.

Fruition.

Koran,
s. 89,
'The Day-
break.'

O thou soul which art at rest!
Return to thy Lord, pleased, and pleasing him.
Enter thou among my servants,
And enter thou my paradise.
And his shall be a life that shall please him well,
In a lofty garden,

S. 69,
'The Inevit-
able.'

Whose clusters shall be near at hand;
Eat ye and drink with healthy relish, as the meed of what ye sent on before in the days which are past.

DCCXXXVI.
Crime Suicidal.

A king having commanded an innocent person to be put to death, he said, 'O king! seek not your own injury by venting your wrath on me.' The king asked in what manner. He replied, 'This torture will cease with me in an instant, and the crime thereof will remain with you for ever. The space of life passeth away, like the wind over the desert; bitterness and sweetness, deformity and beauty, all shall cease. The tyrant imagineth that he committeth violence against me; but it remaineth on his own neck, and passeth over me.' The advice was profitable to the king, who spared his life, and asked forgiveness.. Sádí. Gul.

DCCXXXVII.
Justice.

Justice is so dear to the heart of Nature, that if in the last day one atom of injustice were found, the universe would shrivel like a snake-skin to cast it off for ever. Hindu. (Ancient, but authorship unknown.)

DCCXXXVIII.
Freedom.

    Up, Háfiz! grace from God's high face
      Beams on thee pure;
    Shy thou not hell, and trust thou well,
      Heaven is secure. Persian. Háfiz. (Emerson.)

DCCXXXIX.
Virtue.

Jemshíd introduced distinctions in dress, and was the first person who wore a ring upon the finger. They asked him why he had given the whole grace and ornament to the left, whilst excellence belongs to the right hand? He replied, 'The right hand is completely ornamented by its own rectitude.' Feridoun commanded the Chinese embroiderers to embroider the following words on the outside of his pavilion, 'O man of prudence! do thou good to the wicked, for the virtuous are of themselves great and happy.'

DCCXL.

To-day.

The journey of my existence is accomplished in a few days. It passes as the wind of the desert. And so, for what remains to me of the breath of life, there are two days about which I will not be anxious—the day that is yet to come, and the day that is past.

If the things of this world were not based merely on conventionality, oh! then every day would be a holy festival! If it were not for these vain menaces about the future, each would be able to attain without fear the end and aim for which he longs.

Art thou discreet enough for me to tell thee in the fewest words what man has been in the main? A wretched creature, kneaded with the mire of misery. He has for some days eaten a few morsels of the earth, and then lifted his feet to depart.

O my heart! thou wilt never penetrate the mysteries of the heavens; thou wilt never reach that culminating point of wisdom which the intrepid omniscients have attained.

Resign thyself then to make what little paradise ·thou canst here below; for, as for that beyond, thou shalt arrive there, or thou shalt not.

PRINCIPAL AUTHORITIES.

ABULFAZL, 'ALLÁMÍ. The Aín-i-Akbarí. Translated from the original Persian by H. Blochmann, M.A. (Bibliotheca Indica). Calcutta. 1868.
Alabaster, Henry. The Wheel of the Law. Buddhism illustrated from Siamese sources. London : Trübner & Co. 1871.
Albitis, F. The Morality of all Nations. Manchester. 1850.
Alger, Rev. William R. The Poetry of the Orient. Boston : Roberts & Brothers. 1866.
Ali, Syed Ameer, Moulvie, M.A., LL.B. A Critical Examination of the Life and Teachings of Mohammed. London : Williams & Norgate. 1873.
Ali, Syed Keramut, Moulvie. Makhaz-i-uloom, or a Treatise on the Origin of the Sciences. Translated into English by Moulvie Obeyd-Olla, Al-Obeydee, Arabic Professor, Hooghly College, and Moulvie Syed Ameer Ali, B.A., graduate of the University of Calcutta. Calcutta. 1867.
American Oriental Society, Journal of the (Annual). New Haven, Conn., U. S. A.
Apocrypha (Old Testament). Edition of the Society for Promoting Christian Knowledge. London.
Ardá Víráf, The Book of. The Pahlavi text prepared by Destur Hoshangje Jamaspje Asa. Translated by Martin Haug, Ph.D., and E. M. West, Ph.D. Bombay : Government Book Depôt. London : Trübner & Co. 1872.
Asiatic, Royal, Society. Journal (1816-74).
Asiatic, Royal, Society. Journal of Ceylon Branch. Colombo, Ceylon.
Asiatic Researches. 1801, *et seq.*
Attar. Mantic uttair. Le Langage des Oiseaux. Garcin de Tassy. Paris : Dubuisson & Cie. 1856.

BEAL, Rev. Samuel. A Catena of Buddhist Scriptures, from the Chinese. London : Trübner & Co. 1871.
Bible. The Holy Bible, containing the Old Testament. Translated out of the original Hebrew, and with the former translations diligently compared and revised. And the Greek New Testament, printed from the text, and with the various readings of Knapp. New York : J. C. Riker. 1845.

Bible. The Holy Scriptures of the Old Testament, in a revised translation by the late Rev. Charles Wellbeloved; the Rev. George Vance Smith, B.A.; and the Rev. John Scott Porter. London: Longmans, Green & Co. 1859.
—— The New Testament; translated from the Greek text of Tischendorf, by G. R. Noyes, D.D., late Hancock Professor of Hebrew and other Oriental Languages, &c., in Harvard University. Boston: American Unitarian Association. 1869.
Brockie, William. Indian Philosophy. London: Trübner. 1872.
Buddha. Buddhagosha's Parables. Translated from the Burmese by Captain Rogers; with an Introduction, containing Buddha's Dhammapada, or 'Path of Virtue.' Translated from the Páli by Max Müller. London: Trübner & Co. 1870.

CARLYLE, J. D., Professor of Arabic in the University of Cambridge. Specimens of Arabian Poetry. Cambridge: University Press. 1796.
Channing, Rev. W. H., D.D. Religions of China: an Address delivered before the Free Religious Association of America. Boston. 1870.
Child, Lydia Maria. The Progress of Religious Ideas through Successive Ages. 3 vols. New York: Francis & Co. 1855.
Childers, Professor Robert C. Khuddaka Pátha. A Páli text, with translation and notes. R. A. Soc. 1869.
Clarke, Rev. J. Freeman, D.D. Ten Great Religions: an Essay in Comparative Mythology. Boston: Osgood & Co. 1871.
Colebrooke, H. T. Miscellaneous Essays. 2 vols. London. 1837.
Cole, Robert. The Madras Journal of Literature and Science.
Collie, Rev. David. The Chinese classical work commonly called 'The Four Books.' Translated by the Rev. David Collie, Principal of the Anglo-Chinese College, Malacca. Printed at the Mission Press.
Confucius. The Chinese Classics. With a translation, &c., by James Legge, D.D., of the London Missionary Society. 7 vols. Trübner & Co.
Costello, Louisa. The Rose-Garden of Persia. London. 1845.
Cowell, Professor E. B. On Two Kasídahs of the Persian Poet Anwarí. By E. B. Cowell and E. H. Palmer. Journal of Philology, vol. iv. Cambridge: Macmillan & Co. 1872.

DÁBISTAN, The. The School of Persian Sects. Calcutta. 1809.
Desátír, The; or, 'Regulations.' Purporting to be a collection of the Persian Prophets, fifteen in number, of whom Zerdusht or Zoroaster was the thirteenth, and ending with the Fifth Sásán.

Translated by Mr Duncan, formerly Governor of Bombay, and Mulla Firuz Bin Kaus. Bombay. 1818.
Duperron, Anquetil, Zendavesta. Paris. 1771.

EMERSON, Ralph Waldo. The Dial : a Magazine for Literature, Philosophy, and Religion. Edited by R. W. E. and S. Margaret Fuller. 4 vols., 1841-4. Boston: Munroe & Co.
—— Poems. Munroe & Co. 1847.
—— May-Day, and other Pieces. Boston : Ticknor & Fields. 1867.
—— The Gulistan, or Rose-Garden. By Muslee-Huddeen Sheik Sádi of Shiraz. Translated by Francis Gladwin. With an Essay, &c., by James Ross. Preface by R. W. Emerson. Boston : Ticknor & Fields. 1865.
El Wardi, Ebn, Lamia. Madden. History of the World (in Persian).

FAUCHE, [Hippolyte. Mahábháráta. Poéme epique de Véda Vyasa. Traduit completement en Français. Paris. 1863-5.
—— Le Rámáyana. Traduit en Français. Paris. 1864.
Fausböll, V. Ten Jatakas. Copenhagen. 1872.

GALLAND, A. Les Paroles Remarquables, les Bons Mots, et les Maximes des Orientaux. À la Haye. 1694.
Gogerly, Rev. D. The Friend. Colombo, Ceylon. 1839.
Gouer, Charles E. The Folk-Songs of Southern India. Madras. 1871.

HÁFIZ. Sammlung von E. F. Daumer. Hamburg. 1846.
Hammer, Joseph Von. Geschichte der Schönen Redekünste Persiens, mit einer Blüthenlese aus 200 Persichen Dichtern. 4to. Wien. 1818.
—— Motenebbi der Grösste Arabische Dichter. Wien. 1824.
Haug, Dr Martin. Essays on the Sacred Language, Writings, and Religion of the Parsees. Bombay. 1862.
Hubschmann, Dr H. Ein Zoroastriches Lied, mit Rücksicht auf die Tradition. München. 1872.

JOHNSON, SAMUEL. The Sympathy of Religions. Boston. 1873.
Jones, Sir William, The Life and Works of. 13 vols. London. 1807.

KHÈYAM, OMAR. Les Quatrains de Khèyam. Traduits du Persan par J. B. Nicolas. Paris : L'Imprimière Imp. 1867.
—— The Rubáryát of Omar Khayyám, the Astronomer-Poet of Persia. Translated into English verse by E. Fitzgerald. London : Quaritsh. 1859.

MADDEN, R. R. Travels in Turkey, Egypt, Arabia, and Palestine. London. 1829.
Manning, Mrs. Ancient and Mediæval India. London: Allen & Co. 1869.
Mitford, A. B. Tales of Old Japan. London: Macmillan. 1871.
Muir, J., D.C.L., &c. Original Sanskrit Texts on the Origin and History of the People of India, &c. London: Williams & Norgate. 1857.
—— Metrical Translations from the Hymns of the Veda, and other Indian writings. For private circulation. 1873.
Müller, F. Max. Rig-Veda-Sanhita: the Sacred Hymns of the Brahmans.
—— Chips from a German Workshop.
—— Introduction to the Science of Religion, &c. London: Longmans. 1873.

NAOROJI, Dadabhai, Professor of Gujaráti in the University of London. The Parsee Religion. London: Straker & Sons. 1864.
Noyes, George R. A new translation of the Book of Job, with an Introduction and Notes. Second Edition. Boston: Munroe & Co. 1838.

ORIENTAL FABLES. London: T. Cadell. 1797.

PALMER, Professor E. H., Oriental Mysticism: a Treatise on the Sufiistic and Unitarian Theosophy of the Persians. Compiled from native sources. Cambridge: Deighton, Bell, & Co. 1867.

RAPP, Dr Adolf. Die Religion und Sitte der Perser. Leipzig. 1865.
Richardson, Frederika. The Iliad of the East. Legends from the Rámáyana. London and New York: Macmillan & Co. 1870.
Rodwell, Rev. J. M. The Koran, translated from the Arabic, the Suras arranged in chronological order. London: Williams & Norgate. 1861.
Rogers, Mary Eliza. Domestic Life in Palestine. London: Bell & Daldy. 1863.

SÁDI OF SCHIRAZ. The Gulistan. Translated by E. B. Eastwick.
—— The Gulistan. Translated by Francis Gladwin.
—— Selections from the Bóstán. Translated into English verse by D. M. Strong. London: Trübner & Co. 1873.
Saint-Hilaire, J. Barthélemy. Le Bouddha et sa Religion. Paris. 1860.
Sale, George. The Koran; with preliminary dissertation. London: Charles Mason. 1836.
Schlagentweit, Emil. Buddhism in Thibet. Leipzig and London. 1863.
Spiegel, F. Avesta, die Heiligen Schriften der Parsen. Vienna. 1860–3.

PRINCIPAL AUTHORITIES. 465

Spiegel, F. Commentar über das Avesta. Leipzig. 1864.
Steele, Thomas, Ceylon Civil Service. Kusa Játakaya. Trübner. 1871.
Sturleson, Snorro. The Heimskringla; or, Chronicle of the Kings of Norway. Translated from the Icelandic by Samuel Laing, Esq. 3 vols. London : Longmans & Co. 1844.
Stevenson, Rev. J. Sanhita of the Sáma Veda. London. 1842.

TIRUVALLUVA. The Cural. Books I and II. Translated by the Rev. W. H. Drew. Madras. 1840.

UPHAM, Edward. The Mahávansa; the Rájá-Ratnacari; and the Rájá-Vali. The Sacred and Historical Books of Ceylon. Translated from the Singhalese. London. 1833.

VÉMANA, Verses of. Translated by Charles Philip Brown, of the Madras Civil Service. College Press, Madras. 1829.

WEST. The Book of the Mainyó-i-Khard, 'Spirit of Wisdom.' Translated by E. W. West. London : Trübner & Co.
Wilkins, Charles. Bhágavat Geeta. London. 1785.
Wilson, H. H., M.A., F.R.S., &c., &c. Rig-Veda-Sanhita. Translated from the original Sanskrit. Edited by E. B. Cowell, M.A., Professor of Sanskrit at Cambridge. Trübner & Co.
—— MSS. :—Padma Purána. Four volumes. Vishnu Purána. Two volumes. Agni Purána. Two volumes. Brahma Vaivarta Purána. Five volumes. Siva Purána. Mahábháráta Sábha Párva. Mahábháráta Adiparva.
Windischmann, Friederich. Zoroastriche Studien. München. 1863.

ZIPSER, Dr. The Lesson on the Mount. Reviewed in an Essay on the Talmud and the Gospels by Rev. Dr Zipser, Chief Rabbi of Alba, Hungary. Office of the *Jewish Chronicle*, London. 1852.

2 G

CHRONOLOGICAL NOTES:

CHINESE.

Lao-Tsze. B.C. 604. (At No. CCV., B.C. 17th has been by mistake inserted, instead of 7th.)
Confucius. B.C. 479. Many of the passages in the 'Analects,' and other works associated with him, are quoted from books of great antiquity; *e.g.*, ' The Four Kings,' the oldest of books.
Mencius. *d*. B.C. 313.

PARSÍ.

Zoroaster, or Zerdusht, supposed author of most of the hymns in the Zendavesta, lived certainly as early as B.C. 1200, and some (as Spiegel) think B.C. 2000. The books of the Avesta are not all of equal antiquity, but all previous to the time of Darius.
Dábistan, by Mohsan Fani. A.C. 17th.
Desátír, of apocryphal authorship, and date in Christian era uncertain.
Mainyó-i-Khard ('Spirit of Wisdom'), of uncertain date, but written in one of the earlier centuries of the Christian era, probably the 6th.
The Book of Ardá Víráf. A.C. 1321.

HINDU.

Rig-Veda-Sanhita. B.C. 1500. Some of the hymns dated by Dr Haug B.C. 2400.
Sáma-Veda. B.C. 800.
Yágur-Veda. B.C. 800.
Mahavansi. About B.C. 477-459.
Rájá-Ratnacari. B.C. 4th century.
Rájá-Vali. B.C. 4th century.
Manu. This lawgiver (who must not be confused with the Manu—*i.e.*, Father of Man—in the Vedas) lived about B.C. 1200. The Code with which his name is identified grew in extent

CHRONOLOGICAL NOTES. 467

until collected into a form somewhat like that which it bears at present, probably about B.C. 4th century.
Rámáyana. Dated by Professor Weber of Berlin at the Christian era, but by native scholars ascribed to a much earlier period.
Mahábháráta. B.C. 2d century. (The Bhágavat-Gita is an episode of this work.)
Hitopadesa. This work is founded on the Pańkatantra Tales. The latter, though translated from the Sanskrit about A.C. 6th century, contains tales and maxims known to have existed B.C. 500.
Cúral. Ziruvalluva, the author of the first Book, lived about A.C. 3d or 4th century. His sayings were collected later, and most of the second Book belongs probably to A.C. 9th century.
Verses of Vémana. This author lived, probably, about A.C. 12th century. The verses seem to have been collected from time to time, and to have appeared in their present shape about A.C. 17th century.
Puránas. Though containing myths, records, and hymns of much earlier date, these works were composed within a period stretching from A.C. 10th to 8th century.
Pattanathu. This poet lived in A.C. 10th century.

BUDDHIST.

Buddha (Gotáma) was born B.C. 622.
Játakas. Purporting to have been related by Buddha himself, but when written down doubtful.
Dhammapada. B.C. 246.
White Lotus of the Good Law. B.C. 246.
Wheel of the Law. B.C. 3d century.
Khuddaka Patha. B.C. 250.
Kathá Chari. B.C. 3d century.

HEBREW.

The Pentateuch. Date and authorship of the several books uncertain. The tendency of modern criticism is to the conclusion that a large number of very ancient fragments—historical, legendary, and poetic—were sifted, fused, or, to use Ewald's expression, compounded, into the books which we now have ; and that they assumed their present shape in the 11th century B.C.
The later Historical Books. There is reason to believe that these passed through a process similar to the above, and that, while preserving many earlier records, they were (with certain exceptions) put together at various periods between B.C. 800 and

B.C. 550. The Books of Chronicles cannot be much, if any, earlier than B.C. 330.

The Book of Job. Late in 6th century B.C. A version probably of a Persian form of a Brahmanical story of similar character. For accounts of the Indian Job, Hárictshándra, see Weber, Zeitschrift, vii. ; Schlottman's Introduction to Job ; Roberts' Oriental Illustrations.

Book of Ruth. B.C. 6th century.

The Book of Proverbs is a collection of the proverbs and maxims of a nation, and any attempt at dating them is out of the question ; but there is reason to believe that a collection—much increased since—was made early in the 10th century B.C.

The Book of Psalms contains, with hymns of immemorial antiquity, others that belong as late as the 5th or 4th centuries B.C.

The Major Prophets. Approximate dates :—Isaiah, B.C. 8th ; Jeremiah, B.C. 7–6th ; Ezekiel, B.C. 6th centuries.

The Twelve Minor Prophets were combined into a single volume about B.C. 300.

The Septuagint Translation. B.C. 250.

Apocrypha. Approximate dates are :—Ecclesiasticus and Book of Wisdom, B.C. 250–300 ; Esdras, the four books ranging from B.C. 150–31 (the latter date plausibly identified by Gutschmid as that of the Fourth Book of Ezra, or Esdras).

The Books of the Talmud date from B.C. 220 to A.C. 200. The Codex was completed at the close of the 5th century. Perhaps in this connection it may be well to mention the half-mythical Egyptian priest Hermes Trismegistus, the works attributed to whom are apocryphal, but contain passages which cannot have been written far from the Christian era.

CHRISTIAN.

The periods to which the Four Gospels are to be referred are subjects of warm controversy. The results of modern criticism indicate that Matthew—the most primitive—was, in its present form, composed early in the 2d century, and Luke somewhat later in the same century ; that John was written somewhat later than A.C. 160 ; and Mark at a still later period.

The Book of Revelation, the Book of Acts, and the Epistles of Paul, belong to the 1st century of the Christian era, and are the earliest Christian documents that we have.

The Epistles to the Ephesians, Galatians, Colossians, Hebrews, and to Timothy, and those attributed to John, Peter, James, and Jude, are all of uncertain date and apocryphal authorship.

ARABIAN.

The Sabæan Books. The Arabs regard the Sabæans as an extinct tribe of their own race. Their scriptures are known only by two extracts from them, preserved by El Wardi, the Persian writer, in his 'History of the World,' and these books are assigned a date anterior to the Christian era.

Mohammed was born A.C. 570.

The Mishkát, or Traditional Anecdotes of and Discourses by Mohammed, run from the 6th to the 8th centuries.

Shems Almaali (who should have been named as author of No. DXLV. in the present volume) ascended the throne of Georgia in the latter part of the 7th century A.C.

Ali Ben Ahmed. *d.* about A.C. 900.

Ahmed Ben Soliman (called the Sabæan heretic). A.C. 10th.

SCANDINAVIAN.

The Elder Edda. This consists of ancient ballads of extreme antiquity, collected by Sœmund, a Christian priest of Iceland, in the 11th century.

The Heimskringla (or 'Circle of the Earth'). An Icelandic book, written by Snorro Sturleson in the 13th century A.C., recording early traditions of the Sea-Kings, and of the introduction of Christianity into the North.

PERSIAN POETS.

Sasán. A.C. 7th.
Jemshíd. A.C. 9th.
Firdausi. *b.* at Khorassan A.C. 916.
Shikebí. A.C. 10th.
Faizí. A.C. 10th.
Miyan Káli. A.C. 10th.
Kayáti. A.C. 10th.
'Urfí. A.C. 10th.
Omar Khèyam, the Astronomer-poet. A.C. 11th. (No. CXXX. should have been attributed to this poet.)
Saad of Homa. A.C. 12th.
Nizámi. A.C. 12th.
Amik of Buchara. A.C. 12th.
Sádi. *b.* A.C. 1175, at Shiraz. (No. CLXXVII. should have been credited to this poet.)
Enwarí. A.C. 12th.
Jelaleddin Rúmi (the Moolah of Rúm). *d.* A.C. 1233.

Attar. *b.* A.C. 1226.
Attar (Mohammed Ben, or son of preceding). *d.* A.C. 1376.
Amir Khusraü. A.C. 13th.
Julai-ud-din. A.C. 13th.
Háfiz. *b.* at Shiraz A.C. 14th.
Ebn el Wardi. A.C. 14th.
Kassim-ol-Enwar. *d.* A.C. 1431.
Jámi. *d.* A.C. 1492.
Mani. *d.* A.C. 1517.
Saiyid Nímat-ullah, Walí. *b.* in Kirmán ; *d.* A.C. 1424.
Abul Fazl'. A.C. 16th.

ABBREVIATIONS EXPLAINED.

Ab. = Abridged.
A.C. = The Christian era.
Apoc. = Apocryphal.
B.C. = Before the Christian era.
b. = Born.
Bha. = Bhágavat.
Budh. = Buddhist.
cent. = Century.
comp. = Compiled—*i.e.*, various sentences from a book or chapter brought together.
Col. = Epistle to the Colossians.
Cor. = Epistle to the Corinthians.
d. = Died.
D'Herb. = D'Herbelot.
Deut. = The Book of Deuteronomy.
Ep. = Epistle.
Eph. = Epistle to the Ephesians.
Exod. = Book of Exodus.
Ezek. = Book of Ezekiel.
Gal. = Epistle to the Galatians.
Gen. = Book of Genesis.
Gul. = Sádi's 'Gulistan, or Rose-Garden.'
Heb. = Hebrew.
Is. = Island.
Isa. = Book of Isaiah.
Jer. = Book of Jeremiah.
Lev. = Book of Leviticus.
Lit. = Literally.
Matt. = Gospel of Matthew.
MS. = Manuscript.
Neh. = Book of Nehemiah.
Par. = Paraphrased.
Phil. = Epistle to the Philippians.
Prov. = Book of Proverbs (Heb.)

Ps.	=	Book of Psalms.
Pur.	=	Purána.
R.	=	Rabbi.
Rev.	=	Book of Revelation.
Rom.	=	Epistle to the Romans.
S.	=	Sura, of the Koran.
Sam.	=	Book of Samuel.
Scand.	=	Scandinavian.
Siam.	=	Siamese.
Singh.	=	Singhalese.
Thess.	=	Epistle to the Thessalonians.
Tim.	=	Epistle to Timothy.
Tr.	=	Translated.

INDEX.

ACCOMPLISHMENTS (Chinese), 304
Action (Arabic), 458
—— Determinative (Hindu), 383
Actions, the Heaven of (Hindu), 378
—— The Beauty of (Persian), 385
—— The Heart of (Burmese), 234
Adoration (Hindu), 112
Advice to a Son (Persian), 349
Affection (Persian), 315
—— Filial (Persian), 251
Age (Hebrew), 315
—— and Youth (Persian), 356
—— The Spirit of the (Hindu), 71
Agitator, The (Hebrew), 361
Agriculture (Scandinavian), 381
Aid, Seasonable (Chinese), 299
Altar-Flowers, Mystical (Hindu), 113
Altruism (Persian), 225
Ambition (Persian), 334
Angels (Persian), 161
Anger (Hindu), 306
Animals, Kindness to (Hindu), 218
Appearances (Hebrew), 25
Apprehension (Hindu), 313
Artist, The (Persian), 266
Asceticism (Hindu), 43
—— (Siamese), 43.
Ascription (Egyptian), 94
Assent and Action (Chinese), 378
Attainment (Hindu), 36
Avarice (Hindu), 309

BEATITUDES (Christian), 14
—— (Hebrew), 14
Beauty, Supreme (Persian), 85
Beginnings (Persian), 374
Being and Seeming (Christian), 22
Benevolence (Hindu), 220
Best, The (Persian), 72
Blame (Burmese), 307
Blood, The Voice of (Hebrew), 426
Body, The (Persian), 308
Books (Egyptian), 158
—— (Persian), 274

Bountifulness (Persian), 217
—— (Turkish), 232
Brahma, Hymn to (Hindu), 64
Brotherhood (Christian), 221
—— (Hebrew), 355, 371
Bush, The Burning (Persian), 263

CANDOUR and Detraction (Persian), 219
Captivity (Hebrew), 360
Cares, Selfish (Hindu), 308
Catholicity (Christian), 37
Cause and Effect (Singhalese), 425
—— Demand of a (Christian), 186
Certainty, Ignorant (Persian), 73
Character (Chinese), 286, 385
—— Domestic (Hindu), 220
—— Individual (Hindu), 296
—— Knowledge without (Persian), 210
Charity (Arabic), 216, 235, 241
—— (Christian), 215
—— (Hindu), 235
—— (Persian), 232
—— (Siamese), 219
—— (Singhalese), 232
—— (Syrian), 417
Childlikeness (Chinese), 323
Childlike, The Child and the (Christian), 322
Children (Hindu), 253
Christ, The Ideal (Christian), 55
Church, The Established (Christian), 145
Churches, Faithless (Christian), 150
Circumstance (Hebrew), 386
Clemency and Justice (Persian), 359
Company, Good (Persian), 247
Compassion (Chinese), 216
—— (Hindu), 217
Compassionateness (Christian), 223
Compliance (Chinese), 172
Conscience (Christian), 58
—— (Hebrew), 438
—— A Bad (Persian), 425
—— The Voice of (Christian), 203

2 H

Considerateness (Persian), 243, 251
Contentment (Hindu), 309
—— (Persian), 300, 316, 318, 332
Continuity (Christian), 344
Convention (Christian), 141
Conviction and Task, The Individual (Hindu), 294
Counsel (Hebrew), 313
Counsels (Arabic), 288
Courage (Christian), 55
—— (Persian), 296
—— (Scandinavian), 313
—— Moral (Hebrew), 178
Covetousness (Christian), 440
Crime Suicidal (Persian), 459
Culture (Christian), 442

DANCE, The Mystical (Persian), 109
Danger (Persian), 446
Daughters (Chinese), 165
Dawn (Hindu), 264
—— God as the (Hindu), 71
Day and Night (Arabic), 259
Death (Hebrew), 421
—— (Hindu), 421
—— (Persian), 416, 417
Deeds (Parsi), 382
Deity, The Living (Persian), 70
Dejection (Hebrew), 388
Delusion (Hindu), 64
Destiny (Persian), 350
Destitute, The (Hindu), 236
Devotion (Hindu), 293
—— Ignorant (Christian), 78
Devoutness (Hindu), 111
Diligence (Burmese), 305
Divination (Persian), 138
Dust to Dust (Hindu), 420
—— (Arabic), 392
Duties (Hebrew), 9
—— (Hindu), 7
—— Graduated (Hindu), 356
—— Royal (Russian), 27
Duty, Filial (Chinese), 254

EARS that hear (Persian), 123
Earth-Song (Hindu), 392
Earth, The (Hebrew), 433
—— The (Hindu), 261, 263
—— The New Heaven and the New (Christian), 56
Economy (Chinese), 216
Ecstasy (Persian), 84
Eminence (Singhalese), 343
Enemies, Learning from (Persian), 125
—— Love of (Christian), 19
—— —— (Hebrew), 19
—— —— (Persian), 225

Enjoyment (Hebrew), 303
Enough (Chinese), 235
Enterprise (Persian), 318
Envy (Hindu), 432
—— (Persian), 457
Equality (Hindu), 355
—— (Persian), 354
Equity (Arabic), 353
—— (Hebrew), 8
Evil (Burmese), 447
—— Good for (Chinese), 240
Evil Men, Exaltation of (Hebrew), 435
Evolution, Spiritual (Christian), 270
Excellencies (Ceylon), 12
Exercises, Religious (Hindu), 140
Experience (Persian), 377
—— (Scandinavian), 314

FABLE (Hindu), 117
Faithfulness (Christian), 345
—— (Hebrew), 247
Fall, The Tyrant's (Hebrew), 371
Falsehood (Hindu), 309
Fame (Persian), 343, 349
Fate (Hindu), 449
—— Inward (Arabic), 60
Fathers, Our (Hebrew), 337
Father, The Divine (Christian), 52
Fear and Boldness (Christian), 187
—— The Right (Hindu), 427
Fidelity (Persian), 211
Fire, Consuming (Arabic), 429
Fire-Worshipper, The (Persian), 93
Firmness (Hindu), 287
Fitness (Hindu), 308
—— (Persian), 127
Flowers, Oracles of (Burmese) 272
Folly (Burmese), 116
Force, Unproductive (Hindu), 302
Forethought (Hindu), 117
Forgiveness (Christian), 221
Formalism (Hebrew), 152
—— (Hindu), 151
Fortune, Inward (Singhalese), 127
Fraternity (Christian), 229, 230
Freedom (Persian), 290, 459
Friends (Hebrew), 25
—— (Tartary), 249
Friendship (Persian), 248
—— (Hindu), 249, 250
—— (Scandinavian), 249
—— (Chinese), 250
Friend, The (Hindu), 59
—— (Singhalese), 248
Frivolity (Hebrew), 303
Fruition (Arabic), 458
Fruits, The Tree known by (Hebrew), 24
Future, The Unknown (Hindu), 422

INDEX. 475

GENTLENESS (Hebrew), 247
—— (Hindu), 254
—— (Persian), 169
Gifts, Varied (Christian), 227
Glad Tidings, The Bringer of (Hebrew), 178
God (Arabic), 63
—— (Hindu), 76, 103
—— (Persian), 75, 83, 95
—— (Sabœan), 74
—— in all (Hindu), 75
—— Nature a Mirror of (Persian), 82
—— Seeking (Hebrew), 66
—— the Blinding Glory (Persian), 85
—— The House of (Persian), 101
—— The Near (Hebrew), 89
—— —— (Persian), 90
—— The Veil of (Persian), 72
—— Union with (Hindu), 58
Gods (Hebrew), 83
Good for Evil (Egyptian), 226
—— Imperishable (Persian), 457
Goodness (Chinese), 46
—— Divine (Hebrew), 87
Good Things (Persian), 305
—— Will (Singhalese), 350
Government (Chinese), 352
Gratitude (Hindu), 252
Greatness (Hebrew), 338
—— in Adversity (Chinese), 339
Grey Hairs (Hebrew), 162
Growths, Slow (Persian), 319
Guilelessness (Hebrew), 436

HAPPINESS (Burmese), 302
—— and Misery (Koran), 446
Haughtiness (Arabic), 328
Helpfulness (Hindu), 368
Help, Harmful (Persian), 126
Health (Hindu), 30, 295
Heart, In my (Tamil), 68
—— The (Christian), 51
—— The (Hebrew), 161
—— The (Persian), 39
Heaven and Hell (Persian), 424
Heresy, Ancient (Hindu), 134
Honour (Persian), 342
Hope, A Nation's (Hebrew), 366
Hospitality (Hindu), 237, 238, 239
—— (Scandinavian), 238
Humanity (Hebrew), 10
—— (Chinese), 354
—— The Christ (Christian), 222
Humility (Arabic), 332
—— (Chinese), 216, 327
—— (Christian), 324, 325
—— (Hebrew), 330
—— (Hindu), 320, 327
—— (Persian), 320, 322, 335

Hypocrisy (Christian), 20, 146
—— (Hebrew), 22, 152
—— (Hindu), 155
—— (Persian), 156

IDEALISM (Hindu), 268
Ideals (Chaldæan), 48
Ignorance (Hindu), 309
—— (Persian), 163
Illumination (Chinese), 126
Implora pace (Persian), 377
Inclinations, Four Virtuous (Siamese), 2
Independence (Hindu), 298
—— (Persian), 316, 317, 375
Indifference (Christian), 196
Industry (Hebrew), 380
Ineffable, The (Persian), 74
Inevitable, The (Burmese), 419
Injustice (Arabic), 11
Innocence (Chinese), 311
Inspiration (Persian), 167
Instability (Hindu), 389
Instruction (Hindu), 164
Intelligible, The (Egyptian), 98
Intellect, Piety of (Persian), 193
—— (Singhalese), 119
Intelligence, Ascent of (Persian), 166
Intention, Pure (Persian), 133

JEWELS, Three (Singhalese), 349
Joy (Persian), 283
—— Fountain of (Hebrew), 88
Judgment (Hebrew), 357
—— (Singhalese), 356
—— and Charity (Christian), 450
Justice (Arabic), 5, 353
—— (Hindu), 11, 448, 459
—— (Persian), 373
Just, The most (Persian), 86
—— Rebuke of the (Hebrew), 436

KINDNESS (Persian), 236
—— and Truth (Hebrew), 182
King, The (Hindu), 364
Knowing and Being Known (Chinese), 166
Knowledge (Arabic), 137
—— (Hindu), 163, 164
—— (Persian), 169, 170
—— (Tartar), 164
—— (Turkish), 158
—— and Action (Christian), 26
—— —— (Hebrew), 25
—— Use of (Persian), 128

LABOUR (Chinese), 380
—— (Hindu), 381
Law, Give ear unto the (Hebrew), 152
—— Higher (Christian), 202

Laws (Hebrew), 1
—— (Sabœan), 7
—— Lives that are (Arabic), 31
—— Universal (Nepaul), 31
Leaders (Christian), 344
Learning (Hindu), 159, 162
Least and Greatest (Burmese), 287
Leasts, Power of (Christian), 440
Liberality (Arabic), 231
—— (Christian), 229
—— (Persian), 242
Liberation (Christian), 149
—— (Hindu), 162
Life and Death (Arabic), 423
—— —— (Persian), 419
—— Interior (Hindu), 49
—— Rules of (Parsî), 28
—— Short, Art Long (Hebrew), 418
—— Simplicity in (Christian), 297
—— The Inner (Hindu), 59
Light (Christian), 80
—— Inner (Christian), 39
—— —— (Persian), 82
—— The (Arabic), 91
—— Unrecognised (Christian), 443
Limitation (Persian), 306
Litany (Persian), 104
Living, True (Hindu), 292
Love (Christian), 52
—— (Persian), 50, 218, 244
—— Divine (Christian), 77
—— —— (Hindu), 72
—— —— (Persian), 80
—— Grades of (Persian), 244
—— (Hindu), 245
—— The Power of (Japanese), 255
—— The Highest (Persian), 241
—— The Law'fulfilled in (Christian), 17
—— The Law of (Christian), 18
—— —— (Hebrew), 18
Loving much (Christian), 254
Lowliness and Grandeur (Siamese), 341
Lowly, Ornament of the (Persian), 335
Lying (Persian), 313

MAGNANIMITY (Hebrew), 347
Majorities (Chinese), 368
Majority, The (Christian), 191
—— With the (Hindu), 297
Man (Persian), 281
—— and Animal (Persian), 277
—— Aspiring (Persian), 282
—— Possibilities of (Egyptian), 285
—— The Good (Hebrew), 42
—— The Just (Hebrew), 289
—— The True (Burmese), 35
Manhood (Persian), 294
Mankind (Chinese), 284
Martyrdom (Christian), 191, 197, 201

Martyrdom (Icelandic), 173
Marvels (Christian), 142
Maxims (Arabic), 312
Mean, The (Persian), 308
Measure for Measure (Christian), 21
—— (Hebrew), 23
Mediators (Persian), 263
Meditation (Hindu), 103
Mercifulness (Arabic), 242
—— (Hindu), 233
Mercy (Persian), 376
—— and Forbearance (Singhalese), 358
—— Misplaced (Persian), 372
Mind, The Good (Persian), 174
Minister, Charge to a (Christian), 207
Ministers, Bad (Persian), 367
Ministry (Christian), 206
Modesty (Arabic), 329
Morality (Hindu), 3
Morals (Christian), 231
Morning (Hindu), 93
Moses, Last Words of (Hebrew), 32
Mother, The Divine (Hebrew), 72
Mystery (Persian), 171

NATURE (Arabic), 265
—— (Persian), 211, 273
—— Human (Chinese), 275
—— Love in (Persian), 111
—— Mind in (Hindu), 76
—— Temple of (Persian), 259
—— The Genius of (Hindu), 261
Natures, Bountiful (Hindu), 349
Nature's Voice (Hebrew), 260
Nearest, The (Arabic), 70
Necessity (Scandinavian), 449
Necromancy (Hebrew), 139
Night, In the (Hebrew), 369
—— Songs in the (Hebrew), 433
Nobility (Chinese), 339

OBEDIENCE (Persian), 39
Observances (Hindu), 99
Office (Chinese), 359
Offices and Duties (Christian), 15
Old and New (Christian), 27, 133
Opportunity (Arabic), 452
—— (Christian), 441
—— (Hebrew), 417
—— (Persian), 306
Optimism (Hebrew), 270
—— (Persian), 54
Ordeal (Christian), 188
Orphan, The (Persian), 374
Others, Living with (Scandinavian), 301

PAIN, The Teaching of (Persian), 389
Pantheism (Hindu), 69
—— (Persian), 80

Paradise, The Present (Persian), 273
Parents (Arabic), 253
—— Reverence for (Chinese), 252
Path, The Eightfold (Siamese), 3
—— The Middle (Singhalese), 45
Paths, Old (Hebrew), 35
Patience (Chinese), 314
—— (Hindu), 289
—— (Persian), 334
—— (Persian), 428
Peace (Chinese), 360
—— (Hebrew), 361, 362
—— False (Hebrew), 438
Peacefulness (Christian), 362
Peaceful, The (Singhalese), 358
Pearls before Swine (Hindu), 312
Permanence (Persian), 422
Pilgrimage, The Spiritual (Persian), 106
Pleasure, Transient and Permanent (Hebrew), 430
Poets (Persian), 287
Politeness (Persian), 313
Poverty and Wealth (Parsí), 431
Power (Persian), 375, 377
—— Passive (Hindu), 291
Prayer (Persian), 175
Prayers, Ancient (Hebrew and Christian), 105
Pride (Hebrew), 328, 331
Priest and Prophet (Christian), 142
Priestcraft (Hebrew), 154
Principles (Old English), 26
Problems of Life (Hebrew and Persian), 393
Progress (Arabic), 423
Progression (Chinese), 168
Prohibitions (Siamese), 2
Prophet and People (Christian), 183
—— The (Arabic), 212
—— The (Persian), 42, 177, 180
—— The Faithful (Arabic), 211
—— The False, and the True (Hebrew), 179
—— The Rejected (Hebrew), 179
—— The Unrecognised (Christian), 185
Prosperity (Hindu), 300
Proverbs (Turkish), 307
Prudence (Russian), 164
Punishment, Capital (Chinese), 358
Purity (Chinese), 311
—— (Hindu), 311
Purposes (African), 12

QUALITIES (Arabic), 283
—— Current (Persian), 295
—— Rare (Hindu), 290

RADICALISM (Chinese), 370, 379
—— (Christian), 439

Rank (Hindu), 290
Reality (Persian), 428
Reason (Chinese), 129
—— (Persian), 282
—— Supreme (Chinese), 83
Reciprocity (Chinese), 6
—— (Hindu), 158
Recoil (Hebrew), 427, 447
Rectitude, Repose on (Hebrew), 88
Reformer, The (Hebrew), 370
Refuge, The (Hebrew), 90
Rejected, The (Arabic), 193
Reliances, False (Parsí), 3
Religion (Hebrew), 33
—— (Hindu), 195
—— Practical (Christian), 41
—— The Essence of (Arabic), 53
Religions, Sympathy of (Parsí and Sufi), 33
Renunciation (Hindu), 390
Repentance, Love without (Persian), 47
Reproof (Hebrew), 182
—— (Hindu), 313
—— (Persian), 317, 453
Reputation (Chinese), 299
Responsibility (Persian), 452, 457
Resting (Chinese), 341
Restoration (Arabic), 450
Retribution (Hebrew), 436
—— (Hindu), 456
—— (Persian), 456
Requital (Hebrew), 434
Reverence (Hebrew), 330
Reward, The (Hebrew), 437
Rich and Poor (Chinese), 299
Riches (Hindu), 299
—— (Persian), 319
Rosary, The (Persian), 96
Rule, The Golden (Hebrew), 24
—— The Golden (Hindu), 26
Ruler, The Righteous (Hebrew), 366

SATISFACTIONS (Hindu), 248
Saturn, Hymn to (Persian), 273
Sayings, Pauline (Christian), 54
Scepticism (Christian), 187
Science (Arabic), 159
Sects (Sabœan), 134
Seed and Fruit (Hindu), 4
Seeking (Persian), 284
Seeming and Being (Persian), 453, 454
Self (Burmese), 296
—— and Sect (Persian), 156
Self-control (Hindu), 431
Self-delusion (Hebrew), 437
Self-discipline (Hindu), 288
Self-judgment (Turkish) 425
Self-righteousness (Persian), 321
Self-surrender (Christian), 49, 186

Selfishness, Pious (Persian), 57, 58
Sense, Common (Scandinavian), 122
Sentiment and Principle (Hebrew), 40
Serpents, Two (Persian), 428
Servants (Hindu), 237
Service, Loving (Christian), 228
Servility (Christian), 298
Service (Persian), 332
Servility (Christian), 298
—— (Hindu), 309
Shadows (Persian), 387
Shadow, The (Persian), 456
Signs (Arabic), 268
Silence (Persian), 130
—— (Scandinavian), 314
—— and Speech (Hebrew), 241
—— (Persian), 131
—— and Sufferance (Hebrew), 179
Sinai, The Inward (Hebrew), 1
Sins, The Covered (Persian), 217
Skill (Chinese), 380
Slander (Persian), 251
Slavery (Scandinavian), 448
Sloth (Persian), 122
Society, Low (Singhalese), 248
Sower, The (Christian), 182
Sowing and Reaping (Christian), 445
—— (Persian), 30, 451
Sorrow (Persian), 388
—— and Death (Burmese), 390
Soul, The Supreme (Persian), 63
Speech (Persian), 121
—— Sweet (Hindu), 239
Spirit, The Lowly (Hebrew), 328
State, A Happy (Hebrew), 359
Stone, The Rejected (Hebrew), 92
Strength (Persian), 335
—— Inward (Christian), 198
Stronghold, The (Hebrew), 47
Study, The Supreme (Persian), 92
Substance, Size and (Persian), 210
Sufferance (Christian), 190
—— (Persian), 213
Sun, Hymn to the (Persian), 264
Sun, The (Hebrew), 84
Superstition (Chinese), 155
—— and Silver (Christian), 147
Sustainer, The (Hebrew), 87
Sympathy (Chinese), 233, 365

Taciturnity (Persian), 381
Teaching (Hindu), 165
Temperance (Persian), 170
—— (Scandinavian), 314
—— (Persian), 316, 455
Temples (Persian), 101
Temptation (Siamese), 172
Theism (Hindu), 81
Things, Difficult (Chinese), 171

Thinker, The Timid (Hindu), 176
Thirst, The Soul's (Hebrew), 93
Thorns (Persian), 424
Thought (Burmese), 130
—— Word, Deed (Persian), 383
Time (Hindu), 415
—— (Persian), 455
—— The Present (Christian), 38
Timidity (Christian), 190
To-day (Persian), 460
Toil, Fruitless (Persian), 128, 170
Toleration (Arabic), 34
—— (Christian), 17
—— (Persian), 61
Tradition (Christian), 146
Traditions (Christian), 141
Transition (Christian), 175
Treasure, The Hid (Singhalese), 292
Trial (Christian), 189
Trust (Hebrew), 434
Truth (Hebrew), 160
—— (Hindu), 49, 451
—— (Persian), 306
—— Fidelity to (Christian), 181
—— (Hebrew), 181
—— Rejected (Christian), 443
—— Speaking the (Persian), 214
—— The Crown of (Christian), 198
Truthfulness (Hebrew), 43
—— (Hindu), 177

Unchangeable, The (Arabic), 90
Unchanging, The (Arabic), 449
Undefiled, The (Hebrew), 46
Union (Hindu), 368
Unity, The Divine (Persian), 82
Unknowable, The (Egyptian), 65
—— The (Hebrew), 66
—— The (Hindu), 66
—— The (Persian), 111
Unrecognised, The (Persian), 69
Unsearchable, The (Christian), 66

Values (Christian), 224
Vanity (Persian), 376
Virtue (Chinese), 291
—— (Hindu), 340
—— (Persian), 293, 459
—— Reward of (Persian), 458
Virtues Immortal (Burmese), 422
—— Royal (Buddhist), 346
—— Saving (Persian), 30
Vishnu, Hymn to (Hindu), 65
Vision, Earth-bound (Christian), 20

Waiting (Hebrew), 94
War against War (Hebrew), 363
Wavering (Chinese), 168
Wealth (Hindu), 310

Wealth, Superfluous (Persian), 318
Wife, The (Hebrew), 245, 246
Wisdom (Burmese), 116
—— (Hindu), 118
—— (Hebrew), 115, 118
—— (Parsi), 117
—— (Persian), 123
—— Hidden (Christian), 119
—— in Obscurity (Hebrew), 321
—— and Folly (Hebrew), 119
—— —— (Persian), 124
—— Worship of (Hindu), 96
Within, The Kingdom (Christian), 146
Woes (Hebrew), 445
Work (Persian), 381
Words (Chinese), 307

Words and Actions (Chinese), 379
Word, The True (Christian), 196
World, The (Burmese), 455
—— The (Persian), 416
—— The, Divine (Persian), 267
—— The Inner (Hindu), 283
Woman (Arabic), 342
—— (Hindu), 310
Women, Devotion of (Christian), 192
Worship (Hindu), 97
—— (Persian), 100, 102
Worth, Essential (Hindu), 287
Wrongs (Hindu), 369

YOUNG, Rules for the (Persian), 326

www.ingramcontent.com/pod-product-compliance
Lightning Source LLC
Chambersburg PA
CBHW020834020526
44114CB00040B/757